1987 REPRINT

~~43.00~~

1st US EDITION

12.50

HAUNTED HOUSES

By CAMILLE FLAMMARION

Author of "DREAMS OF AN ASTRONOMER," Etc.

D. APPLETON AND COMPANY
NEW YORK MCMXXIV

PRINTED IN THE UNITED STATES OF AMERICA

CONTENTS

HAUNTED HOUSES

INTRODUCTORY

SPIRITUALISM AND MATERIALISM: A REPLY TO CAMILLE SAINT-SAËNS

SINCE, in spite of the most decisive observations, the battle between psychists and anti-psychists is still raging, it seems to me that the following article, published in the *Nouvelle Revue* of December 15, 1900, may usefully be prefaced to this book, especially as it presents the arguments of the two opposed camps side by side. My friend, Camille Saint-Saëns, had just published an article extolling the faculties of the brain as opposed to the theory of a personal soul. On comparing the terms of this article with the letters published in *La Mort et son Mystère* (vol. ii, p. 34, and iii, p. 8) it will be seen that in the nineteenth century we had not yet become intimate friends. In spite of our different points of view, our relations became more and more cordial until his death, which took place on December 16, 1921. Seekers after truth who keep their mental independence may learn to esteem and love each other in spite of their differences of opinion. They are incapable of intolerance. This article, written in the last year of last century, forms a fitting prologue to what follows:

MY DEAR FRIEND,

I have just read your well-informed and attractive article in the *Nouvelle Revue*—a little late in the day, perhaps, but, as you know, I spend more time in the Heavens than on Earth—and it struck me like one of those powerful symphonies of which you have the secret, and in which science and art compete to produce in our minds the maximum effect. You seem in this article to touch but lightly on the subject under discussion, but in reality you show us glimpses of all its depths.

You are absolutely right in saying that the words spiritualism and materialism are really only *words* nowadays, since the essence of things is unknown to us, and since recent scientific discoveries base the visible world upon an invisible world, which forms, so to speak, its substratum. I thank you for having drawn attention to my modest excursion into the domain of the "Unknown," but I ask your permission to reply to your interpretation. You seem to fear that the etymology of the word "psychic" had influenced my mind. The facts marshalled in my book do not, according to you, establish the existence of a soul. The facts, which, with good reason, you accept as authentic, would only prove this: "That the unknown force which produces thought has the power of projecting itself beyond the limits of the body, so that a brain might act on other brains at a distance. It does not follow that this force has a spiritual nature independent of the brain."

That is the argument I should like to examine and dissect.

Let us, if you please, take a fact and analyse it. A young woman, Mlle. Z., brought to my office in Paris the following story, in which I suppress the names:

On the day of our first meeting I was twenty years of age and he was thirty-two. Our relation lasted seven years, and we loved each other tenderly.

One day my friend told me sorrowfully that his circumstances, his poverty, etc., obliged him to marry; and among his embarrassed explanations I perceived a vague desire that our relation should not thereby be altogether broken off.

I cut short this painful interview; and, in spite of my great sorrow, I did not see my friend again, as I had no wish, in my unique and absolute love, to share this man I loved so much willingly with another.

I heard afterwards indirectly that he was married and the father of a child.

Some years after this marriage, on a night of April, 1893, I saw a human form entering my room. The form, tall in appearance, was enveloped in a white veil, which hid nearly the whole of the face. I saw with terror how it advanced and bent over me. I felt its lips touching mine. But what lips! I shall never forget the impression they made upon me. I felt no pressure, nor movement, nor warmth, only cold—the cold of a dead mouth!

Yet I felt a relief and a sense of well-being during this long kiss, but never during this vision did the name or the image of my lost lover present themselves to my spirit. After waking up I did not think of my dream, until, towards noon, I happened to look at a paper and read: "We hear from X. that the funeral took place yesterday of M. Y." (here followed the description of the deceased). The article ended by attributing the death to an attack of typhoid fever, caused by the overstrain of conscientious work.

"Dear friend," I thought, "when you were released from worldly conventions you came to me to tell me that you had loved me, and would still love me after death. I thank you, and I love you still."

MLLE. Z.

That is the fact as it took place. The old and convenient hypothesis of a simple hallucination no longer satisfies us to-day. What we must explain is the coincidence of the death with the apparition. Manifestations of this kind are so numerous that the coincidences can no longer be regarded as fortuitous, but must be taken to indicate a cause and effect.

Both you and I, being free from prejudice, admit that Mlle. Z. saw and perceived the presence of her lover at the critical moment of his departure from this world. Hundreds of examples of the same kind exist. But our interpretations differ. You only see a cerebral action of a dying person. I see a psychic action.

(I asked myself whether the narrator might have seen the paper the night before without remembering it, and whether the association of ideas had produced her dream, but she assures me it was only the next day that she read the paper. That hypothesis must, therefore, be excluded. There had been a real communication between the two beings.)

It is, of course, always difficult to distinguish between that work which belongs to the spirit or the soul from that which belongs to the brain, and in our appreciations and judgments we are naturally guided by the inner feeling produced in us by the discussion of the phenomena. Now have we not in this case what is essentially a manifestation of the spirit? Two hypotheses present themselves. Either the lover, as indicated by the narrative, was already dead when he acted thus, or he was still alive, and at the moment of death this man thought of that woman, of his friend of sunnier days, and felt a regret, a remorse perhaps, and possibly a hope for the Beyond. That telepathic communication was perhaps not perceived at once during the daily routine, but was postponed to the hours of sleep and tranquillity. It was not, of course, a case of a phantom transported from one city to another. It was a mental transmission, of which wireless telegraphy furnishes us a physical image. The distance was sixty-two miles, and we know that such a distance does not count.

The mental communication took the form described by the narrator. Such is the impression made by an examination of all the facts, and it becomes more convincing as we advance in the study of these phenomena. Let us take another case:

When a student at the University of Kieff, and already married, I had gone to spend the summer with my sister, who lived in the country not far from Pskow. While returning through Moscow, my beloved wife suddenly fell ill through influenza, and, in spite of her extreme youth, she was quickly broken up. Heart-failure, like a stroke of lightning, carried her off.

I shall not attempt to describe my pain and my despair. But I must submit to your competent judgment a problem which I sincerely hope to have solved.

My father lived at Pultowa. He knew nothing of the illness of his charming daughter-in-law, and knew that she was with me at Moscow. What was his surprise on seeing her beside him as he was leaving the house, and accompanying him for an instant! Seized with fear and anxiety, he at once sent us a telegram to assure himself of the health of my dear one. It was the day of her death.

I should be grateful to you all my life for an explanation of this extraordinary fact.

WENECIAN BILILOWSKY
21, NIKOLSKAJA, KIEFF. *(Student of Medicine).*

Here, also, the observation was made after death.

Have we not in this example also the impression of a non-material origin of the phenomenon, of a moral or mental cause, indicating not only the existence of unknown faculties in the human being, but even the existence of an intelligent agent? I cannot find in this class of facts anything pertaining to anatomy, animal physiology, or organic chemistry.

Let us take another example, different from the two preceding ones, but still belonging to telepathy. This is the narrative:

In the first days of November, 1869, I left Perpignan, my native town, to continue my pharmaceutical studies at Montpellier. My family consisted of my mother and my four sisters. I left them very happy and in perfect health.

On the 22nd of the same month my sister Hélène, a fine girl of eighteen, the youngest and the greatest favourite, assembled some girl-friends in her mother's house. About three o'clock in the afternoon they started with my mother for the Promenade des Plabanes. The weather was beautiful. After half an hour my sister was suddenly taken ill. "Mother," she said, "I feel a queer shudder all over my body. I am cold, and my throat hurts me. Let us go home."

That night, at 5 a.m.,[1] my beloved sister expired in my mother's arms, strangled and laid low by an attack of diphtheria which two doctors were unable to master.

I was the only man who could have represented the family at the funeral, and my family sent me one telegram after another to Montpellier. But by a terrible fatality, which I still deplore, none reached me in time.

In the night from the 23rd to the 24th I had an awful hallucination.

I had returned home at 2 a.m., with a light heart and full of the joy I had experienced in a pleasure party on the 22nd and 23rd. I went to bed feeling very gay, and was asleep in five minutes.

About 4 a.m., I saw the face of my sister. It was deathly pale and bleeding, and a piercing cry, plaintive and unceasing, struck upon my ear: "What are you doing, my Louis? Do come. Do come."

In my nervous and agitated sleep I took a cab, but in spite of superhuman efforts I could not make it go. And still I saw my sister's face and heard her voice in my ear: "Louis, what are you doing? Do come. Do come."

I awoke suddenly, my face congested, my head on fire, my throat dry, my breath was short and gasping, and I perspired profusely. I jumped out of bed, trying to com-

[1] The hours have been corrected from the first narrative after careful examination.

pose myself. An hour afterwards I lay down again, but could get no rest.

At 11 a.m., I arrived at the refectory in a state of profound dejection. Questioned by my fellow-students I told them exactly what I had experienced. They chaffed me about it. At 2 p.m., I went to the Faculty, hoping to pull myself together over some work.

Coming out of the lecture I saw a woman in deep mourning coming towards me. She raised her veil and I recognised my eldest sister. Feeling anxious about me, she had come, in spite of her distress, to find out what had become of me. She told me of the fatal event which nothing could have led me to expect, since I had had the best news of my family on the morning of the 22nd.

I assure you on my honour that this story is absolutely true. I express no opinion, but only state facts.

Twenty years have passed, but the impression is still vivid, especially now, and if the features of my Hélène do not appear with the same clearness, I still hear her plaintive, oft-repeated, and despairing cry: *"Que fais-tu donc, mon Louis? Mais viens donc, mais viens donc."*

LOUIS NOELL
(Pharmacist at Cette).

There is the narrative of the psychic phenomenon. If you, my dear friend, do not feel that the body of the dead girl, twenty-three hours after her death, cannot have caused the impression; that there was something apart from the material organism; that, whether M. Noell's spirit was wafted in his sleep to his dead sister, or that some telepathic action emanated from her, we are face to face with an action of the soul and not of the body; that we are driven to think of the soul as personally existing, and not as an effect, a function, or a secretion of the brain: if you do not feel that, it is because you, the artist and thinker whom I know, have not given yourself time to weigh the problem.

What do you suppose the girl's brain did after

her death? Any "material" hypothesis is improbable. We might suppose that she called her brother before her death, and that the call remained latent in her brother's spirit until an hour of quiet enabled his brain to perceive it. On the other hand, we may suppose that the appeal was made after her death. We must consider everything.

The simplest expedient would be to deny, and to declare that the young student simply had a nightmare which accidentally coincided with the death of his sister. That is indeed very simple. But does it satisfy you? Does it satisfy you when you are faced with hundreds of cases of the same kind? Does it satisfy you also in the cases where the narrator has "seen" at a distance all the details of a death, a suicide, an accident, or a fire? No. You have too scientific and rational a mind to be satisfied with this old hypothesis of chance, and you know that the calculus of probability renders it inacceptable. What then?

Then it follows that the psychic problem is set, and we may as well acknowledge it.

I do not claim to explain it. Science has not advanced so far. To admit and to explain it are two different things. We are forced to admit the facts even when we cannot explain them. A man passes the corner of a street and gets a flower-pot on his head. He is bound to admit the fact without guessing at once how it came about, and how the horizontal and vertical just met at the point occupied by his head.

No indeed, what we call matter and its properties does not suffice to explain these facts, and therefore they are of another order, of an order which we have every right to call "psychic," and which leads us to admit the existence of souls, spirits, intelligent spiritual beings, which are not simply cerebral functions. Do not the phenomena of mental transmission, of seeing at a distance without eyes, of seeing things yet to come—do not these bear the same testimony?

Mental transmission is beyond doubt, notably between a hypnotiser and his subject. I could recall a thousand examples. Here is one, surely free from sentiment, but very characteristic, cited by Dr. Bertrand, most competent of experimenters in this field:

> A hypnotiser, much imbued with mystical ideas, had a somnambulist who during his sleep only saw angels and spirits of every kind. These visions confirmed the hypnotiser more and more in his religious belief. As he always quoted the dreams of his somnambulist in favour of his system, another hypnotiser of his acquaintance undertook to disillusion him by proving to him that his somnambulist had the visions described solely because their prototype existed in his own head. In proof of this, he undertook to let the somnambulist witness a reunion of the angels of paradise sitting at table and eating a turkey!
>
> He therefore hypnotised the somnambulist, and after a time asked him whether he did not see anything extraordinary. He replied that he saw a great assembly of angels. "And what are they doing?" asked the hypnotiser. "They are sitting round a table eating." But he could not tell the dish of which they were partaking.

That is an example of mental suggestion, of which you know many cases. The will of the hypnotiser acts upon the subject without the aid of words. We can, of course, call it the action of one brain upon another, but does it not seem as if the brain were only an instrument of the will? I should not congratulate the brain upon its thought any more than I should congratulate a telescope upon its view of Saturn. Is not the brain the organ of thought as the eye is the organ of sight?

And what about seeing at a distance, or in dreams?

Does it not bring us face to face with a spiritual being endowed with special faculties? A mariner writes to me from Brest:

From 1870 to 1874 I had a brother employed at the arsenal of Foochow, in China, as a fitter. A friend of his, a mechanic who came from the same town (Brest), and was also employed at the Foochow arsenal, came one morning to see my brother at his lodgings, and told him the following story: "My dear friend, I am much upset. I dreamt last night that my little child died of croup on a red eiderdown." My brother ridiculed his fears, spoke of nightmares, and in order to dissipate the impression invited his friend to lunch. But nothing could divert him. For him his child was dead.

The first letter he received from France after that event was from his wife announcing the death of their child from croup after great suffering, and, strangely enough, on a red eiderdown, on the very night of the dream.

On receipt of this letter he showed it, weeping, to my brother, from whom I heard the story.

Do not such facts, which are very numerous, indicate something in man other than the body?

And what do you think of this vision?

My father had a friend of his youth, General Charpentier de Cossigny, who had always evinced much affection towards me. As he had a nervous trouble, which rendered his humour very eccentric, we were never surprised at his paying us several visits in quick succession, and then ceasing to visit us for months. In November, 1892 (we had not seen him for about three months), I had a sick headache and went to bed early. I had just begun to doze when I heard my name, pronounced at first in a low tone, and then rather more loudly. I listened, thinking it was my father calling; but I heard him in the neighbouring room, and his breathing was very regular, as of a person asleep for some time. I dozed again, and had a dream. I saw the stairs of the house where the general lived (7, Cité Vaneau). He appeared leaning on the handrail of the first-floor landing. He descended, came to me, and kissed me on the forehead. His lips were so cold that the touch woke me up. I then saw distinctly in the middle of the room, with the light of the street lamp, the fine, tall outline of the general as it receded. I was not asleep, as I heard eleven o'clock strike on the Lycée Henri IV. and counted the strokes. I could not get to sleep, and the cold impression of the lips of our old friend remained on my forehead all night. In the morning, the first word to my mother was: "We shall hear some news of General de Cossigny; I saw him last night."

A few minutes afterwards my father saw in the paper the news of the death of his old comrade, which happened the previous evening as the consequence of a fall downstairs. None of us had seen the paper.

JEAN DREUILHE.

36, RUE DES BOULANGERS, PARIS.

As in the previous case, and all similar ones, it is difficult to deny that the spirit sees at a distance. It is neither the eye, nor the retina, nor the optic nerve, nor the brain.

You must also have heard of the case of Marshal Serrano, as told by his wife:

For twelve long months a grave malady, which eventually proved fatal, undermined the life of my husband. Feeling that the end was near, his nephew, General Lopez Dominguez, went to the Prime Minister, Señor Canovas, to obtain permission to bury Serrano in a church like the other Marshals.

The King, then at the Prado, refused the request of General Lopez Dominguez. But he added that he would prolong his stay in the royal demesne so that his presence in Madrid should not hinder the rendering of military honours due to the rank of the dead Marshal and to his place in the army.

The sufferings of the Marshal increased every day. He could no longer lie down, but remained always in an easy chair.

One morning at dawn my husband, who was entirely paralysed owing to the use of morphia, and who could not move without the help of several assistants, suddenly rose alone, strong and upright, and in a more resounding voice than he had had in all his life cried in the silence of the night: "Let an orderly officer mount his horse and ride to the Prado; the King is dead!"

He fell back exhausted in his chair. We all thought of delirium, and hastened to give him a calming draught. He dozed off, but some minutes afterwards he rose again. With a weak and almost sepulchral voice he said: "My uniform, my sword; the King is dead!" It was his last flicker of life. After receiving, with the last sacrament, the Pope's benediction, he expired. Alphonse II. died without those consolations.

This sudden vision of the King's death by a dying man is true. The next morning all Madrid learned with consternation of the death of the King, who was almost alone at the Prado.

The royal corpse was taken to Madrid. Owing to this circumstance Serrano could not receive the promised honours. It is well known that when the King is in his palace at Madrid all honours are solely for him, even after his death, as long as his body is there.

Was it the King himself who appeared to my husband? How did he learn the news? There is some matter for reflection.

Countess de Serrano
(Duchess de la Torre).

Here we have a man at the point of death, and doubly disabled by the use of morphia, announcing an unexpected death unknown to anybody. Here again, how can we escape the conclusion that his soul, his spirit, perceived in some way what had happened?

Seeing at a distance, especially in dreams and in somnambulism, is proved by such a considerable number of observations that it is *incontestable.* I cannot find in it an argument in favour of hypotheses called materialistic. On the contrary, I find in every case an argument for a psychic state endowed with special faculties.

But what will you say of premonitory dreams and of the accurate spiritual prevision of events which have not yet happened? It is with these I may fittingly crown this reply.

Take the following dream, commonplace enough, and ill-adapted to transcendental philosophical theories:

I was going to college as an external student, and in my dream I saw myself crossing the Place de la République in Paris with a novel under my arm, when, just in front of the Magasins du Pauvre-Jacques, a dog passed me pursued by a horde of boys, who maltreated it. I saw their precise number. It was eight. The employees were beginning to display the goods, and a greengrocer woman passed with her cart full of fruits and flowers.

Next morning, on going to the college, I saw in the same place the scene which I had seen in my dream. Nothing was wanting. There was the dog in the gutter, the eight urchins pursuing it; the greengrocer woman passed with her cart going up to the Boulevard Voltaire, and the employees of the Pauvre-Jacques arranging their goods in the shops.

D. HANNAIS.

10, AVENUE LAGACHE, VILLEMONBLE, SEINE.

If the brain, a physical organ, is capable, with all its imaginable secretions, of thus perceiving all the details of an event which has not yet happened, we must suppress in our Institute the Academy of Moral

Sciences and replace it by the Academy of Medicine or, even more simply, by any clinic.

To see the future! Are we not there in pure psychism? Bear in mind that these premonitory dreams are not very rare either. I have quoted a number of them; I know many others. Do you remember this one, told to me by the father of the charming pensioner of the second Théâtre Français?

In 1869, at the time of the plebiscite, I had a dream, or, rather, a terrible nightmare.

In this nightmare I saw myself as a soldier. We were at war, and I underwent all the trials of a soldier's life—marching, hunger, and thirst. I heard the words of command, the fusillade, the cannon shots. I saw the dead and wounded falling around me, and heard their cries.

Suddenly I found myself in a country and in a village where we had to sustain a terrible attack of the enemy. There were Prussians and Bavarians and some cavalry (Baden Dragoons). Please note that I had never seen these uniforms, and that there was no question of war at the time. At a certain moment I saw one of our officers mounting a steeple with a field-glass to ascertain the movements of the enemy. He then descended, gave the word to sound the charge, and flung us with fixed bayonets on to a Prussian battery.

At this moment of my dream, fighting hand to hand with the artillerymen of that battery, I saw one of them aim a sabre-cut at my head. It was such a fierce cut that it split my head in two. I then woke up, and found myself out of bed, with a sharp pain in my head. In falling out of bed I had knocked my head against a small stove.

On October 6, 1870, this dream came true: the village, the school, the mairie, the church, our commander ascending the steeple to inspect the enemy position, descending, and, to the sound of "charge," throwing us and our bayonets on to the Prussian guns. In my dream at that moment I had had my head split with a sabre-cut. In reality I expected the same, but I only received a blow with a mop, probably intended for my head, which, however, I warded off, so that it struck me on my right thigh.

RÉGNIER
(Retired Sergeant-Major of the Neuilly Company of Francs-tireurs).

23, RUE JEANNE-HACHETTE,
HAVRE.

We might suppose, with Alfred Maury, that the shock produced the dream, but this hypothesis has nothing to do with premonition.

It is often objected that such dreams have been modified and arranged after the event, though quite sincerely, in the imagination of the narrators. Of course, it is quite possible that diverse modifications may be produced in the remembrance. But this objection is demolished by the observer's own impression, for it is just the impression of having seen it before which strikes him most. Besides, some are so simple that no modification is possible. For instance:

I dreamt that I was going on an errand on my bicycle, when a dog ran across the road and I fell down, breaking the pedal of the machine.

In the morning I told my mother of my dream, and, knowing how often my dreams had come true, she induced me to stay at home. I made up my mind not to go out; but about eleven o'clock, as we were about to have a meal, the postman brought a letter, saying that my sister, who lived five miles away, had fallen ill. Forgetting my dream, and only anxious to have news of my sister, I hurried over my lunch and started off on my bicycle. I proceeded without a mishap until I came to the place where I had seen myself the previous night rolling in the dust and breaking my machine. Hardly had my dream occurred to me when an enormous dog suddenly jumped out of a neighbouring farm and tried to bite my leg.

Without reflecting I tried to kick him, but at that moment I lost my balance and rolled over on my machine, breaking the pedal, and thus realising every detail of my dream. Please note that this was, at least, the hundredth time I had ridden that way without having met with the slightest accident until then.

AMÉDÉE BASSET
(Notary at Vitrac, Charente).

And the following:

In 1868, when I was seventeen, I was employed by an uncle who was a grocer at 32, Rue Saint-Roch. One morning, while still under the influence of a dream, he told me that in that dream he was on his doorstep, when, looking in the direction of the Rue Neuve-des-Petits-Champs, he saw approaching him a town omnibus of the Northern Railway Company, which stopped in front of his shop. His mother alighted from it and the omnibus drove on, taking away another lady who sat in the omnibus with his grandmother. The lady was dressed in black, and held a basket in her lap.

We both laughed at this dream, so far removed from reality, for *never* had my grandmother ventured to come alone from the Gare du Nord to the Rue Saint-Roch. Living near Beauvais, when she wanted to spend some time with her children in Paris, she preferred to write to my uncle and he met her at the station, whence he always brought her home in a cab.

Well, on the afternoon of that day, as my uncle stood watching the passers-by from his doorstep, his eyes glanced mechanically towards the corner of the Rue Neuve-des-Petits-Champs, and he saw an omnibus of the Northern Railway Company turning the corner and stopping at his shop.

In the omnibus were two ladies, one of them my grandmother, who alighted, while the vehicle continued on its journey with the other lady, whom he had seen in his dream, and who was dressed in black and held a basket on her knees.

Imagine the general astonishment! My grandmother thinking to surprise us, and my uncle telling her of his dream!

PAUL LEROUX.

LE NEUBOURG, EURE.

I make an end of these witnesses, because one need only bend down to pick up as many as one could wish for. The most precise and positive sciences are only established on conclusions from our reasoning, and Astronomy itself, that queen among the sciences, is based upon the theory of gravitation, of which Newton, its founder, said simply: "Things happen *as if* the heavenly bodies attracted each other directly in proportion to their masses, and inversely as the squares of their distances apart." Well, face to face with the phenomena of telepathy, with the examples of mental vision at a distance, without the aid of corporeal organs, with the still more mysterious and incomprehensible fact of seeing the future in accurate detail with spiritual eyes, I say: "Things happen *as if,* in the human organism, there existed a psychic, spiritual entity, endowed with perceptive faculties as yet unknown." This entity, this soul or spirit, acts and perceives through the brain, but it is not a material function of a material organ. This seems to me a logical conclusion arrived at by a sound and exact method. It seems to me superior both to negations and affirmations devoid of proof and founded on blind faith. Faith, the so-called miracles, even martyrdom, have never proved anything, for they have been at the service of all causes, both political and religious, even the most varied and contradictory, and sometimes the most absurd. Science alone can really enlighten humanity.

CAMILLE FLAMMARION.

Such is the article which I published in the last year of last century, nearly a quarter of a century ago. As I said before, my friend Saint-Saëns did not bear me a grudge for this opposition to his system. On the contrary, for our relations became more intimate and our friendship closer. He did not change his opinions, but he was not unaware of psychic phenomena, as proved by the following letter of July, 1921:

On reading for the *n*th time your last volume [2] a memory arises, and I shall not wait till to-morrow before communicating it to you.

It was in January, 1871, on the last day of the war. I was at an outpost of Arcueil-Cachan. We had just dined off an excellent horse, of which we had made a stew with dandelions we had gathered ourselves. Our dinner had entirely satisfied us, and we were as gay as one could be in similar circumstances, when I suddenly heard in my head a plaintive musical theme of dolorous chords—which I have since used for the commencement of my *Requiem*—and I felt in my inmost being a presentiment of some misfortune. A profound anxiety unnerved me.

That was the very moment when Henri Regnault was killed, to whom I was very much attached. The news of his death caused me such grief that I fell ill, and had to remain three days in bed.

I thus proved the reality of "telepathy" before the word was invented. You are indeed right in saying that classic science does not know the human being, and that we have everything to learn.

CAMILLE SAINT-SAËNS.

I cannot but repeat here what I wrote to my illustrious friend:

You are the mightiest of musicians, the glory of the Institute, one of the profoundest thinkers of our time—but you are not logical.

---

[2] *La mort et son mystère*, vol. ii.

And I found him all the more illogical because he had communicated to me his very characteristic personal observations, which I published in the same work (pp. 35, 36).

Is it not the spirit which acts in these phenomena? How can we find in them the properties of matter? My readers know that these psychic phenomena are too frequent to be attributable to chance coincidence. Their reality is mathematically proved by the calculus of probability.

It seems to me that this bygone exchange of ideas between two independent searchers is a very fit prologue to the present volume. I may add that Saint-Saëns himself gave an example of the independence of the soul relatively to the body. He died on December 16, 1921, aged 86 years. On the previous 16th of October he had lunched at my table at the Juvisay Observatory, and we had all been charmed by his conversation; his spirit was as young as it had been at twenty, yet he complained of the failure of his organism, and could not ascend to the tower to observe Venus and Arcturus in the company of our colleagues of the French Astronomical Society, including Prince Bonaparte, Count Gramont, Count de la Baume Pluvinel, General Ferrié, and other friends who had strongly insisted upon it. He suffered from his legs. At the same time, *Le Ménestrel* published (October 21) an article full of the spirit of youth from his pen, on Berlioz. While his body perished his soul remained in full force. And such a difference between the physical and the spiritual element is not rare.

CHAPTER I

EXPERIMENTAL PROOFS OF SURVIVAL

Preliminary reply to certain criticisms—Ascertaining the facts—Blind and prejudiced denials—Laplace and the calculus of probabilities—The choice of precise observations.

SERIOUS and competent readers who know exactly the state of our problem, and appreciate the value of the results achieved towards its solution, will perhaps consider it superfluous if I devote the first chapter of this volume to the task of answering objections, devoid of intrinsic value, raised by uncompromising sceptics who do not want to admit the existence of metapsychic phenomena at any price. But it seems to me that a clear reply to these negations is not superfluous, for the mass of human beings is inevitably ignorant of these phenomena, and therefore disposed to pass them by. And if I but convinced one reader out of ten of the error of those blind critics, it would be rendering a signal service to general information.

If we wish, by our own personal conviction, to acquire a rooted and permanent opinion concerning the reality, the nature, and the interest of psychic phenomena, we must first of all know that illusions of sight, of hearing, of touch, and, indeed, of all the senses, occur easily, and may be due to a thousand unexpected causes, so that we must guard against every possible error. Generally, we observe badly, we do not see below the surface, we are content with mere approximations. The scientific *method* is here called for more than elsewhere if we personally desire a well-founded conviction. Once we have taken those preventive precautions, none of the opinions of millions of other people avail to impede our free appreciation of observed facts. Let that be understood once for all!

As regards fraud, both conscious and unconscious, I have dealt with that in a long discussion (fifty pages) in my work *Les Forces Naturelles Inconnues*, so that I need not go over it again.

I am inclined to think, with Emile Boirac, that the chief reason for the bias and mistrust encountered by psychic science among some of our contemporaries lies in the form in which it was originally clothed, and from which it has not been sufficiently liberated. It was originally called Occult Science, or it at least formed part of that confused mass of empirical observations, traditions, hypotheses, and speculations which are known under that name, and which are mixed up with astrology, alchemy, chiromancy, magic, and other embryonic sciences of antiquity, of the Middle Ages, and of the Renaissance. It is barely two centuries since psychic science began to emerge from that mass, and among those who devote themselves to it there may remain some of the mystic spirit of the old adepts. It is one more reason why we should take care to introduce, with increasing ardour and vigour, the true spirit of modern science. It is thus that astronomy has finally arisen out of astrology, and chemistry out of alchemy, and neither one nor the other has retained the blemish of a sort of original sin. In the same way psychic science, cradled, so to speak, in magic and sorcery, deserves already, and will deserve more fully in the future, being described as an effective and positive science, thanks to the steady employment of the experimental method.

Here we study the greatest of problems. The knowledge of the soul, the enquiry into our destiny, is an all-absorbing pursuit. A biographer has just said that if my life, after being devoted to the investigation of the astronomical world and the demonstration of universal life, had only served to prove the existence of the human soul, it would have contributed to the progress of humanity. I devoutly hope so.

We require careful discussion nowadays. The publication of the third volume of my metapsychic trilogy, *Death and Its Mystery,* which deals with manifestations "after death," has raised a tempest of recriminations from ignorant publicists, some of whom, while apparently sincere and well-balanced, recover, like other people, lightly and irresponsibly, while others show signs of bad faith and acrimony, which is as strange as it is useless.

Is it not astonishing? Our legitimate and natural wish to know the nature of the soul, to know whether it really has a personal existence, whether it survives the inevitable destruction of the body, that wish, I say, makes enemies and adversaries for us, who spend their ingenuity inventing a thousand obstacles to this free and independent research and in retarding it in every possible way! This systematic opposition is hardly conceivable, and yet it exists.

It is opportune just now to examine the subject with special attention, applying the principles of the positive scientific method. Let us take up the discussion at the original incidents which provoked it.

On June 16, 1922, *Le Journal* did me the honour to publish at the head of its columns the following article I had sent in:

Manifestations of the Dead

Researches on the nature of the soul and its existence after death must be conducted according to the same method as is used in any other science, without prejudice or preconceived opinion, and apart from any sentimental or religious influence. Are there, or are there not, manifestations of the dead? That is the question. Now I declare that there are. The *Journal,* to which I had the honour of contributing in the days of its founder, my spiritual friend Xau, having called attention to the solution of this long-standing problem, I bring before its readers one of two facts which have most convinced me of such a survival, and I defy the most sceptical of my antagonists to explain it without assuming an action by the deceased person. Let them try, indeed.

There was an engineer who owned two factories, one in Glasgow, and the other in London. In his service in the Scottish factory there was a young lad called Robert Mackenzie, who was particularly devoted and bore a deep feeling of gratitude towards him. The employer did not live in Glasgow but in London.

One evening, a Friday, the Glasgow workmen gave their annual ball. Robert Mackenzie, who had no taste for dancing, asked permission to serve at the refreshment stall. All went off well, and the entertainment was continued on the Saturday.

On the next Tuesday evening a little before eight, in his house at Campden Hill, the engineer saw a manifestation which he relates as follows: "I dreamt that I was sitting at a desk engaged in conversation with an unknown gentleman. Robert Mackenzie came towards me. Rather annoyed, I asked him whether he did not see that I was engaged. He retired with a dissatisfied air, then came again as if he strongly desired an immediate conversation. I reproached him even more rudely with his want of tact. Just then the person to whom I was talking took his leave, and Mackenzie advanced again. 'What does this mean, Robert?' I said in a tone of some irritation. 'Don't you see that I was engaged?'

"'Yes,' he replied, 'but I must speak to you at once?'

"'What about? What is the hurry?'

"'I wish to tell you, sir, that I am accused of something I did not do. I want you to know that and to forgive me for what they accuse me of, for I am innocent.' Then he added: 'I did not do what they say I did.'

"'What is that?' I asked.

"He repeated the same words. Then I asked, naturally: 'How can I forgive you when you do not tell me what you are accused of?'

"I shall never forget the emphasis of his response with its Scottish accent: 'You will know soon.'

"My question was repeated at least twice, and the reply three times in the most expressive manner. I woke up, with a certain anxiety regarding this singular dream. I asked whether it had any meaning, when my wife came rushing into the room in great agitation, an open letter in her hand. She cried: 'Oh, James, a dreadful thing has happened at the workmen's ball. Robert Mackenzie committed suicide.' I then understood the meaning of my dream and said quietly with an air of certainty: 'No, he has not killed himself.' 'How do you know?' 'He has just told me.'

"When he appeared—to avoid interrupting the narrative I did not mention this detail—I had been struck by his queer appearance. His face was a livid blue, and on his forehead were spots resembling drops of perspiration.

"This is what had happened. Coming home on the Saturday night, Mackenzie had taken a bottle containing nitric acid thinking it was a bottle of whiskey. He had poured out a small glassful and emptied it at a gulp. He had died on the Sunday in terrible agony. He was believed to have committed suicide, and that is why he had come to tell me that he was innocent of the accusation brought against him. Now the remarkable thing, of which I had no idea, is that when I looked up the symptoms accompanying poisoning by nitric acid, I found they were just about those I had noticed on Robert's face.

"It was soon found that the death had been attributed

to suicide in error. I heard this next day through my representative in Scotland.

"This apparition, in my view, was due to the profound gratitude of Mackenzie, whom I had taken out of a deplorable state of misery, and his ardent desire to retain my esteem."

That is the story told by the Glasgow manufacturer. Does not the fact of this workman coming, after his alleged suicide, to reveal the truth to him prove survival?

We have hundreds of similar observations, made by responsible people who simply relate what happened to them. The only way to evade all explanation is to say that the stories are not true, that they are imagined or invented, that the alleged witnesses are not telling the truth. Now the Glasgow manufacturer was a personal friend of Gurney, one of the founders of the English Society for Psychical Research, known to him as a sincere and upright man, and his veracity is beyond doubt. Well, if we do not accuse all the observers of imposture if we do not think that they were feeble-sighted and that everybody is more or less mad or subject to hallucination, we must admit these facts just as we are bound to admit a strange and unexplained flash of lightning. One cannot deny everything. We must frankly acknowledge that we have here a whole region of things unknown to scientific investigation. In the particular case which I have just related, the young man, poisoned by mistake in the night from Saturday to Sunday, at Glasgow, appeared the following Tuesday in London to his employer, who did not know of his death, to declare that he had not committed suicide. He was, therefore, forty-eight hours dead. We cannot here admit the coincidence of any dream with such a detailed occurrence, nor chance, nor anything else.

Those who deny these facts are ignorant, or illogical, or insincere, for if they know them I cannot imagine how they eliminate the action of the deceased person.

CAMILLE FLAMMARION.

That was the article published in the *Journal.* I admit that, against my usual custom, I had employed a rather aggressive style, in order to provoke discussion and see what happened. The effect came soon. The next day, our comrade, M. Clément Vautel, who is particularly sceptical in these matters, replied by the following radical denial:

MY FILM

In the year 1861, on a fine summer evening, Mr. Harry Cower was sitting in his dining room at Sydney, Australia. He had no appetite and could not dispel the melancholy ideas which crowded upon him.

Suddenly he heard a crisp and very faint noise. The mirror over the mantelpiece had split. "That is queer!" said Mr. Harry Cower. Some weeks afterwards he heard that at the moment when the mirror broke, his old aunt, Mrs. Dorothy Elizabeth MacClure, had suddenly died at Minneapolis, Minnesota, U. S. A.

Does this authentic fact not prove in an undeniable fashion the reality of manifestations from Beyond?

Another time it is a certain Archibald B. Blackburn of Chicago, who in 1874, at Woodston, Ohio, saw appear before him his friend John William Hercules O'Sullivan, of New Tipperary (Mass.). O'Sullivan's face was convulsed. He seemed to breathe with difficulty and made queer gestures. "What is the matter?" asks Mr. Blackburn. "Help, I am drowning," says O'Sullivan, and disappears.

Blackburn, much distressed, goes home. And, eight days afterwards, he hears that his friend is drowned in the Missouri, at the time and on the day when his phantom called for help.

Those who deny these eloquent facts, says M. Flammarion, are either ignorant, or illogical, or insincere.

Well, then, I deny them.

I deny them all, *en bloc,* in the most categorical fashion.

I have read in the psychic books of M. Flammarion and other mystery mongers innumerable cases which strangely resemble the story of Harry Cower and Archibald B. Blackburn. I consider them devoid of any kind of documentary value. They all occurred at a fabulous epoch, and guarantees are absolutely lacking. When I think that we cannot be trusted to describe exactly a street accident which we saw, I say to myself that it is foolish to base a whole philosophy, a sort of religion, on ancient anecdotes told in their own way by people we know nothing about.

Besides, there is too much English spoken in these stories of another world. The spirits, spectres, phantoms, etc., are never natives of Pontarlier or Romorantin; it is always in England or America that they indulge in their little manifestations. Is the Beyond also an Anglo-Saxon colony?

Why, for instance, did not the late Bessarabo appear to the President of the Assize Court, to the Jury, or even to Maître de Moro-Giafferi, to tell in what circumstances he took up his quarters at the bottom of a trunk?

That would more surely overcome our scepticism than the collection of *psycho-canards* collected by the gentle and pensive Camille Flammarion.

CLÉMENT VAUTEL.

It is by these pleasantries, this playing with words, etc., that our *confrère* of the Grand Press thinks he can explain the posthumous apparition of Robert Mackenzie! I venture to remark that this "solution" bears no relation to the problem. It is equivalent to these simple words: "There is nothing in it." "Nothing"—that is, very little, considering all the facts established beyond a doubt.

As M. Clément Vautel declares that they "all

occurred at a fabulous epoch, and guarantees are absolutely lacking," I brought him up against a fact observed in France, and not at the Antipodes, and neither an ancient anecdote nor belonging to a fabulous epoch. Here is the fact. It is an observation by Mr. Frederick Wingfield, made at Belle-Isle-en-Terre (Côtes-du-Nord):

On the night of March 25, 1880, he writes, I dreamed that I saw my brother Richard sitting on a chair in front of me. I spoke to him. He simply nodded in reply, then rose and left the room. I awoke, and found that I was standing with one foot on the floor by my bed and the other on the bed, and I was trying to pronounce the name of my brother. The impression that he was there was so strong, and the whole scene so vivid, that I left the bedroom to look for my brother in the drawing-room, but found nobody.

I then had the idea of an impending calamity, and I noted the "apparition" in my diary, with the remark: "God forbid it!" Three days afterwards I received the news that my brother had died that day, at 8.30, of the consequences of a fall while hunting.

The death had therefore occurred several hours before the clear vision.

The very Parisian and very subtle sceptic of the *Journal* kindly acknowledged the receipt of this communication in a quite amiable letter, from which I quote only the following lines:

This took place in the Côtes-du-Nord. True, but your personages are Anglo-Saxons. Richard Wingfield, Baker, is not very Breton. Now this story, like *all* the others, I deny. Illusion. Vanity. Humbug.

This very characteristic observation is of no value, because the narrator is not French! If he were French, it would be just the same. It is "humbug," and there is nothing but humbug in all these stories: Death, mourning, pain, despair, all this does not count, and we can only laugh. This explanation of unexplainable things is extremely simple! Let us add that all this is just as usual. All the sciences had that sort of treatment when they began.

Besides, the objection itself is valueless, inasmuch as an observation made in London or Rome is as respectable as one made in Paris. These facts are observed in the whole world, and France has no monopoly of them.

Some days afterwards, June 18, the following letter was sent to me from Bologne, as a really French observation:

I read your article of June 16 (Manifestations of the Dead). I also read the "film" of our amusing Clément Vautel (17th), who denies the facts you mention on the excuse that they always take place in distant countries. Very well, I shall quote one which happened in Paris, in 1911, and you may communicate it to our Clément Vautel.

My father died of the consequences of an operation at the Cochin hospital in February, 1906. My mother not possessing at the time the money necessary to bury him, the hospital undertook the expense, and my father was buried in the *fosse commune* of the Bagneux cemetery.

Five years later I was at home and living in the Rue Etex. One morning I was walking up and down in my room. I turned towards the kitchen to have my early breakfast (it was 7 a.m.). I suddenly saw my father, standing upright in the kitchen, his right hand resting on the rim of the sink. It was he, indeed, with his calm manner which he always had during his life.

Some months passed and I told nobody about the occurrence. But one evening I found myself on a visit at my sister's and told her. She said: "Look here. That was just the day on which father was exhumed!"

Not knowing this, I asked why I had not been told.

"Because we thought you would not come at such an early hour." "What hour?" "Seven in the morning."

And it was just at seven that I had seen my father.

Why did he appear to me? Was it to reproach me for not being there when his grave was changed? Yet I was not guilty, because I had not been told.

At that time I believed nothing, for I had not been brought up in any religion, but I assure you that since the day when I saw my father I have believed in God and the immortality of my soul.

Please accept my declaration of the most scrupulous sincerity.

MLLE. H. H. (my name for you only).

We may still assume a hallucination without cause. But how account for the coincidence of the vision with the exhumation of the narrator's father? That is where the problem arises. Can it be vanity, humbug? What do you think? Is it not better to confess that we know nothing, but that there is "something in it," and that we ought to admit the facts?

(M. Vautel has a good sense of humour. So had Voltaire. The great spirits of science—Copernicus, Galileo, Newton, Columbus, Gutenberg, Denis Papin, Fulton, Volta, Ampere—were less humorous, but progress owes its existence to them.)

Here is an observation in which the hypothesis of hallucination is not even admissible, for there are two independent witnesses. It was sent to me from Strassburg, on June 17 of the same year, 1922:

My brother, Hubert Blanc, was Almoner of the Marist Brethren at Saint-Paul-Trois-Châteaux (Drôme). There was in the monastery a Brother who had been bedridden for a long time and was then *in extremis*. My brother went regularly to pass some minutes at his bedside. One day, in the course of conversation, the sick man said: "You know, Mr. Almoner, I shall not depart hence without taking leave of you." "I should hope not," said my brother in a tone of pleasantry.

Two or three days afterwards, my mother and my brother, having retired about 10 p.m., were hardly in bed when they heard at the same time, though their rooms were at a distance from each other, a well-marked noise of a key in the front door of the house, and then the steps of someone walking in the hall. Greatly disturbed, my mother called her son as loudly as she could, saying: "Hubert, somebody is in the house."

My brother, who had heard the same noises, arose at once, went through the rooms, found the hall door shut and nothing out of the ordinary. But hardly had that visitation taken place when the telephone bell sounded. "Hullo, hullo, Mr. Almoner, come quickly, so-and-so is dying." My brother hurried up and found in fact that the patient was breathing his last sigh.

This event, related by witnesses whose good faith cannot be doubted, produced a sensation in the monastery. The story was told me often by my mother and my brother. I authorise you to publish it if you think fit. My brother died at Grignan (Drôme) where he was parish priest.

MARIUS BLANC

(Technical Director of the Biscuit Works, "La Cigogne," Strassburg).

These manifestations and noises, the cries, the key in the lock, the steps in the hall, etc., are unexplained, and yet they were undoubtedly and incontestably observed. There are thousands like them. They cannot have been invented. (Those I have received number more than 5,600, and there are more in other countries.) It is nonsense to ascribe them all to practical jokers.

Out of the numerous letters received in connection with the article in question, I shall select the following, which I give *verbatim:*

DAMPIERRE, SEINE-ET-OISE.
June 16, 1922.

MONSIEUR ET ILLUSTRE MAÎTRE,

I pray you will excuse my indiscretion and importunity. Having this day read your article in *Le Journal,* I have remembered the following fact which I can certify as being true. I take the liberty of reporting it to you.

My grandfather, now deceased, who used to be a district surveyor, had retired. He descended one morning from his room and said: "Last night I dreamed a strange dream: M. J. P., our cousin, appeared to me and told me he had just died and asked me to accompany him to the notary, where he would communicate his will to me."

As my grandfather was saying this, the postman brought a telegram announcing the death of this cousin, whose illness had been unknown to us. We were very much struck by the coincidence. The subsequent reading of the will of M. J. P. astonished his family. He did not leave any of his goods to those he had loved. The heir was even accused of a forgery. Had M. J. P., when he appeared in the dream, wanted to call attention to the strangeness of his will? If you will read these lines you will, illustrious master, be able to draw a conclusion.

Je vous prie, etc.
PAUL BRUSTIER
(Of Dampierre, Tax-collector).

To these unexplained (and inexplicable) observations we could add a large number of similar ones. One may try to understand them by telepathic or unconscious transmission. But to deny them is absurd.

What is the explanation?

Before assuming the action of an intelligence outside ourselves, all normal hypotheses must be exhausted, not only that of an unconscious activity of the spirit, but also that of a memory from which nothing escapes. This vigorous procedure is necessary.

But let us go back to the case, above cited, of Robert Mackenzie and its interpretation. Let us analyse and dissect it. This demonstration is of such importance that all possible objections must be examined and rigorously weighed. The dream apparition of Robert Mackenzie, coming to defend himself against an imagined attack, raises several of these.

I shall mention at once that the account is extracted from my book *After Death,* slightly abridged for *Le Journal,* and that among the possible objections I pointed out in the book, that of "retarded suggestion." Since the public is, generally speaking, unacquainted with these studies, I did not mention it in the article. Let us here examine the hypothesis of a thought transference made by the dying person before his death to his employer, which remained latent in the brain of the recipient, and only manifested itself after the calm of a night of sleep. A reader sends me his comments which specify this objection very clearly, and also deal with the transmission of thought by the reading of the letter received by the engineer's wife.

It is possible [writes my honourable correspondent] that Mackenzie, in the course of his long agony, perceived the guesses of those about him without being able to answer them. The honest and timid youth was haunted in his delirium by the fixed idea to undeceive his benefactor, and to cry out the truth to him. And since his thought, being gagged, could not express itself in words, his instinct would no doubt seek, and possibly find, such means of communication as are admitted in the phenomena of telepathy, and which you do not deny. Would a message launched into space get through at once to the person intended, if he were not warned? In the first place, the factory owner, much absorbed in business—even in his dream, as the story shows—shows himself recalcitrant to the interview. Perhaps he had already several times dismissed this importunate buzzing. But the night, appeasing one by one the other dissonant voices, may have made his unconscious self more amenable to the imperceptible appeal. Harassed by the insistence of the phantom, he would at last give it audience. You know the rest.

But on what grounds can you maintain that it represents a being returning from the Beyond rather than one who was still living at the time of emission? Examples of retarded communications are quoted and accepted by you in analogous cases (see especially *Avant la Morte,* pp. 137 and 162). Why exclude them in the present case?

Besides, another hypothesis presents itself, inspired by your narrative itself: We know that a letter was already on its way, though unknown to the engineer. It brought him details of this tragic end. Its context was therefore of a nature to furnish his dream with the first elements of the scene, and the imagination—more imaginative than ever in the dream state—could easily bring out the dramatic element in the apparition. The remark, "You will know it soon," repeated three times by the phantom, does it not seem to you to be a clear and direct allusion to the imminent arrival of the letter which suggested it at a distance? And thus we come back to the rather less discussed phenomena of second sight, telepathy, etc. And these, to those who accept them, do not conclusively prove survival, which, after all, is the sole object of the controversy.

Your interpretation, dear master, is not excluded by mine. Both can subsist parallel to each other. But the fact that yours allows room for concurrent hypotheses makes it indecisive in itself.

GEORGES IZAMBARD.

NEUILLY, SEINE.

The above letter must be taken seriously (unlike the article of Clément Vautel). It puts forward two hypotheses towards an explanation. Let us examine the first of these. I can deal with it the better for having studied it for a long time.

Since the commencement of my enquiry in 1899 I have received more than 5,600 different psychic observations, and I had received 500 before I decided upon the enquiry. Of the quantity of psychic facts reported by societies devoted to such studies in France, England, Italy, Germany, or other countries I estimate that an equal number has come to my knowledge. This gives ten or eleven thousand at least. Among these there was none which equalled in all its aspects the case of Mackenzie. The narrative which approaches it most closely, and concerns a retarded cerebral impression, is that which can be read in vol. II. of *Death and its Mystery,* and which is specified above (p. 6): the sister of Louis Noell, a beautiful girl of eighteen, suddenly attacked by diphtheria during a walk at Perpignan, dying after a cruel agony and appearing after her death to her brother, a student at Montpellier. I have enumerated this fact, which is absolutely authentic and undeniable, among telepathic communications between the living, and not the dead, while leaving the door open for the latter hypothesis, for we must look for an explanation first in the mentality of the living. Frederick Myers, the discoverer of the "retarded latent impression," who studied it with so much care, admits that the retardation can only extend over a few hours, twelve at the most (*Human Personality,* vol. ii, p. 13), and that it is explained by the daily occupation of the brain which does not allow the impression to manifest itself until the spirit is sufficiently rested. On the day of the catastrophe, the student had been at a pleasure party. His sister was attacked on the afternoon of November 22 and died the next morning. The student did not get home until the evening of the 23rd, or rather at 2 a.m. next morning, went to bed quite elated, and at 4 a.m. saw in his dream his sister, pale and despairing, and calling him plaintively again and again. The hypothesis of retarded reception logically presents itself. The young man was not in a condition to receive his sister's appeal sooner. We therefore conceive this retardation of twenty-three hours after death, if we suppose that his sister desired his presence near her until she expired, feeling herself entirely lost.

Given the special situation of the percipient, it seems to me that we have a right to prolong the retardation of the impression felt, though it is usually limited to a few hours. Can we use this experience to explain the Mackenzie case? We cannot, since this sort of explanation no longer fits the reality.

I repeat that, among the thousands of cases, that of Louis Noell is the only one which to my knowledge can be compared with that of Mackenzie. Yet, what a difference! Let us examine it and analyse it.

Louis Noell feels the impression as soon as he is capable of it, the *first* night after the appeal, two hours after the moment when sleep commenced to liberate his brain.

The dream of Mackenzie's employer only took place the *second* night, forty-eight hours after the death. To apply the retardation hypothesis to this dream, it would be necessary to assume that the employer had not slept the night before—a pure assumption. There is no question of it in the account published by Myers himself (*Human Personality,* vol. ii, p. 52, "Phantasms of the Dead"), and there is no suspicion of a latent impression, though he himself originated that hypothesis. We should also have to suppose that the brain was unfit to perceive until after a second whole night of sleep, at the hour of waking. It therefore seems to me we must eliminate that explanation and that for retardation the Noell case is unique. There is a limit to the possible interval between emission and reception. The action of the deceased himself remains the most probable and admissible hypothesis.

As regards an explanation by thought transference on the arrival of the letter addressed to the engineer's wife, it is even less admissible, since that letter announced the suicide and not the error of interpretation. We should have to suppose that the reader of that letter had not believed it, but had imagined an error—another pure assumption. A telepathic reading of the letter by the sleeping engineer and combinations in his spirit? More hypotheses! There is no question of this in the direct original narrative. Note that Frederick Myers, the author, with Gurney and Podmore, of the celebrated work *Phantasms of the Living,* did not arrive at *Phantasms of the Dead* till after ten more years of contradictory discussions. And I am in the same case, as I did not accept manifestations of the dead until I found it impossible to explain the facts by acts of the living. The other hypotheses will not stand a rigorous and complete analysis.

Among the numerous letters written in search of a possible explanation based upon acts of the living or dying person—among others by Messrs. Grandmougin, Geoffriault, Clément de Saint-Marcq, Kontz, de Schildknecht, and Flobert—the majority invoke a thought transference due to the letter received by the engineer's wife. As we have seen, these two hypotheses do not apply. I have recalled them here to show once again that we look for the fullest light. It is a good example of a discussion in the French Press and is worthy of being referred to here, in spite of its great extent.

I may add that the cadaverous aspect of the "suicide"—livid flesh and spots symptomatic of fatal poisoning—supports better than all the other arguments the reality of this posthumous manifestation.

We may differ as to explanations and theories to account for the facts; but to deny the facts would be an inexcusable error.

Our first tendency is to attribute these various manifestations of the dead to telepathy among the living. But in some cases this interpretation breaks down. The authors of *Phantasms of the Living* quote in this connection (vol. i, p. 365) the case of Mrs. Menncer, who twice in the same night dreamt of seeing her brother headless, standing at the foot of his bed, with his head placed on a coffin beside him! She did not know where that brother was. His name was Mr. Wellington, and he was travelling abroad. In reality he was then at Sarawak with Sir James Brooke, and he was killed there during a Chinese insurrection. He had been taken for the son of the Rajah. His head was cut off and carried in triumph, and his body was burnt with the house of the Rajah. The date of the dream coincided approximately with the date of the murder. It is almost certain that his head was cut off after his death, for those Chinese were not soldiers but coolies in a gold mine who, having armed themselves with anything they could lay their hands on, could certainly not kill a European on the defensive by cutting off his head. We must therefore conclude that the impression made on the sister took place *after his head was cut off*.

The same volume of the *Phantasms* quotes another case, quite as conclusive, against the hypothesis of a telepathic communication before death. Here it is:

Mrs. Storie, of Edinburgh, when living at Hobart town, in Tasmania, one night had a strange, confused dream, resembling a series of distinct visions. She saw her twin brother sitting in the open on high ground and illuminated by oblique moonlight. He raised his arm, calling out: "The train! the train!" Something struck him, he fell down senseless, and a large black object passed by whistling. Then she saw a compartment in a train, in which she recognised Pastor Johnstone. After that she again saw her brother passing his right hand across his forehead, as if he were in suffering, and finally she heard an unknown voice announcing that her brother had just died.

That same night her brother had been killed by a train passing near the place where he had sat down to rest.

The details of this dream agreed with reality. The Rev. Mr. Johnstone was in the train which killed her brother. This fact was not known to the victim of the accident while he lived. The vision must, therefore, have been produced by the deceased who, at the moment when the train passed, acted upon his sister and let her see the fatal accident. It is not *before* his death that he acted thus, but at the moment of death, and after the fatal blow.

Logically and normally we must seek to attribute the phenomena to faculties of the living being as yet unknown to science, and I for one am the more inclined to do so, since Astronomy tells of stars which may no longer exist, but from which we receive to-day rays which have been emitted by them thousands of years ago. They are dead, yet they speak. But we must not be content with insufficient reasons.

It is quite natural—and, indeed, it is our duty—

to doubt the manifestations of the dead so long as there is no proof. We have a tendency to cast suspicion on all stories of manifestations of the dead, and in this attitude we are justified by their apparent improbability and the rarity of positive proof. In the first place, the sincerity of the narrators may be doubted. There are liars and jokers. In the second place, even when there is perfect sincerity, memory is not always faithful, and arrangements and exaggerations are possible. Besides, the problem is so grave in itself that we cannot and must not admit any observations but those which are indisputable. Furthermore, we must know how to interpret these observations, to show that they cannot be accounted for by known human faculties, and not to admit the action of deceased persons unless no other hypothesis is possible. All these elements of study can only be combined in the observer if he is himself well acquainted with this class of facts and, so to speak, knows what he is talking about.

In this connection I may point out that generally the strangest confusions creep into metapsychic studies among the public. To take a recent example, it appears that certain experiments undertaken in 1922 by three professors of the Sorbonne on the production of ectoplasm having led to a negative result, or, rather, an incomplete result, the conclusion has been drawn that there are no manifestations of the dead. What singular reasoning! What have any organic products issuing from the mouth or the nose of Miss A. or Miss B. to do with the immortality of the soul? Yet thousands of readers of the daily papers have agreed with such conclusions, which are as stupid as they are ridiculous.

Yes, we must know what we are talking about. If anybody came to me and said: "I have just been present at a railway accident. I saw the dead and wounded, and I assure you that the moon does not revolve round the earth," I should ask myself by what false reasoning that person may have proceeded from the train to the moon. But aberrations of this kind are of daily occurrence.

The observations which have been communicated to me by unknown persons do not differ from those sent in by persons whom I have known for a long time, and in whom I have as much confidence as I have in myself. If these are true there is no reason why the others should not be equally true. The class of practical jokers is small when it comes to the loss of a relative, a father, a mother, a wife, or a child. Those are sorrows which, as a rule, are not treated with loud laughter. These subjects are not played with. And sincerity has its own accent. "The style is the man," as Buffon said.

With these correspondents I am in the same case as I am with those who constantly send me from every part of the globe their various observations on astronomy and meteorology.

When a person writes that he has observed an eclipse, an occultation, a meteorite, a shooting star, a comet, a change on Jupiter or Mars, an aurora borealis, an earthquake, a storm, a peculiar lightning flash, a lunar rainbow, etc., I consider the communication to be made sincerely and in good faith, which does not hinder my examining and judging it. It may be objected that the situation is not identically the same, for an astronomical or meteorological observation may be made at the same time by other persons, and that gives a sort of control. No doubt. But, as regards my opinion of the observer's sincerity, the case is precisely the same: I give it the benefit of the doubt and reserve all rights of free examination.

In the case of telepathy and such cases the same human beings are in question. They have the same intellectual faculties. They are in a normal mental state and prove it by their own reflections. *A priori,* I have no more reason to distrust a savant, a professor, a magistrate, a priest, a clergyman, a manufacturer, or a farmer when he tells me of a psychic fact than when he speaks of a physical observation. Yet, because these phenomena are rarer and less credible, I set about investigating a large number, gathering information, and making enquiries which have almost always resulted in the direct confirmation of the narratives received.

That was also the practice of the Psychical Research Society of London. And in spite of certain variations in the narratives, certain obscurings of the memory, it is always found that the original fact is real and not invented.

But, if impostors are rare, illusions are plentiful. Their name is legion in this class of facts. The extent of human credulity is incredible! The style is also very characteristic. Yet, false money does not disprove the existence of the real article.

What is perhaps most difficult is for a man to be entirely independent, to say what he thinks and knows without considering what opinion is held of him by others. *Vitam impendere vero,* "to consecrate one's life to Truth." It was a noble device of Juvenal and Jean-Jacques Rousseau, but it usually produces nothing but enemies. For humanity is, above all, a coarse, barbarous, ignorant, cowardly, and hypocritical race.

What is perhaps yet more curious is that the free search for truth is distasteful to everybody, for every brain has its little prejudices which it will not give up.

If I say, for instance, that the survival of the

soul, already rendered probable by philosophy, will soon be experimentally proved by psychic science, more than one sceptic will smile at my contention.

If, on the other hand, I say that the spiritualist who calls up Socrates or Newton, Archimedes or Saint Augustine, to his little table, and imagines he is conversing with them, is the victim of an illusion, there is quite a crowd which will collect stones to stone me.

Well, even though the trail of projectiles flung at me continue, I shall declare as follows: *The human being is not yet known to naturalists, nor to physiologists, nor to philosophers.*

A person who dies at Marseilles can appear at the same moment at Paris, at Algiers, in America, or in China, and can do so without changing place.

A young girl waltzing with a beloved fiancé can suddenly see her dead mother enter the drawing-room and call out that she is dying a thousand miles away.

A man passing along a street under the windows of his mistress can appear to the latter in her room without leaving the street.

Thought can act upon the thought of another person without the help of the senses.

One may see in a dream a country he has never seen before, and see himself in that country as he will be ten years later.

The Future is perceptible, like the Past. The Present alone does not exist, since scientific analysis reduces it to less than a hundredth of a second.

Space and time, as presented to us by our measuring instruments, do not exist. Instead, there is infinity and there is eternity. The distance between here and Sirius is not a greater part of the infinite than the distance between your right hand and your left. Electricity has already accustomed us to rapid transmissions over great distances. Light and electricity do not take as much as two seconds to traverse the distance between the earth and the moon.

Matter, also, is not what it appears to us to be.

On the whole, the science of all the academies of the globe represents an immense ignorance.

We know nothing exact, precise, or absolute about anything, and we are surrounded by forces as yet unknown; let nobody, therefore, have the presumption to say, "This is impossible," or "That is possible." We have only one right—that of being modest, especially as to what concerns life and death. We live in the middle of the unknown. But it is beautiful, it is good, it is useful to seek.

Laplace reasoned exactly when he wrote in his *Analytical Theory of Probability:* "We are so far from knowing all the agencies of nature, and their various modes of action, that it would be unbecoming in a philosopher to deny the phenomena simply because they are inexplicable in the present state of our knowledge. Only we must examine them with an attention which is the more scrupulous the more difficult it appears to be to admit them. And the calculus of probabilities becomes indispensable for determining how far the observations must be multiplied in order to obtain in favour of the agents indicated by them a probability superior to the reasons one may have for rejecting them."

This argument of the immortal French astronomer confirms the ruling spirit of our present work on metapsychical problems. Let us also remember that he published those remarks in connection with animal magnetism and the divining-rod. I ask my readers to weigh that last phrase in applying it to the *number* of observations already specified. With Laplace we are in good company. Let us continue.

Certain objections end by becoming annoying. Among these is the observation that, in order that an observation be of scientific value, we must be able to renew it at will. It amounts to saying that a lightning flash has not existed because one cannot have it over again; that the fall of a meteorite is inadmissible because we cannot reproduce it at will; that an eclipse is a fable because it is necessary to await certain luni-solar conditions for its recurrence; that an earthquake has not occurred because we cannot repeat it. It is confusing two orders of things which are entirely distinct: observation and experiment. We observe a spontaneous phenomenon; experimentally we manufacture a chemical compound. Now it is not rare to find this sort of fallacy even among men used to scientific methods. Astronomy and meteorology are observational sciences. Mechanics is an experimental science.

Must the manifestations of the dead be admitted to the class of facts scientifically demonstrated by means of sufficient observations? That is the question, and it is useless to complicate it by bringing in side issues.

The amount of armour which was buckled on against manifestations of the dead on the occasion of the publication of my third volume of my work induces me to insist upon the certain reality of those manifestations. The witnesses are innumerable. To refuse to admit them means accusing the narrators of malobservation, of illusion, or even of falsehood. These accusations are sometime applicable, but not generally. Let us examine, coolly and carefully, some of these accounts of manifestations of the dead. We may begin with one of the oldest.

This ancient testimony, already known to my readers because they saw it in *Uranie,* is from a writer greatly esteemed for the strictness of his judgment and the care he bestowed upon all his writings. It is the history of the two travellers of Megara, related by Cicero.[1] Here it is:

Two friends arrived in Megara and went to lodge separately. Hardly had one of them gone to sleep when he saw before him his travelling companion, who told him, with an air of dejection, that his host had decided to murder him, and asked him to come to his aid as quickly as possible. He awoke, but concluding that he had been misled by a dream, he soon went to sleep again. His friend appeared again and implored him to hasten, as the murderers were entering the room. Feeling more concerned this time, he marvelled at the persistence of the dream and prepared to go to his friend. But reason and fatigue triumphed, and he lay down again. Then his friend showed himself for the third time, pale, bleeding, and disfigured. "Unhappy one," he said, "you did not come when I implored you to do so. The deed is done. Now you must avenge me. At sunrise you will meet at the gate of the town a cart filled with dung. Stop it and order them to empty it. You will find my body hidden in the middle of it. See that the honours of sepulture are paid to me and pursue my murderers." Such tenacity and such consistent details left no room for hesitation. The friend arose, ran to the gate indicated, found the cart, arrested the driver, who showed confusion, and after the first search the body of his friend was discovered.

That is the narrative of the famous Latin author. What must we think of it? We may object that perhaps the story did not happen as told by Cicero; that it has been amplified and exaggerated; that two friends arriving in a strange town might well fear a mishap; that fear for the safety of a friend, after the fatigues of a journey, in the middle of the night, might induce one to dream that he is the

[1] *De Divinatione*, i., 27.

victim of a murder. As regards the episode of the cart, the travellers might have seen one in the yard of their host, and association of ideas might bring it into the dream. All these explanatory hypotheses might be made. But they would only be hypotheses.

Are they satisfactory? I, for one, am not satisfied at all, and it seems to me that Cicero would not have told this story as an example of divination in dreams, had he not had good reason to believe it. Without astonishment, he adds: "What could be called diviner than this dream?"

It is difficult to suppress this passage of Cicero with a stroke of the pen. Those most opposed to survival do not dare to do so, and even refer to the narrative as a special curiosity, Brière de Boismont as a "hallucination," Charles Richet as a "metapsychic phenomenon," etc. But what do these words teach us? Do they not simply hide the truth we want to discover? If we admit the narrative as it stands, we must assume that the murdered friend really announced his death as well as the circumstances leading up to it.

I shall be told: "This is not certain." Agreed. It is not as certain as if you received a blow with a fist on the nose or a revolver bullet in your heart, and that is why I wrote that there are gradations between probability and certainty. But the strict duty of every sincere man is to exercise his judgment freely. Of the reader I only ask attention and sincerity. We can suppose that Cicero *invented* this story.

Well. Observations of this kind are numerous. To attribute them to hallucination or to chance coincidence is not a satisfactory explanation. It explains nothing.

A mass of ignorant people, of every age and every calling, people of private fortune, commercial people, sceptics by temperament or by inclination, simply declare that they do not believe these stories and that there is no truth in them. That is not a serious solution either. Minds accustomed to careful study cannot be satisfied with such light-hearted denials.

A fact is a fact. We cannot help admitting it, even when it is impossible to explain in the present state of our knowledge.

It is true that medical records show that there are hallucinations of more than one kind and that certain nervous organisations are misled by them. But between that fact and the conclusions that all unexplained psycho-biological conclusions are hallucinations there is an abyss.

The scientific spirit of our age rightly seeks to free all these facts from the deceptive mists of supernaturalism, since nothing is supernatural, and since nature, whose kingdom is infinite, includes everything.

We see at the present time journalists, either in ignorance or in bad faith, declare that all these recitals of apparitions and manifestations of the dead are made by people of no intellectual value. Can we thus describe Cicero? Or Montaigne, or La Rochefoucauld, or Goethe, or all who have dealt with our subject?

Here is another observation, also well known to my readers, and due to Lord Brougham, reported by that eminent personage himself, who was, as everybody knows, a member of the Institut de France and a Fellow of the Royal Society.

People of my generation saw that fine old man in Paris or at Cannes, where he died in 1868. (He was born in Edinburgh in 1778.) This thinker wrote his autobiography and published the following extract from it on October 16, 1862. The accuracy of this recollection, which dates back to 1799, has never been placed in any doubt; the celebrated English politician and historian was only 21 then and was travelling in Sweden.

> The weather was cold [he writes]. Arriving at Gothenburg in a comfortable-looking inn, I asked for a hot bath, and then I was the subject of an adventure so curious that I must tell it from the beginning.
>
> I had a college friend at the High School, called G., whom I particularly liked and admired. We often conversed on the great subject of the immortality of the soul. One day we were so foolish as to make an agreement, written in our own blood, which declared that whichever of us died first should come and manifest himself to the other in order to dispel any doubt we might have retained concerning the continuation of life after death. G. left for India, and I almost forgot his existence.
>
> As I have said, I had plunged into my bath, and was enjoying the delicious warmth which heated my stiffened limbs, when, on preparing to get out, I glanced at the chair on the which I had left my clothes, and what was my amazement at seeing, seated on that chair, my friend G., who was gazing at me quietly! How I got out of the bath I cannot say, for when I recovered my senses I found myself lying on the floor. The apparition, or whatever the phenomenon was which simulated my friend, was no longer there. I was so much impressed that I wanted to write down all the details at once, with the date, which was December 19.

Lord Brougham adds that on his return to Edinburgh he found a letter from India which announced the death of his friend. It took place on December 19.

It seems to me that Lord Brougham is no more a negligible quantity than Cicero, and that this observation must also be taken seriously. I agree that it only represents a probability, but does not that probability approach certainty? I first thought of an illusion suggested by the arrangement of the clothes on the chair; but (1) the resemblance was both striking and unexpected, and (2) the coincidence of the death with the promise made strongly supports the vision.

One of the most learned members of our Metapsychic Institute, Professor Richet, does not accept survival, though it does seem to follow from these observations. Yet he himself, in his monumental *Traité des Métapsychique*, quotes several facts which, like the two last, point to the same conclusion. Here is one of them:

> M. Belbéder, of the 6th Colonial Regiment, had gone to spend his holidays with friends at Ribérac (Dordogne). At the moment of going to sleep he saw a white transparent shadow which came from the fireplace, advanced towards the bed, and said to his inner ear: "Always be a friend to my son." As the shadow rose slowly he recognised the mother of one of his best friends, whom he had left in good health. He got up to find if it had been an illusion. There was no moon, and the night was very dark. The person whom he had recognised had, in fact, died two hours before.

Well, if that mother had died two hours previously, why attribute this observation to a mysterious cryptæsthesia, a word which requires previous definition? Are we not often satisfied with *words?* To say that one "sees what is hidden" is no more an explanation than "lucidity."

Another example from the same author:

> Miss Beale, then fourteen years of age, saw coming into her room in the middle of the night the figure of a man in a flowing dressing-gown. He seemed to feel his way with his hand; then he disappeared. Miss B., much frightened, called one of her companions who slept in the

same room. The latter said: "That is my brother C., no doubt." Next morning at breakfast the brother said he had not come, but he had also seen at the same time a form which he had recognised as the shadow of a friend (who was in bad health, but not supposed to be in danger) who had once said to him: "Whichever of us dies first shall come and see the other." In reality, that friend had died the same night, as was found afterwards.

The deceased had come to redeem a promise. Why not admit it? Cryptæsthesia, or lucidity, do they explain the act? Has death nothing to do with it? That is what we want to know.

Another example quoted in the same work, and which I also published (*Death and Its Mystery,* iii, p. 144):

Miss Stella, then seventeen years of age, saw coming into her room a young friend of the same age, a fraternal comrade. The door opened [she writes], and I saw him enter. I rose to offer him a chair near the fire, for he seemed to be cold and had no overcoat, although it was snowing. I began to scold him for going out without wrapping up properly. Instead of replying, he placed his hand on his chest and on his head. I was still talking when Dr. G. came in and asked to whom I was talking. "Here," I said, "this troublesome boy without an overcoat, with such a bad cold that he cannot speak. Lend him an overcoat and send him home." I shall never forget the horror and amazement shown on the face of the doctor, for Bertie had died barely twenty minutes before. I had heard the latch of the door turn and the door open. He had walked into the room and sat down while I lighted the candles.

The young man had certainly died. Miss Stella did not know it. He had really shown himself to her. That is what must be explained.

It is alleged that our proofs are insufficient, but no allowance is made for the fact that the proofs we can, and must, demand in these researches are not of the same order as those to which we are accustomed in our laboratories and our physical experiments. The dead are not at our disposal. We are forced to rely on the good faith of the narrators, on their honesty and their conscience. If a good woman writes to me, with the tears from her eyes falling on the paper, that she has seen a vision of her husband who was buried the night before, I can imagine an illusion of sight, but not a story invented by her to trap me, nor that the advice she asks for her consolation in her distress is pure comedy. If a person falls ill as the result of an apparition, I cannot see in that circumstance a snare for my credulity, and so on. None of these objections are serious. When our information shows that we have to do with honest people, does not the simplest common sense enjoin upon us to accept the narratives, to control them as best we can, and to interpret them with attentive care, after eliminating cases of illusion and hallucination? I have too often published the precautions taken against practical jokers and impostors to be obliged to specify them again. As a rule, they are unaware of their own superficial and incompetent contradictions.

Nothing remains seriously admissible but the illusive hypothesis, which is only rarely applicable and often inadequate from every point of view, as in the following case:

On Friday, August 22, 1890, at 10 a.m., a certain Mr. Russell, precentor of the Church of St. Luke, San Francisco, fell down in the street with a stroke of apoplexy, at the corner of Sutter Street and Mason Street, and was taken to his house, where he died at 11 a.m. He was to have gone the next day, Saturday, to practise a certain piece of music. Now on this Friday afternoon, the music master, Mr. Reeves, looked for the piece of music to be sung on the following Sunday, when, on leaving his room, he saw the precentor on the staircase, holding a sheet of music in one hand and raising the other to his forehead. "He seemed so real, so living," said Mr. Reeves, "that I went forward at once to shake hands and bid him welcome. But he evaporated, like a cloud disappearing in air." (For details see *Death and Its Mystery*, iii, p. 73.)

The startled observer cried out: "Oh, my God!" His sister and niece rushed forward, and he wanted to tell them what he had seen, but he could not speak. He was ill for several days in spite of his normally sound health, his strong constitution, and his very sceptical temperament. He did not know of the death, which had happened three hours before. His cry was heard by three witnesses. The vision was seen in a perfectly normal state, awake in broad daylight, and not in a dream, so that a hypnotic hallucination cannot even be imagined.

This narrative, accurate in its smallest details, and confirmed by the Rector of St. Luke's, Mr. Davis, who sent it to Professor Adams, of Cambridge, can hardly be treated as "humbug" or as "stuff and nonsense," as many critics wish me to do. Does not common sense authorize us simply to turn our backs on these people? To deny such an observation is to deny everything.

We are often told that we must not believe everything we hear, and that there are tricksters and impostors about. This I have said myself a dozen times. But there are cases when invention is not imaginable, and this is one of them.

The word "coincidence" also often comes from the lips of critics. I should like to know what business that word has here. Is there no such thing as cause and effect? Is not the defunct person the cause of the apparition?

Do you not think, dear readers, that it is time to become positive in our statements and to declare definitely the proved truth: *The dead continue to live.*

Let us now go into the following observation:

I had a friend of the name of Charles, a young man of sixteen [writes a correspondent]. It was in 1908. One evening, on coming home, I heard my name called several times very clearly, and I recognised the voice. It was troubled, imploring, but very soft.

Much concerned in spite of myself, I only got to sleep very late, and almost immediately afterwards I was awakened by a touch on my forehead and a voice calling me. I distinctly saw Charles at my bedside and he said: "Good-bye, good-bye, I am all right; console my people," and he slowly disappeared. Then, nothing more!

In the morning I rushed round to our friends. They were much perturbed, as Charles had not come home that night.

Instinctively, for some unknown reason, I thought of a little property they had in the country, and, confiding my fears to the family I took them there. In the garden, in an arbour, we found his body on the ground. In his right hand he held a flask, which contained traces of cyanide.

He had died by his own hand and had told me by that manifestation.

That, dear master, is what I can guarantee as being exact, and which you may investigate if you like.

Henry Bourgeois
(Of Mâcon).

The connection between the manifestation and the act of suicide is certain.

To invoke the subconscious, or the subliminal, or anything else you please, does not furnish us the solution of this vision or audition. We can find no other explanation but the act of the suicide himself. And he acted *after his death.*

I should also like to know how one can explain —and what right one has to deny—the following observation, due to my colleague of the Royal Astronomical Society of London, the Rev. Charles Tweedale:

On Friday, the 10th of January, 1879, having awakened out of a first sleep, I saw the moon shining in by a southern window and lighting up my room. My eyes were attracted towards the panels of a cupboard let into the wall, which served as a press. I suddenly saw a form appearing before me on the panels of the cupboard. Dim at first, it became gradually clearer, until I recognised my grandmother's face. I observed her for several seconds, when the vision slowly faded and disappeared. A peculiarity struck me and engraved itself on my memory. It was that my grandmother's head was covered in the old fashion with a gophered bonnet. I was not at all startled, but thought that I was the victim of an illusion due to the moonlight, so I turned over and went to sleep again.

The next morning at breakfast I commenced to tell the story of the nocturnal apparition, when, to my great surprise, my father abruptly left the table in great agitation and went out of the room. I asked my mother for an explanation. She motioned me to be silent. When the door was closed she said to me: "Charles, I am going to tell you the strangest story I ever heard. This morning your father told me that he awoke in the night, and that he saw his mother standing by his bedside, but that when he tried to speak to her she was gone."

This conversation took place about 8.30 on the morning of Saturday, January 11. Before noon we received a telegram to say that my grandmother had died in the night. But that was not the end of the story, for my father heard afterwards that my sister, who lived twenty miles away, had also seen my grandmother appear. Thus, three persons, independently of each other, had the same vision. My father noted the exact hour—2 a.m.

I am certain that the moon was not far from the meridian at the time of the apparition, and that it was about two, which is a notable confirmation of the time noted by my father. My aunt also put the instant of the apparition she had witnessed *after* the death, which took place at a quarter past twelve. Hence we may conclude that the deceased, though apparently dead, was sufficiently alive some hours afterwards to manifest herself to different persons separated from each other by considerable distances.

On the subject of the "apparel of spirits," I wrote to my uncle asking him for information on certain points. Here is an extract from his reply:

"You ask me whether the sketch of the bonnet which you send me has any analogy with the mortuary head-dress of the deceased. The resemblance is striking. It is, indeed, the gophered bonnet which your grandmother wore all the time she was ill, and your whole description of the phantom agrees with the aspect of the dying person at the moment of her death. That is the plain truth, and I can, if necessary, give you my oath to it."

The fact I have related has so many guaranties of authenticity that it cannot be treated with any suspicion.

CHARLES TWEEDALE, F.R.A.S.

I considered it useful to give the above narrative in full. It is noteworthy in that it records an observation made an hour and three-quarters after the death, and seen independently by three persons. The death took place a quarter of an hour after midnight, and the apparition was seen at two o'clock.

What is the explanation?

It is obviously impossible here to imagine any sort of fraud.

Illusion or hallucination of those independent witnesses seems to me inadmissible. The narrator declares that for him and for his father the phantom was there objectively, and the bonnet is adduced as proof. It seems to me that the reality of the apparition may be interpreted in the sense that the deceased acted upon the spirits of her children, and that this suggestion translated itself into an image.

A dead person can act at a distance upon a living being, and can manifest in some form or other, no doubt, by producing an impression on the brain.

Whatever may be the interpretation, the apparition itself cannot be denied.

Next we have a ghost, clearly seen and well examined by the observer, and the narrative is given by the witness himself:[2]

In 1880 I succeeded a Mr. Q. as librarian of the X. Library. I had never see Mr. Q., nor any photograph or likeness of him, when the following incidents occurred. I may, of course, have heard the library assistants describe his appearance, though I have no recollection of this. I was sitting alone in the library one evening late in March, 1884, finishing some work after hours, when it suddenly occurred to me that I should miss the last train to H., where I was then living, if I did not make haste. It was then 10.55, and the last train left X. at 11.5. I gathered up some books in one hand, took the lamp in the other, and prepared to leave the librarian's room, which communicated by a passage with the main room of the library. As my lamp illumined this passage, I saw, apparently at the further end of it, a man's face. I instantly thought a thief had got into the library. This was by no means impossible, and the probability of it had occurred to me before. I turned back into my room, put down the books, and took a revolver from the safe, and, holding the lamp cautiously behind me, I made my way along the passage—which had a corner, behind which I thought my thief might be lying in wait—into the main room. Here I saw no one, but the room was large and encumbered with bookcases. I called out loudly to the intruder to show himself several times, more with the hope of attracting a passing policeman than of drawing the intruder. Then I saw a face looking round one of the bookcases. I say looking *round*, but it had an odd appearance, as if the *body* were *in* the

[2] Frank Podmore, *Apparitions and Thought Transference*, p. 312, 1894.

bookcase, as the face came so closely to the edge and I could see no body. The face was pallid and hairless, and the orbits of the eyes were very deep. I advanced towards it, and as I did so I saw an old man with high shoulders seem to *rotate* out of the end of the bookcase, and with his back towards me and with a shuffling gait walk rather quickly from the bookcase to the door of a small lavatory, which opened from the library and had no other access. I heard no noise. I followed the man at once into the lavatory, and to my extreme surprise found no one there. I examined the window (about 14 inches by 12 inches), and found it closed and fastened. I opened it and looked out. It opened into a well, the bottom of which, 10 feet below, was a skylight, and the top open to the sky some 20 feet above. It was in the middle of the building, and no one could have dropped into it without smashing the glass, nor climbed out of it without a ladder—but no one was there. Nor had there been anything like time for a man to get out of the window, as I followed the intruder instantly. Completely mystified, I even looked into the little cupboard under the fixed basin. There was nowhere hiding for a child, and I confess I began to experience for the first time what novelists describe as an "eerie" feeling.

I left the library, and found I had missed my train.

Next morning I mentioned what I had seen to a local clergyman, who, on hearing my description, said, "Why, that's old Q." Soon after I saw a photograph (from a drawing) of Q., and the resemblance was certainly striking. Q. had lost all his hair, eyebrows and all, from, I believe, a gunpowder accident. His walk was a peculiar, rapid, high-shouldered shuffle.

Mr. Podmore adds:

Later enquiry proved he had died about the time of the year at which I saw the figure.

This observation is equally inexplicable without the hypothesis of a personal action of the deceased. Is it, then, possible that the dead sometimes continue their terrestrial habits? There is more than one example of it, but the mystery remains, because their visibility is the outstanding problem. Podmore frankly admits that an extension of the hypothesis of thought transference "has seemed to some extravagant." But to go so far as to suppose that some unknown person at that very moment had thought of the old librarian, and that this thought had given birth to the vision of his successor, who followed the shade walking the library and disappearing at the end of the passage, is an hypothesis of an audacious temerity much farther removed from probability than the admission of the phantom as an image projected by the thought of the deceased, a very clear phantom, and sufficiently material to be taken for a thief and pursued by the observer, armed with a revolver.

I also submit to the imperial reader's most serious attention the following observations extracted from Richet's *Traité de Métapsychique* (p. 403):

A certain Mr. L. V., of Bordeaux, sitting at his desk, has the sensation that the door opens. He turns a little in the direction of the door, and sees for a very short time his uncle G. A quarter of an hour afterwards a telegram arrives to say that his uncle has committed suicide. The warning came at 9.30, while the suicide was at 5 o'clock. The telegram had reached the Bordeaux post office at 8 o'clock.

There is an observation made, not in a dream, but in quite the normal state. (I regret once more that people dare not give their names in full, but we must take the world as we find it.) This uncle appeared to his nephew four and a half hours after his death. This is what we must admit and explain.

Another observation (p. 409):

Madame X. sees, on December 28, 1906, at 11 p.m., at her bed the form of a woman, whose features and details of dress she can clearly make out. This form said, with a muffled voice: "I am Hélène Ram. I shall come and take you away, and we shall be together in the next world." Mme. Hélène Ram had died at Hyères on December 28, at 4 a.m. So it was nineteen hours after the death that the apparition took place. The details of clothing were exact. Mme. Ram had not been ill, and Mme. X. knew her but slightly.

I have too great a respect for Professor Richet's sincerity to refrain from expressing the difficulty in reconciling his negation of survival with the examples quoted by himself. As regards explaining the apparitions, that is another matter.

I shall also ask my illustrious friend how he accepts the following observation, which he also quotes (p. 436) without also admitting the cause of the apparition:

Miss K. was caressing a kitten in her lap, when suddenly the animal got restless, rose, spit, and arched its back with every sign of terror. Then Miss K. saw in an easy-chair close beside her, an old hag, with an ugly, wrinkled face, fixing an evil gaze upon her. The kitten went wild, and jumped frantically against the door. The terrified lady called for help. Her mother came, but the phantom had disappeared. It had remained visible for about five minutes. It appears that in the same room an old woman had once hanged herself.

Once more, how can we accept all these facts without associating them with the dead? We shall be reduced to seeing in them nothing but hallucinations without a cause, which yet coincide with deaths which took place a more or less long time before.

And this further observation made by two witnesses. An Italian reader, Countess Carandini, gives me this fact:

One evening, towards 9 o'clock, when everybody was still busy, my sister, aged seventeen, in passing along the corridor of our dwelling, was amazed to see, standing close to her under the gas light, a tall and beautiful girl, dressed like a peasant, whom she did not know. She cried out, and the phantom disappeared. She wept with terror, and her mother scolded her. Next morning the cook, a girl of about twenty-five, came to tell my mother that the evening before, when she had gone to bed, she had heard a breath and felt something like breathing on her face. Opening her eyes, she had seen, standing by her bed, one of her friends from the country, a tall and beautiful girl, dressed in peasant garb. This pretty girl, said the cook, had behaved badly, and she had often given her good advice. She had died the day before.

The old and rather trite hypothesis of hallucination, does it apply here also? Surely not. There are two independent impressions without assignable cause, since the death was unknown. We can always assume that it was not true, that the story was invented, that the first girl was under an illusion, and the second girl a liar, etc. But when these stories are numbered by thousands and come from every country in the world, we are called upon to examine them seriously.

Let us approach this examination with an open mind.

The apparition of the dead can no longer be denied. Let us recapitulate the last observations described, without enumerating any preceding ones:

1. The story told by Cicero.
2. Lord Brougham's story.
3. The mother of M. Belbéder's friend, dead two hours.
4. The deceased person appearing to Miss Beale.
5. The companion of Mlle. Stella, dead for twenty minutes.

6. The precentor Russell, dead in an accident.
7. Charles, who committed suicide.
8. The grandmother of the astronomer Tweedale.
9. The English librarian.
10. The apparition of an uncle to his nephew at Bordeaux.
11. The apparition of Mme. Hélène Ram, twenty hours after her (unknown) death.
12. The old woman seen by the kitten.
13. The double observation reported by Countess Carandini.

A total of thirteen observations, to which we can only oppose arbitrary undemonstrable negations. Let us admit that the two first are less radically established than those which follow them; they yet compel our attention.

If we only consider these thirteen cases we find that their degree of probability is equal to what in all human affairs is called a certainty.

And how many other examples could we not add to this small selection, if only that of the mother, dead for several weeks, who appeared to her children as they played in a passage and stopped them at the moment when they were approaching a pit into which they would have fallen (vol. iii, p. 251). This is another quite typical proof of survival. But I need not repeat here what has been said and proved in vol. iii.

He who denies the reality of psychic phenomena proves his ignorance or untruthfulness. So wrote Victor Hugo after his Jersey experiences. The dilemma is a radical one. There is no escape from it. One must be either ignorant or dishonest to deny these phenomena. All independent people who have wished to observe them without prejudice have confirmed them with certainty. They can be imitated or fraudulently simulated, just as one may say a mass without believing in it, or take the place of a priest in the confessional, or as one can cheat at cards, or make false coins. But these practices prove nothing against truth, and they only serve to spread slanderous and absurd interpretations among the public.

Instead of denying all these facts and ridiculing them, it would be wiser to look for the best interpretation, to discuss them freely, to respect and study them, and obtain guidance towards the solution of what is—especially now—the greatest of problems.

These determinations are of the highest philosophical import. I should like to say of psychic phenomena what the mathematician Henri Poincaré said in 1911 of the spiral nebulæ: "This spiral form occurs much too often to suppose it is due to chance. It is clear how incomplete is any cosmogonic theory which ignores it."[3] In the same way, psychic phenomena can now no longer be eliminated or neglected by any philosophical theory. They must form an integral part of the study of man.

Formerly the spiral nebulæ were unknown. They have only slowly and gradually been discovered and studied. At first they were not believed in, but attributed to instrumental illusions. When, in the year 1858, I entered the Paris Observatory at the age of sixteen as an astronomer in training, I heard them say that they were false images due to the telescope of Lord Rosse, which was probably moulded on optical curves producing those images. At present they are becoming the essential element of sidereal astronomy. It seems to me that psychic phenomena holds the same position as regards the

---

[3] Henri Poincaré, *Leçons sur les hypothèses cosmogoniques*, p. 24.

complete knowledge of the human being and his destiny.

The sphere of human reasoning is, in general, very narrow.

There is no case of a savant sceptical with regard to these phenomena who took the trouble to examine these phenomena to a sufficient extent who did not arrive at a conclusion in their favour: Crookes, the physicist; Wallace, the naturalist; Lord Lindsay; Varley, the engineer; Zöllner, the astronomer; Richet, the physiologist; Lombroso, the physician; Morselli, the university professor; Professor Sir Oliver Lodge, and many others, bear eloquent testimony.

The critics who, from the height of their ignorant greatness, judge the seekers occupied in scrutinising psychic phenomena, and treat those who admit the existence of the soul as simpletons, remind me of those geologists who, after examining the surface of the terrestrial globe to the thickness of a mile, make a classical determination of the interior of our planet, whose diameter is 8,000 miles, and fix the thermometric degrees of heat at the centre of our globe!

Science advances and progresses in all its branches. We have just quoted the opinion of Victor Hugo. We may read in his *Postscript of My Life*: "From Francœur to Flammarion, telescopic stars have increased from 60 millions to 100 millions." The poet died in 1885. If he were still alive, what would he say now? Francœur's *Uranographie* dates back to 1830, my own *Astronomie Populaire* to 1880. Astronomical discoveries have been multiplied tenfold since that last epoch, as have those of physics and those of metapsychics. We have seen determinations relating to survival which are forced upon our attention and upon our philosophy. Yes, progress is there; but how many obstacles on the way!

The readers of my books on this vast subject who know the considerable number of observations received (letters on the subject alone amount to more than 5,600 to date) know that the complete publication of these observations and their verification would represent some twenty volumes of the dimensions of this one, and that I have therefore only been able to give summaries and extracts. But apart from the lack of space for publishing these confirmatory attestations, it should be noted that these confirmations are often refused for reasons of sentiment and family scruples. Thus we may read in the chapter of the *Inconnu* (p. 181) devoted to the manifestations of the dying:

> One of my cousins was seriously ill of typhoid fever; his parents never left his bedside, and watched him day and night. But one evening, when they were both at the end of their strength, the nurse constrained them to take a little rest, promising to call them on the slightest alarm. They had just fallen into a deep sleep when they started up on hearing the door opening. My uncle called out: "Who is there?" My aunt, convinced that they were being called, got up at once; but she was hardly seated on her bed when she felt somebody embracing her closely and saying: "It is myself, mother; I am going away. Do not weep. Good-bye." And the door closed quite softly. Barely recovering from her emotion, my aunt ran into her child's room, whither her husband had preceded her. There she learned that my cousin had just breathed his last.
>
> MME. ACKERET.
>
> ALGIERS,
> *April* 25, 1899.

In accordance with my scientific method, I made an enquiry from the person who had sent me that narrative, explaining to her that illusions and hallucinations are always possible, and that it would be advisable for her to consider the value of the story. Here is her reply:

ALGIERS,
May 3, 1899.

DEAR MASTER,

In spite of my great wish to satisfy you by asking my aunt to give you an account of the fact I related herself, I cannot do so. My aunt has always desired to keep that memory of her son to herself, thinking that perhaps she would profane it by speaking of it to strangers, and she has only mentioned it to her family. It is a joy to these poor people to think of the last leave-taking of their son. I do not wish to tell her that I have committed this little indiscretion in your favour, as I only did it to benefit your noble work and to enable you to add one more example to the very conclusive ones you have already made known. Certainly there has been no hallucination or illusion. My uncle and aunt, who live in the country in Alsace, were quite incredulous in all these matters. On hearing similar stories they would laugh and treat the people as fools. Now they laugh at those who do not believe it, and this memory is always to them a tender emotion, as they are sure that their dear son did not wish to leave them without saying good-bye.

M. ACKERET.

This is not the only case. It is ten times, fifty times, a hundred times that similar reservations have been made with respect to the desired confirmations. Do these reservations hinder us from acknowledging the authenticity of the narratives? Surely not. They are worthy of respect. I am the more grateful to those strong souls who knew how to dominate their sorrows and to yield their precious testimony for the advancement of science.

Doubtless these posthumous allegations astonish us, and seem improbable. But reality often is improbable. Boileau said it before: "The truth may sometimes not be probable."

If I were to say that I am the contemporary of a lady whose husband spoke to Louis XIV. it would naturally cause surprise. Well, Dr. Legrand showed us that in 1862 the Duchess de Richelieu could say to Napoleon III. in the course of light conversation: "Sire, Louis XIV. said to my husband . . ." That was in 1710. In 1786, at the age of sixteen, she had married the Duke de Richelieu, who was then ninety, and she herself was ninety-two in 1862. The Duke was born in 1696, and Louis XIV. died in 1715. The Duke, a grand-nephew of the Cardinal, had been presented to the great king at the age of fourteen, on the occasion of his first marriage. I myself was twenty years of age in 1862, and I could easily have heard with my own ears a person connected with a contemporary of Louis XIV. So indeed, truth may sometimes be improbable. I write these lines in 1923. Let us never deny anything.

French writers of the nineteenth century, and even of the twentieth century, generally show a complete ignorance of psychic phenomena. There are but two exceptions, and they accept them: Victor Hugo and Guy de Maupassant. I do not speak of philosophers or special authors, but of literary and scientific men. Generally they disdain these facts. They even take a sort of pleasure in ignoring them.

I have no other object but to convince my own readers, and I only claim their attention, their thirst for knowledge, their freedom of conscience, and their desire to know the truth. It seems to me that their conviction is now fixed. The survival of the soul is proved by positive experimental observation. For the present, at least, we find no other explanation of the facts in the state of our knowledge to date. We seek sincerely and with complete independence of spirit. The science of the future has perhaps some unexpected discoveries in store, which may transform our whole philosophic structure.

What is the duration of this survival? Does it amount to the immortality of the soul?

In principle, there is no reason to suppose that, if it survives the body by virtue of its own nature, it should be destined to a future destruction. That is a metaphysical question outside the realm of scientific observation to which this work is confined. Observation can only prove that which is contemporaneous with it. In the present researches we do not prove immortality, but only survival for a certain time.

In the thirteen cases enumerated above we only encounter a short survival, amounting to some minutes in Cicero's story, some hours for Lord Brougham's case, and some hours for the other observations. We see that in general the manifestations closely follow the death. This is what we already saw in vol. iii.

The essential condition for investigating natural phenomena, says Claude Bernard, is to preserve in our studies an entire liberty of spirit, based on philosophic doubt. From this principle we must never depart.

The study of the soul is far from being completed. It has hardly been begun, especially in the experimental field, in which the ground has barely been cleared. Now that the principle of survival is established on proofs which cannot be logically refuted, we can go a little further in our metapsychic excursions. And here arises a question, that of Haunted Houses. (The last but one of the preceding thirteen observations is a case in point: what is the shade of an old woman perceptible to a kitten and seen by a girl?) In vol. iii (p. 442) I announced that supplementary documents could be added to the numerous proofs already furnished. We shall try.

NOTE.—"Seek and ye shall find." Several readers have asked me to indicate the origin of this quotation from the words of Jesus Christ published on p. 10 of my book *After Death.* They are found in the beautiful Sermon on the Mount, Matt. vii, 7. That sentence, which belongs to the Old Testament (Chron.), is written in Hebrew. The last cry of Jesus on the cross: *"Eli, Eli, lama sabachthani"* is in the Aramaic language, the language current in Palestine at that time. It was the cry of despairing man: "My God, my God, why hast Thou forsaken me?"

CHAPTER II

HAUNTED HOUSES: A FIRST SURVEY OF THE SUBJECT

Truth and falsehood—Proved realities—Ancient and contemporary observations—Legal recognition of haunted houses—Broken leases—Certainty of phenomena of haunting.

WHO can believe in haunted houses? Feeble and credulous minds. They are but nurses' fables, good for frightening small children. Such is the general opinion—and such, it would seem, must be the verdict of common sense. How much is true? How much is false? *Quod gratis asseritur gratis negatur,* as Renan said to me one day as we were talking about the new dogma of Papal Infallibility which had just been affirmed by the Council of the Vatican (1870). What is asserted without proof is simply denied. If haunted houses were not established by irrefutable proofs it would be our right, and even our duty, to deny their existence.

An old proverb assures us that there is no smoke without fire. No doubt there is often much more smoke than fire, but the popular adage remains true.

Even the most absurd legends have some origin.

Now it is remarkable that haunted houses are as old as the history of humanity itself.

In a large number of cases, especially in recent and contemporary times, criticism and judicial enquiries have found nothing in these ghost stories but purely human actions.

In the final analysis they often resolve themselves into more or less conscious hysterical deceptions, mystifications, comedies, farces, and amusements, which sometimes degenerate into sinister tricks. Somebody wanted to frighten the inhabitants, to avenge an injustice, to discredit a dwelling in order to buy it cheaply, or simply to annoy poltroons and timid dupes.

But not all the cases can be thus explained. And besides, what was the first haunted house? Nothing is imitated but that which exists already. The tricksters only renew the scenes which have already terrified people. Those scenes may have been real ones. On the other hand, they may have been nothing but timorous interpretations of very elementary accidents, such as unknown noises, amplified by the silence of the night, and frightening the awakened sleepers. Originally, there may have been but a movement of stray animals, dogs, cats, rats, mice, night birds, or nothing but the wind blowing through dilapidated rooms, doors and shutters banging, a bit of wall crumbling without apparent cause, etc.

If the stories of haunted houses could be reduced to these explanations, such commonplaces would not deserve a special chapter in this work. But that is not the case. We must examine the facts without prejudice, without any preconceived idea, but with the most severe circumspection. We shall then be able to arrive at a considered judgment.

What has not been written about these stories? What has not been written against them? For my part, I have been for many years [1] examining, com-

[1] See among other documents in the Report on Spiritualism of the London Dialectical Society (London, 1871), my article, pp. 349-354, and in this volume the two haunted houses of Port Glasgow and Stradey, pp. 97 and 162.

paring, analysing, discussing so many observations, narratives, and commentaries that even twenty years ago I had, for my personal instruction, composed a large volume which has remained unpublished.

There are real haunted houses. There are also spurious ones. There are genuine bank-notes. There are also spurious ones. There are truthful people. There are also liars. There are honest people and rascals. There are serious people and boobies. There are intelligent and unintelligent people.

To reject without examination all that has been said about haunted houses would be as foolish as to accept everything without examination.

Old traditions and proverbs must not always be despised. "He roams about like a spirit in torment" is so ancient a saying that it is lost in the mists of antiquity. Whence did it come? What is its origin?

Not all accounts must be rejected, despised, or suppressed. It is not all error, illusion, or imposture. Here, as elsewhere, if we wish to learn, we must examine things without prejudice.

It is in this state of mind that we shall investigate this curious problem. An eminent man of science whose judgment is highly appreciated by all who know him, General Berthaut, late Director of the Army Geographical Service, and a former Member of Council of the Paris Observatory, recently wrote me a long letter, of which I shall, with his permission, publish the beginning:

DEAR MASTER,

Haunted Houses? It does not surprise me that they have encroached upon you. You distrust them, and you are right, a hundred times. Not that they are more improbable than any other psychic manifestation, but because there is a greater likelihood of interested parties and because they almost always lend themselves to fraud. There are too many reasons why living persons should wish to discourage people from inhabiting such and such premises for the haunted house to remain free from suspicion. There are too many facilities for combining noises, displacements of objects, and even so-called apparitions for a free acceptance of all that is told. And, apart from trickery, there are sometimes natural sources, not of a psychic character, but difficult to particularise. Finally, there is humbug and more or less morbid pleasantry of a doubtful taste, which can play their part even if no interests are engaged. I can, if you like, give you an example of this, a story of a haunted house or rather a flat, told by my friend Vibert, the painter, who died in 1902. It took place in Paris, I know not where or when—I have forgotten the names, but I have kept the remembrance of the facts. The police were notified, but their search proved unavailing, and it was discovered quite by chance that the whole thing was a joke perpetrated by a studio full of painters.

Human ingeniousness is great! I do not consider it sufficient, for establishing the reality of haunting, that the manifestations observed should remain unexplained, that the phenomena should be incontestable, recognised, and not, in the general opinion, due to any assignable cause. For this only proves that nobody knows the natural cause, not that the natural cause does not exist.

I consider that the only facts worth retaining are those which prove their own extra-natural origin, both in the category of haunted houses and in all other varieties of psychic phenomena.

I am quite of the opinion expressed by the learned General. And, after all precautions have been taken, we shall soon have here under our eyes typical and rigorously observed examples, into which no doubtful element can have entered.

Having had occasion for more than half a century

to examine these more or less strange and confused observations of haunted houses, which are often annoying and absurd, I believe I have the right to affirm here, somewhat crudely perhaps, but clearly, that the people who jeer at stories of haunted houses and deny their reality suffer from a special form of myopia, so that their horizon does not extend much beyond the tip of their nose.

I have just said that I have studied these special phenomena for a long time. I shall commence this chapter with a memory which goes back sixty-three years.

In the course of 1860, coming back from the Observatory daily towards the Seine, I often passed by a street which has been absorbed by the Boulevard Saint-Germain, then just planned out. It was the Rue des Noyers, celebrated just then as the object of a judicial enquiry made at the request of the tenant of a haunted house, who had been obliged to take refuge elsewhere (M. Lesage, housekeeper of the Palais de Justice). The tenancy was broken by order of the court. That is a first point of fact not generally known, and it is valuable.

I have received hundreds of accounts of haunted houses and of occult phenomena. But whatever the number of narratives addressed to me and to others who collect these strange phenomena, it is certain that nobody is in a hurry to make them known. To quote but one example, while I was busy comparing the manifestations of dying persons, I received the following card in reply to my enquiry of the *Inconnu*:

VENDOME,
March 30, 1899.

My reply to both your questions is in the negative. Yet I have been a witness, and my house, which I inhabit alone, has been the scene of absolutely inexplicable occurrences, which I have correlated with the greatest care, because I should have been unable to find any servants to help me.

ANNA PROUBAT.
(*Letter* 59).

The time has gone by when the phenomena of haunting could be treated as imaginary tales. There are too many of them. Examples are as numerous as they are varied. They are generally incomprehensible, and often of a comic appearance.

But let us return to the case of the Rue des Noyers just mentioned.

Well, in the course of the year 1860, when I was an astronomer-apprentice at the Paris Observatory, returning every day to my relatives (then living in the Boulevard des Italiens), I often passed through the Rue des Noyers. There was then a house known to be upset by a rapping spirit, a very turbulent spirit indeed. The following narrative embodies what was said about it. Under the heading "A Scene of Sorcery in the Nineteenth Century," the journal *Le Droit,* in its issue of June, 1860, told the following:

Very strange things are happening just now in the Rue des Noyers. M. Lesage, housekeeper at the Palais de Justice, occupies a flat in that street. For some time past, missiles thrown from nobody knows where have come and smashed his windows. They have penetrated into his dwelling, hit persons, and injured them more or less seriously. They are large logs of half-burnt wood, or heavy pieces of coal. M. Lesage's servant has received several on her chest and has received severe bruises.

M. Lesage made up his mind to call in the police. Constables were put on the watch, but they themselves were hit by the invisible artillery and they were unable to locate it.

Existence having become unbearable in a house where was a perpetual alarm, M. Lesage asked his landlord to cancel the lease. This request was granted, and it was decided to send for the purpose of registration a bailiff of the name of Vaillant, a name which was particularly appropriate to the circumstances.

The officer of the court had hardly begun his work when an enormous block of coal, thrown with great force, flew in through the window and hit the wall, breaking up into powder. Nothing disconcerted, M. Vaillant took up this powder, as Junot once did the earth thrown up by a bullet, and spread it on the page he had just written. No explanation has been found for this bombardment with various missiles. But it is hoped that the enquiry pursued by M. Hubaut, the inspector of the Sorbonne quarter, will elucidate the mystery.

The "enquiry" elucidated nothing at all, and we may remark that half the time these enquiries have only served to confirm the reality of the facts, without discovering any explanation. Not finding any does not prove that there is no hidden natural cause. But let us not conclude hastily. It should be noted that the objects thrown came from the immediate vicinity and not from a distance. In my prolonged investigations, prompted by a scientific curiosity, I came to the conclusion that a classification is essential if we are to find our way among these rather disconcerting phenomena. These curious throwings of objects have been observed hundreds, nay, thousands of times. Their cause is a conscious and invisible agent. They have often been associated with possible acts of deceased persons, but not always, or rather, we are often unable to discover the existence of a deceased person who might have something to do with them. If the discarnate play a part—and we shall have to enquire into that—the incarnate certainly do also. It appears that the invisible forces act upon the visible world by using the organic faculties of mediums or intermediaries, mainly girls or young women (sometimes youths), whose presence makes the ignorant public—and even certain judges of the same negative value—believe that they are the responsible agents—in other words, practical jokers of a more mischievous type than any of the inquisitors.

In the dwelling of the Rue des Noyers the servant, herself a victim of these happenings, was a young girl.

This first recollection of my youth presents three instructive features: (1) The presence of unexplained phenomena; (2) the cancelling of a lease consequent upon their proof; (3) the presence of a young girl, herself a victim of these occurrences. Now, similar facts had already been observed in 1849, not far away, in the Rue des Grès, near the Sorbonne, and had also been the subject of legal informations. The *Gazette des Tribunaux* of February 2, 1849, brought the following observation:

> An extraordinary event, repeated every evening, every night, for the last three weeks without its cause being discovered by the most active search and the closest and most persistent watch, has been exciting the populous quarter of the Montagne Sainte-Geneviève, of the Sorbonne, and the Place Saint-Michel.[2] What we are about to relate actually took place, although at the earnest request of the public an enquiry, both judicial and administrative, was held for several days without throwing any light on the subject.
>
> During the work of demolition undertaken to make a new street which is to join the Sorbonne to the Panthèon and the Law School, cutting through the Rue des Grès and going up to the old church, the workers arrived at a coal and timber yard where there is an uninhabited house, communicating with the yard and having only one storey with

[2] At that time the Place Saint-Michel was where we now have the Place Médicis; neither the Boulevard Saint-Michel, nor the Rue Soufflot, nor the Boulevard Saint-Germain existed then.

an attic. That house, situated at some distance from the street and separated from the condemned houses by large excavations, has been assailed, every evening and during the nights, by a hail of projectiles, which, by their volume and violence of projection have caused such damage that the house in question has been pierced and its doors and windows reduced to splinters, as if the house had sustained a siege and a bombardment by catapult.

Whence came these projectiles, consisting of paving-stones, fragments of walls demolished close by, even whole mouldings which, owing to their weight and the distance from which they came, could not have been thrown by the hands of a human being? It has been impossible to find out. In vain has a night and day watch been kept under the personal direction of the inspector of police and other competent persons. In vain has the head of the secret service remained on the spot, and in vain have watch-dogs been placed every night in the neighbouring yards. Nothing has given a clue to the phenomenon, which the people in their credulity attribute to mysterious causes. The missiles which continue to rain noisily upon the house are projected to a great height, over the heads of those posted on the roofs of the small neighbouring houses. They seemed to come from some distance and all hit the mark with an almost mathematical precision without deviating from the parabolic line evidently traced for them.

We shall not enter on further details of these happenings, which will doubtless receive a prompt explanation. While congratulating those who have taken the proper measures, we may remark that in similar circumstances, and with a similar sensational effect in Paris, a rain of small coins has fallen every evening in the Rue Montesquieu, attracting all the boobies of Paris. Also, all the bells have been rung in the Rue de Malte by an invisible hand. It was impossible to make any discovery or to find the material cause of the phenomena. Let us hope that this time definite results will be obtained.

Such is the story in the *Gazette des Tribunaux*. Let us add, as before, that the objects come from the vicinity and that all this was extremely well known.

The most minute researches led to no result, neither in 1860 for the Rue des Noyers, nor in 1849 for the Rue des Grès. After losing much time, nobody seems to have worried about the matter. But a piquant circumstance is that the proprietor of the house was accused of himself being the author of the trouble in his own interest, and he gave a violent denial of the allegation, and brought the papers in question before the law courts, the summons being, according to *Le Droit,* in the following terms:

In the year eighteen hundred and sixty, the ninth day of July, at the request of M. Lerible, formerly a merchant in coal and timber, house owner, living in Paris, Rue de Grenelle-Saint-Germain 64, and electing domicile at his dwelling:

I, Aubin Jules Demouchy, a bailiff of the Civil Tribunal of the Seine sitting in Paris, living there at Rue des Fossées-Saint-Victor 43, and undersigned, have called upon M. Garat, Director of the journal *La Patrie,* in the office of the said journal situated in Paris, Rue du Croissant,

To insert, in reply to the article published on the 27th day of June last in the journal *La Patrie,* the following summons made by the plaintiff on the journal *Le Droit,* said plaintiff offering to charge himself with the costs of insertion in the case of his reply exceeding the number of lines which the law authorises him to publish.

I, Aubin Jules Demouchy, a bailiff of the Civil Tribunal of the Seine

Have summoned M. François, in the name and as director of the journal *Le Droit,* in the office of the said journal, situated in Paris, Place Dauphine,

To appear on the 8th day of August, 1860, before and in the audience of MM. the President and Judges comprising the sixth chamber of the tribunal of First Instance, at Paris, at ten o'clock in the morning, for the following cause:

Whereas, in its issue of the 26th June last, and on the occasion of occurrences which are alleged to have taken place in a house in the Rue des Noyers, the journal *Le Droit* reports that similar occurrences took place in 1847, in a house in the Rue des Grès;

And whereas the writer accompanies his observations with explanations which tend to show that the attacks upon the house in the Rue des Grès in 1847 emanated from the occupier of the house himself, and that he brought them about in bad faith, to obtain, by a dishonest speculation, the cancellation of his lease;

And whereas the facts described in the journal *Le Droit* occurred, not in 1847 but in 1849, in the house which the plaintiff occupied at that time in the Rue des Grès;

And whereas these imputations are of a nature calculated to damage the reputation and consideration of the plaintiff;

And considering that they are the more reprehensible as none of the verifications aimed at have taken place, and that those events which, for example, occurred in the Rue des Noyers have remained unexplained;

And considering that the plaintiff was, since 1847, the proprietor of the house and plot which he occupied in the Rue des Grès;

And considering that the supposition put forward by the journal *Le Droit* has no reason and has never been established;

And whereas the terms employed by the journal *Le Droit* constitute a libel and fall under the application of the penalties provided by Law;

And that all the journals of Paris have made use of the article in *Le Droit,* and that the honour of the plaintiff, has, by the fact of this publication, suffered a damage for which reparation is due to him;

For all the above reasons

Let M. François be warned of the imposition of the penalties provided by Law and for his condemnation, even in his own person, to pay the plaintiff the damages which the latter will claim in Court, and which for the present, he declares he will employ for the benefit of the poor, and let him be informed also that the judgment obtained will be inserted in all the journals of Paris at the expense of the defendant, and that he may be condemned to pay costs, without prejudice;

And in order that the defendant may not be in ignorance, I have, at his domicile and speaking as above, served upon him a copy of these presents.

Cost: 3 frs 55c. (Sg.) Demouchy.

Registered in Paris, July 16, 1860.

Received 2 frs. 20c. (Sg.) Duperron.

Declaring to the defendant that, failing his giving satisfaction on the present summons, the plaintiff will proceed by course of Law,

I, at his domicile, and speaking as above, have served upon him this copy.

Cost: 9 frs. 10c. (Sg.) Demouchy.

Legal damages and cancelled leases are things which do not authorise one to laugh childishly about things one does not understand, or to deny everything blindly.

These two observations of the throwing of stones and various missiles, made in 1860 and 1849, have been the object of several enquiries, one of which was published by the Marquis de Mirville, in 1863, in his great five-volume work, *Spirits and their Various Manifestations,* which he had the politeness to send me. The conclusion arrived at was that there was no explanation, and that all those proposed were absurd or ridiculous. But a conclusion which may astonish us is that which confirmed the Marquis de Mirville in his conviction as to the *existence of the Devil!* Let us listen to him for a moment:

We were talking with Lerible, the coal merchant. "Would you believe it," he said, "that they had the nerve to accuse me of all this—me, the owner, who has been more than thirty times to the police to ask them to deliver me, who on the 29th of January went to the Colonel of the

Twenty-fourth, who sent me a platoon of his Chasseurs? I told them, 'You may believe it is myself, if it amuses you —that makes no difference; only tell me how, and catch the person whom I set to work, for you see it is not myself, because I stand before you. Whether it is I or another whom I employ, catch the fellow. It is your business, and you will not find me ungrateful.' But indeed, the poor devils did what they could, and caught nobody. And another thing: Suppose it was I who demolished myself. Should I have furnished the house specially with new furniture, as I did a month before? Should I have had all my furniture spoilt, like this sideboard with mirrors, which the stones seemed to be aimed at? Look here, sir,'' and the poor man showed us all the fragments of his broken crockery, his clock, his flower vases, his mirrors, fragments of things valued at 1,500 francs (and no wonder), and we found his defence altogether valid, especially when he added: ''And what about myself? Should I not first of all have taken shelter? Did not the stones fall upon me as roughly as upon the others? Look at this wound near my temple. It might have killed me. Indeed, sir, we must agree that some folks are funny.''

One very curious detail he pointed out. The room was full of stones and long flat tiles. Their shape struck us. ''How was that?'' we said. ''Oh! that is because I had closed my shutters. Look at that slit; it is very long and narrow. Well, sir, no sooner had I closed my shutters than all the stones had the shape which you see, and all came through this slit, which is just about that width.'' We were astounded by the cleverness of the conjurers, who could aim so well and from such a distance. It was a chance of 1 in 100,000, even at twenty-five paces, not to speak of a mile.

The good man had interested us, but we wished to question his neighbours. We went to several of them, including a large book-seller, who lived at the corner. Like the rest, he found the thing absolutely inexplicable, and the accusation of jugglery more absurd than anything.

We then went to the police inspector. He was away, but his two secretaries were in the office, and his representative said: "The police inspector would tell you, as I do, that in spite of our tireless searches, nothing has been found out, and I can tell you beforehand that nothing ever will be." "Thank you; we were quite sure of it, but it is good to hear you say so."

So speaks the Marquis de Mirville concerning that haunted house of the Rue des Noyers. We agree with Bozzano that this is the story of almost all the enquiries made into such cases.

In fact, the causes of the phenomena remain impenetrable. They force the sceptics to satisfy themselves with more or less absurd conclusions, which, while harmless so long as the manifestations continue in full, acquire consistency and hide the truth when the manifestations stop and the impression of incontestable authenticity gained by onlookers becomes enfeebled.

The remarkable incident of projectiles formed so as to be able to pass through a narrow slit in a shutter, though marvellous, is not at all rare in this series. Indeed, the curious precision with which the projectiles hit their target is similar to many other cases of missiles which systematically and surely hit a certain mark. It is almost the rule in such cases. Everybody will understand the great theoretical importance presented by these episodes, since their origin implies an intention served by supernormal faculties and powers. So we may excuse those who believe that the Devil is mixed up in the affair. Remember also that the Devil is even now associated with all Christian teaching.

Let us at the same time acknowledge the first impression we have in these strange actions, which is their triteness and vulgarity. Whatever the cause, they are peculiar forms of exercise. "Intelligent forces in action!" Surely very poor intelligences.

Let us pass on to other manifestations. Let us learn freely, without preconceived opinion.

These physical exercises, bizarre and incomprehensible, are the same everywhere and always, with some strange variations. Among the many examples in my collection I shall pick out a recent one which offers the most complete analogy with the two described above. It was communicated to me in 1922 by a Protestant clergyman of the Ardèche, M. Laval, and has also been observed with certainty.

Here is this curious narrative, numbered 5,208 in the metapsychic correspondence I commenced in 1899 (see *L'Inconnu,* p. 88, and *Death and its Mystery,* vol. i, p. 15).

SAINT-MICHEL-DE-CHABRILLANOUX.
December 15, 1922.

DEAR MASTER,

The incomprehensible facts which I related to you last year, begging you for an explanation, and which you asked me to verify as far as possible, are unexceptionable. I am sending you an exact plan of the house and its surroundings, as well as the names of these good people, who are much impressed by what has happened to them, and you can locate the spot geographically. I do not see any objection to your publishing my name and address, if you consider it useful for your scientific documentary evidence.

Poor M. R. has suffered a great deal mentally from the stupidity and credulity of the people, who look on him as one sold to the "evil spirits." Perhaps it would be better not to give his name, which I communicate to you personally, as I do not wish to take away from the scientific value of the document.[3]

This M. R. is a farmer in the parish of——, and possesses in a neighbouring village some property comprising an old house, not far from which is another belonging to M. E.

---

[3] The clergyman is right. I only give the initials. Human stupidity being universal, it seems to me equally advisable not to print the names of the places, of which I have the plan before me.

He goes to his farm at the busy agricultural season. The nearest houses to these two are 440 yards away. You have before you a plan of the two houses, with their barns, the streams, roads, and neighbouring meadows; the ploughed fields, vineyards, tobacco fields, and woods on these rural properties. I have marked the rooms into which the stones and apples were thrown from no one knows where; also the place, at the crossing of two roads, where I myself was hit by a stone, which grazed me vertically from head to foot.

The stones first began to be thrown in the early days of September, 1921, and continued (with interruptions) until the end of December. The maximum phase can be assigned to the first ten days of October. *They fell at all hours of the day, and even followed M. R. in the fields,* 220 yards away from the house. The front door was hit, window No. 1 was broken, window No. 2, which gives on to an open space of ground 440 yards long, was the one which received most of the hits. The stones arrived without one being able to tell how: they were not seen until they touched an object. Some fell vertically.

M. R. has three children—Héli, twelve years old; André, aged seventeen; Henri, aged twenty-two—who were very naturally accused. Consequently, they were watched and spied upon as much as possible, but they were not caught in a single suspicious action.

One Sunday M. R. begged me to write out for him a complaint to the Public Prosecutor. I was anxious, first of all, to satisfy myself as to the facts. The next day, at five o'clock in the evening, I was in the farmyard, having two of the children with me, and facing me, when a stone the size of a hen's egg came down vertically, grazing one of the children. A little later another stone grazed me in the same way, about 52 yards from the house. The children were in sight close by me, and they could not have been the cause. The stones fell slowly, and gave one the impression of falling from a height of about 6 feet only. This was often remarked. It is incomprehensible.

I decided to go to bed. Nothing happened in the night. The next day, at seven o'clock, in full daylight, while M.

R., with a friend, M. D., worked in the room adjoining the kitchen, two apples hit the closed shutter of a window and touched M. R. The first apple knocked out an old board in the shutter which was very loose, the others coming in through the space thus created. M. D., believing that I was the perpetrator of the deed, said: "Is it you, M. Laval, who are throwing apples at us?" Imagine my surprise! It is true that just at the moment when the apples were thrown I happened to be outside facing the window aimed at. An extraordinary thing was that I heard something strike the shutter but saw nothing. Convinced that I had not thrown anything, M. D. joined me quickly to see what was happening. Some seconds afterwards two other apples arrived through the same opening into the room and fell at M. R.'s feet. As in the first case, we heard the shock but saw nothing. We were greatly surprised, and M. D., who is a great huntsman, and who the night before had sworn to trace the culprits, told me that he decidedly could not understand it.

The apples came really from the outside. They arrived in a horizontal direction with considerable speed. It would have been humanly impossible for anybody to hide in broad daylight in front of the window, which opens on to an empty field 440 yards long.

The most able man, unless he were quite near the window, would never have succeeded in throwing an apple through a hole of an inch or so, however well he aimed.[4]

While we were outside, we heard a blow on the window, but saw nothing entering from outside.

M. R. called in the gendarmery of Gourdon, which arrived on the spot. During the four months of these happenings there would surely have been ample time to surprise tricks of children.

M. R. the elder suspected his only neighbour, M. E., who has two sons, aged seventeen and twenty-two respectively. I conveyed a remonstrance to the E. family, but they replied: "Yes, we are accused, but we are innocent." The father wrote me the letter appended to my report, and declared he would assist at any enquiry.

---

[4] A similar observation to that made at Noyers, above.

In order to show that he had nothing to do with this affair he gave me an irrefutable proof. This is what he literally declared to me:

(1) On September 25, at noon, my elder son was in the vineyard, and my younger son in bed. At that hour I was nursing my father-in-law, who was dying. M. R., who had stones thrown at him, asked me for the rifle. I went to the house with him and we shot. Some minutes afterwards two stones hit the door. I was then with M. R., and my son was still in bed.

(2) On October 6, at 6 a. m., I was talking with M. R. in his farmyard. We were all together, R. and his sons and my two sons, when two stones hit the roof of the house, and two others the door of the barn.

Does M. R. believe what is said concerning the death of his father? And does he seek to stifle some ancestral fears in ascribing the throwing of stones to his neighbours? It is possible, and what makes me credit it is his regularity in church since the affair at his house.

His father, who lived for many years at X———,[5] was struck in his old age by a mental malady. One day, while his son was away, he left X——— and disappeared. His people searched for him in vain for several weeks, and finally supposed that he had been drowned in the river and his body carried away by the current. Seven months afterwards a chasseur who crossed the bog between—— and —— saw a body floating on the stagnant water. The police were called, and a doctor, M. X., said to M. R.: "As you recognise the body of your father, go on at once with the burial to avoid judicial complications." M. R. obeyed the doctor's injunction, had a coffin made in a hurry, and the deceased carried almost secretly to the cemetery, without the assistance of the priest. The parish priest of ——, a very able man, interpreted the occult phenomena in his favour, and his flock reproached M. R. for having deprived his father of the consolations of religion. Was it not to excuse himself that R. threw suspicion upon the E. family?

M. E. is highly esteemed at ——. For twenty years he

[5] As stated above, I feel bound to suppress all names.

has been town councillor, and was always elected first on the list.

Here is also the declaration mentioned above:

"Having lived for a long time on a good footing with M. R., and having up to now considered him a good neighbour, we declare before our conscience that we had no part in the inexplicable occurrences at his house.—J. E."

"How can we explain these things?" writes Pastor Laval. "Are we, without knowing it, plunged into an unknown psychic environment? Do electro-psychic forces exist which show themselves thus?"

After reading your work, *Les Caprices de la Foudre,* I thought that certain electrical phenomena seemed to be associated with a psychic nature we do not understand. Is common sense right in attributing such things to the spirit of the departed? If so, why are they so queer?

After co-ordinating a certain number of similar facts, do you notice a certain connection between hauntings and suicides, crimes and tragic deaths?

In the district interpretations differ. The majority attribute the facts to the spirits of the dead. Others maintain that the parish priest of —— is an amateur conjurer, and that we are his victims. Others suppose trickery. My father-in-law, an orthodox pastor, summarily regrets the stories in the name of certain Biblical passages. To me, for one, the observations are real, and trickery, as you may see, is inadmissible. Nor is the hypothesis of an hallucination possible; stones and apples are quite objective. These facts seem to me to belong to the domain of the unknown, and to be worth including among those which you submit to the thinking public.

After all, are they more mysterious than those whose nature we can explain? Perhaps they are, only rarer and more difficult to prove. It shows a lack of sane philosophy to regret *a priori* all that is outside the sphere of our ordinary thoughts. The world we see and think about can only be a feeble reflection of objective reality. You have discovered the mysterious link between the magnetic needle and solar storms. Other links, still more mysterious, must join the worlds and beings across all the grades we do not know of. The new forces which we hardly apprehend will form interesting studies for the learned of the future. Such facts, insignificant perhaps in appearance, will one day change our ideas of the world and of life.

I was borne at Treignac, in the Corrèze, in 1885. Lately I heard in my native village that some thirty years ago a house had been the scene of hauntings. (The house, which still exists, is five miles from Treignac.) In the evening stones were thrown among persons sitting round the fire. In broad daylight grains of rye and buckwheat were thrown on the heads of the astonished people.

It must be noted that the owner had killed himself, and the house had been the scene of a tragic event.

I agree with you that we must study everything without preconceived opinions.

LAVAL
(*Evangelical Pastor*).

SAINT-MICHEL-DE-CHABRILLANOUX, ARDÈCHE.

We see that these observations offer the greatest analogy with the previous ones. In the interval between the Rue des Noyers in 1860 and the letter of Pastor Laval in 1922 I have known more than one hundred observations of the same order. The above one was made with particular care.

I thank the author of this narrative for sending it in. It may help us to clear up these problems, more especially as these studies are varied and numerous. In my own case alone, this letter is No. 5,208 of my metapsychic correspondence, commenced in 1899, which had been preceded by a large number of diversified documents. What strikes us most in these doings is their commonplace character, which gives the idea of more or less stupid forces—though occasionally tragic. What also strikes us is that children, and often hysterical girls, are almost always associated with them, and the result is that superficial examinations have nearly always stopped there, and explained the facts on the basis of trickery. Now, the deeper study of the most remarkable cases has proved that unknown forces are in action, and that often these children and adolescents have been the first victims. I have before me at this moment a large number of certified cases of *leases cancelled on the ground that the houses had become uninhabitable.*

As we have already remarked, these throwings of apples are childish games, and seem absurd to us. If, on the other hand, the suicide of the old owner had anything to do with them, and if his shade subsisted, we could perhaps see in these absurdities the posthumous acts of a peasant.

But let us get back to our first glimpses of the sixties.

About that time, and also under our eyes, so to speak, at Poitiers in 1864, and under the observation of an excellent observer, Count d'Ourches, with whom I was in communication, and who was closely occupied with these studies in conjunction with Baron Guldenstubbe and General de Brevern, phenomena just as mysterious and inexplicable as those of Paris were observed. I have preserved of this "haunted house of Poitiers" an account which was published at the time by the *Journal de la Vienne* of January 21, 1864. Here it is:

For the last five or six days such an extraordinary thing has happened in Poitiers that it has become the subject of the strangest conversations and comments. Every evening after six, certain singular noises are heard in a house of the Rue Neuve Saint-Paul, inhabited by Mlle. d'O., sister of the Count d'O. These noises, according to our information, resemble discharges of artillery. Violent blows seem to rain upon the doors and shutters. The first idea was that they were due to some urchins or unfriendly neighbours. A close watch was kept. On the complaint of Mlle. d'O. the police took the most detailed measures, and policemen were stationed both inside and outside the house. The explosions took place all the same, and we are credibly informed that Sir M., a brigadier, was during the night before last surprised by a commotion which he has until now been quite unable to explain.

Our whole town is disturbed about this unexplained mystery. The enquiries made by the police have hitherto been abortive. Everyone is looking for a solution of the riddle. Some persons initiated into spiritism say that rapping spirits are the authors of these manifestations, and that a certain famous medium, who, however, no longer lives in the district, has something to do with it. Others say that a cemetery once existed in the Rue Neuve Saint-Paul, and we need not specify the conjectures they indulge in on that account.

Of all these explanations we do not know which to choose. Meanwhile public opinion is much excited about this event, and last night such a large crowd assembled under the windows of the house of d'O. that the authorities had to requisition a picket of the 10th Chasseurs to clear the street. At the time of writing the police and gendarmes occupy the house.

The first idea which occurs to one is, of course, that of trickery. An enquiry was therefore instituted, but it yielded nothing, and no trickster has been discovered.

Exorcisms have been tried, but without result, for after stopping for some days the noises recommenced with a certain violence. They are said to resemble the noises made by small bombs.

But whence do they come? It is impossible up to the present to determine their direction. They do not come from the cellar, because pistols fired there are not heard on the first floor.

In a third article the same paper attempted to satisfy everybody by publishing the following:

For some time past we have received by every post letters from our subscribers or others asking us to give more particulars of the scenes at the house of d'O. We have said everything we know.

It is quite true that singular noises are heard every evening from 6 o'clock till midnight, in the Rue Saint-Paul, in the house of d'O. These noises resemble those which would be produced by the successive discharges of a double-barrelled gun. They shake the doors, windows, and partitions. Neither light nor smoke is seen, and there is no smell. The facts have been proved by the most distinguished and trustworthy persons of our town and by police and gendarmery investigations made at the request of the d'O. family.

M. H. d'Orange believes in physical causes, such as gases disengaged from an ancient cemetery on which the d'O. mansion is supposed to have been built. However, the house is built on the rock and there is no cellar adjoining it.

For our part, we believe that the strange and as yet unexplained facts which for more than a month have disturbed the repose of an honourable family will not always remain a mystery. We believe it a very clever form of trickery, and we hope soon to see the apparitions of the Rue Saint-Paul appear in the police court.

In spite of this hope, nothing could be found out, and the police court has not had to deal with the unknown forces producing the raps and detonations.

As I said before, these things occurred at the house of Count d'Ourches and his sister. Mlle. d'Ourches was a medium, and was, as I proposed to call it, *dynamogenic.*

In connection with this haunted house of Poitiers, we may add that similar noises had already occurred in the same town and the same quarter. Gorres, the well-known author of a famous work called *La Mystique,* reports that according to Guillaume d'Auvergne, deceased in 1249, who was Bishop of Paris, a "rapping spirit" (*Poltergeist*) had got into a house of the same Saint-Paul quarter at Poitiers, and that he threw stones and broke windows.

Pierre Mamoris, professor of theology and author of the *Flagellum Maleficorum,* has reported the same history. A certain spirit threw stones, moved furniture, broke windows, even hit people, though lightly, without anyone discovering how it happened.

On this occasion Jean Delorme, parish priest of Saint Paul, is said to have gone with some others to visit the scene of these strange exploits, and is said to have passed through all the rooms armed with blessed and lighted candles, holy and Gregorian water, to sprinkle and exorcise.

Note this coincidence of locality: the same town and quarter. Let us proceed.

Here are the manifestations observed at Fives, near Lille (Nord), at the same epoch. We read in the *Indépendant* of Douai of the 6th and 8th July, 1865, the following account of the very grotesque and infantile occurrences observed by the inhabitants of a house at Fives:

1. For the last fortnight some hitherto unexplained things have been happening in the Rue du Prieuré, at Fives, and have caused a profound sensation in the whole district. At certain intervals a hail of missiles arrived in the yards of two dwellings in that street, which breaks the windows and sometimes hits the inhabitants, without anyone discovering the place whence they come nor the person who throws them. Things have come to such a pass that one of the two tenants has had to protect his windows with wire netting for fear of being killed.

At first the persons concerned took to watching, then the police were called in, and they held the closest watch for several days. This did not hinder the bits of brick and coal from falling as thick as ever in the two yards. One policeman even received a missile in his back at the moment when he was trying to explain to a comrade the parabola described by the stones in their fall.

The glazier who repaired the windows broken the night before was also hit in the back. He immediately rushed out, swearing to find out who did it, but was no more successful than the others.

For several days there has been a notable diminution in the volume of the projectiles, but they are more numerous, so that the excitement continues. However, hopes are entertained of soon discovering whatever is mysterious about this singular affair.

2. The curious phenomena which have happened in the Rue du Prieuré, at Fives, since Thursday, June 14, and which we have already described, entered upon a new phase on Saturday.

It is no longer a matter of missiles thrown with extraordinary force at the doors and windows, or more lightly at persons. This is what happens now:

On Saturday eight *sous* and five Belgian 2-*centime* pieces fell into the yard. The lady of the house, seeing at the same time several pieces of furniture moving and chairs upset, went to call in the neighbours. The chairs were picked up, but they fell down again. At the same time a pair of *sabots,* left at the entrance by the servant, jumped about as if attached to the feet of a person dancing.

In the evening a calendar placed on a chimney-piece jumped up and flew about in the air. Shoes placed on the floor also jumped about and fell with the soles upward.

When the night came, the master of the house decided to watch.

Hardly was he alone when he heard a noise. It was a candlestick falling on the chimney-piece. While he was picking it up, a piece of shell work rolled on the ground. He stooped to pick it up, but the other candlestick fell on his back. That went on for a good part of the night.

At the same time, the servant who slept upstairs called for help, and she was found in such a state of terror that her sincerity could not be doubted when she said she had been beaten. She was taken down and put to sleep in a neighbouring room. She was soon heard to cry out again, and one could even hear the blows she received. The girl fell ill and had to go back to her relatives.

On Sunday morning and the next day Belgian *sous* and *centimes* were thrown into the yard.

In the afternoon Mme. X went out with one of her friends after examining the whole house and noticing all in order. The door was carefully locked, and nobody could enter. On coming back, Mme. X found on her bed a large figure of 8 traced out with stockings and socks which had been in a chest of drawers.

In the evening, with her husband, her nephew, and a lodger, the whole party in the house, she visited all the rooms. Next morning, on going up to the room formerly occupied by the servant, she found a curious figure traced on the bed with hats, and on the lower stairs a dozen steps covered with her husband's, nephew's, and lodger's overcoats stretched out and surmounted by a hat.

On sweeping the dining-room, two knives were seen to fix themselves in the floor, and another in the ceiling.

A key fell in the yard, the key of the front door; then the key of the writing-table, then silk handkerchiefs, and handkerchiefs rolled and knotted, which had vanished for some time.

In the afternoon a circle was found on M.M.'s bed, formed of clothes, and in the attic a similar design made with a rolled-up hooded cloak and a game basket.

All these facts are attested by persons of the house, who are of a settled, calm, and deliberate character. It is all the less explicable as the neighbourhood is well inhabited and a close watch has been kept for three weeks.

It may be imagined how the inhabitants of the house suffer from this state of things. After first closing up the windows on the yard side, they have abandoned the rooms where the things happened, and they are now, in a way, camping in two or three rooms, and waiting for the end of their troubles.

These things, like those of the Rue des Noyers, of the Rue des Grès, of Poitiers, have defied the most active watchfulness and the investigations of the police. In presence of these manifold statements and many witnesses, denial is no longer possible. There must be more than one exaggeration. But there must also be accurate facts.

They have been personally vouched for by Colonel Mallet of Douai, a man of real scientific attainments, who has made enquiries on the spot and among the persons concerned. We may be sure of their reality.

Let us admit that they are absurd, idiotic, and unmeaning, that they resemble tricks of mischievous children, and that that, if it applied, would be the most natural explanation. Coins flung, shoes displaced, objects moved, blows given, the same triteness as in previous examples (after all, the lower strata of humanity are not more spiritual). Boys' tricks? Yet one finds nothing, in spite of the severest observation, and we shall see later that these movements are also found in hermetically sealed rooms.

Before going any further, we may say that the intervention of spirits of the dead does not seem indicated at all. One might sooner think of goblins.

We think quite naturally of electrical phenomena, such as lightning, but with a certain rudimentary intention.

The phenomena of haunted houses present to us on the one hand material occurrences without apparent significance, and on the other hand spiritual manifestations, with which certain organic properties of girls, young women, and youths are associated. We see how complex is the problem. Whatever the explanation may be, there are unknown, invisible forces in operation. Should there not be in the atmosphere certain psychic entities entirely devoid of any intellectual or moral value? Our human race is full of them. If the soul is not destroyed, what becomes of the souls of idiots? And animal souls, superior to some human ones?

One of the haunted houses which have been studied with the greatest care is that of Port Glasgow in England, which I had occasion to quote before in connection with the Dialectical Society of London, founded expressly for these verifications. Here is the narrative, made by an eye-witness [6]:

FROM MR. ANDREW GLENDINNING,

IVY BANK,
PORT GLASGOW,
August 30, 1869.

THE HONORARY SECRETARY,
SPIRITUALISM COMMITTEE.

SIR,

I understand you receive written communications bearing upon your late enquiry concerning Spiritualism. If so, and if it is of any interest to you, I will send you particulars of a "house haunting" case in Port Glasgow which happened some few years ago, and which I investigated along with the police.

I am,
Yours truly,
ANDREW GLENDINNING.

[Account forwarded.]

"In April, 1864, considerable excitement arose amongst the people resident in Scott's Lane, Port Glasgow, owing to noises which were heard in an apartment occupied by Hugh McCardle, gardener, and his family. The knockings were heard almost nightly for about two weeks, and after the rumour had spread through the town, large numbers of men and women assembled in the lane from about seven o'clock till ten o'clock every evening. The stair, lobby, and apartments were often crowded, but the police occasionally passed through the lane to ensure order. I visited the house to investigate the matter, and obtained the assistance of Mr. James Fegan, grocer. While waiting in the room for the commencement of the noises, Police Sergeant James McDonald and a constable came

[6] Original English version, from the Report on Spiritualism of the London Dialectical Society, 1873, p. 260.—TR.

in. I told Sergeant McDonald my object, and, as he was anxious to expose the trick—if such it were—he consented to assist me. The knockings commenced about nine o'clock, and continued for more than an hour. The first sounds were similar to what is made by scratching on rough boards; then knocking, as if made with a heavy hammer, on the floor, under the bed, which was situated immediately above the outer stair. Sergeant McDonald and I took a candle and went below the bed, exactly over the spot where the sounds were proceeding from. Mr. Fegan stood in front of the bed. J. F. Anstruther, Esq., and a number of persons were in the room besides the constable. Being informed that knocks had been given as affirmative or negative answers to questions, we asked a good many questions, requesting that three knocks be given for yes, and one for no. The knocks were rapid and loud, and were often given before the question was quite finished. During any pause in the question, the knocks seem to beat to the air, 'There is nae luck about the house'; I whistled that tune, and the knocks became still louder and accompanied my measure. I whistled other airs—'Let us gang to Kelvin grove, bonnie lassie, oh'; 'Scots wha hae wi' Wallace bled,' etc.—and, beginning always with the second line, they kept exact time. We asked some questions in a low tone—quite a whisper—our position being such that no one could see our lips moving, so as to guess the nature of our questions; but it made no difference in regard to the knocks. As ten o'clock struck on the town clock, each stroke seemed supplemented by a sound in the wall above the bed. We got a pickaxe, and tore up part of the flooring at the spot where the knocking was going on; the sounds shifted position for a little, but at times they were the same as if a person were hammering heavily on the edge of the hole we had made in the floor.

"We examined minutely the floor, walls, ceiling, etc.; we got the children (who were asleep) out of the bed, and lifted aside the bed-clothes, mattress, bed-bottom, and, in short, did everything we could think of to discover, if possible, the cause of the knockings; others (amongst whom were police constables and the superintendent) examined the lobby, staircase, and cellars. They likewise tried, by knocking on various places, to produce similar sounds, but without the slightest success.

"(Signed) ANDREW GLENDINNING.

"PORT GLASGOW."

15th October, 1866. The foregoing is abridged from letters written me shortly after the occurrences.

(Initialled) A. G.

16th October, 1866. We solemnly testify that the foregoing statement, drawn up by Mr. Andrew Glendinning, is exactly correct.

(Signed) JAMES McDONALD,
Late Sergeant,
PORT GLASGOW.

JAMES FEGAN,
Grocer.
PORT GLASGOW.

PORT GLASGOW,
October 16, 1866.

These things were seen and heard by some of the strangers and neighbours as well as by ourselves. And we state solemnly that we did not do any of these things, nor cause, nor allow them to be done, and that we have no idea whatever how to account for them, as they were all quite mysterious to us.

For self and family,
HUGH McCARDLE.

PORT GLASGOW,
October 16, 1866.

I have known Hugh McCardle, gardener, for some time, and to the best of my knowledge and belief he is an honest, sober, industrious, straightforward, truthful man.

(Signed) JAMES FEGAN.

Here, again, we have commonplace trivialities, and yet an indication of a thinking entity. These phenomena of haunting present every kind of aspect.

I have considered it appropriate to commence this first survey of the subject we are about to study with these ancient memories, dating back more than half a century, because they have, at all events, the intrinsic value of showing that my study of these queer phenomena is not a thing of yesterday, that my appreciation is based upon a lengthy experience, and that I can only smile at certain publicists who talk about every subject without knowing it and lead the public into error by declaring that the stories of haunted houses are farcical and unworthy of attention. What is unworthy of attention is the superficial mentality of ignorant scribes.

These memories of half a century ago have since been supplemented by hundreds of observations of various kinds, which confirm and develop them in many ways. Two great classes of phenomena challenge our attention. On the one hand, there are noises, agitations, the throwing of missiles, the shifting of furniture, the movement of objects without contact and without apparent cause, the physical facts of *telekinesis* (τελε, distance, and κινησις, movement); and, on the other hand, intelligent manifestations, whether of unknown and unknowable spirits, or deceased persons, or souls in torment. Those are two very different categories. Everything must be studied. We know nothing.

At the time of Descartes science was to be organised upon the direct observation of facts by a method contrary to the dialectics of verbal discussions. At the present time this organisation, far from being finished, must be continued by linking up with physical facts the facts of a psychic order, which are no less important.

Laplace said on his death-bed: "What we know is but little; what we do not know is immense." What was true at the time of Laplace, a century ago, is even truer today, in spite of the progress of science, or rather on account of it, because every advance in the knowledge of things opens new horizons before us.

This applies especially to metapsychics, where we comprehend almost nothing. There we have an entirely new world, which it would be very wrong, I think, to call supernatural. Should Nature not embrace and comprise everything?

We have examined the observations made in Paris in 1860 and 1849, at Poitiers in 1864, at Fives-Lille in 1865, at Port Glasgow in 1864, etc. We shall have to choose among hundreds to lay even the foundation of our studies. Not a year passes without some case or other of a "haunted house." Before going further, let us note a very curious example, which I take for this purpose from the *Revue des Études Psychiques,* edited by the competent and sincere writer, C. de Vesme (August, 1904):[7]

The English poet Stephen Phillips, known chiefly by his plays *Herod* and *Paolo and Francesca,* wishing to obtain the tranquillity necessary for finishing an important work, had rented a country house in the neighbourhood of Egham, a quiet little village near Windsor, on the Thames. "Yet," he says, "although the inhabitants of Egham knew my tastes and my intentions, nobody had the kindness to warn me that the house was supposed to be haunted.

"I had hardly established myself with my family when the most incomprehensible noises began to disturb me. I heard in the night, and sometimes even in the evening, raps, scratchings, the sound of steps, both heavy and light, slow and fast. Cries were added to these noises—choking

[7] Reproduced in *Annales des Sciences Psychiques,* 1907, pp. 211, 551.

and despairing cries—as of a person mad with terror or on the point of being strangled.

"That was not all. We saw, even in broad daylight, the doors open, though no hand was visible. Every time I sat down at my desk and started work I was disturbed, as if somebody had entered and had walked in the room. I turned round, I *saw the door opening,* moved by an invisible force, and I heard as usual the steps coming closer and receding in turn.

"I was never afraid of anything, but these phenomena finally annoyed and impressed me. The quiet I had desired was not given to me. And as for work, I could not think of it.

"I was not alone in hearing these noises. My family and servants were more disturbed than I. One evening my little daughter called out and said she had seen in the garden a little old fellow, a sort of dwarf, who had quickly disappeared."

The poor poet could not bear up long against sleepless nights. He had never lived in that neighbourhood, but he made enquiries, and succeeded in extracting from the careful peasants an avowal that a story was current about that house. It was said that on the site of the house, fifty years before, an atrocious crime had been committed. A passing tramp had one night strangled a woman and a child.

When the people of the house knew the story their fear became general. The servants one day suddenly left their employment, without even taking away their belongings. It was only at his departure that Mr. Phillips heard that he had not been the only victim. All the preceding tenants of the house had left it precipitately like himself.

"I believe," says the author of *Herod,* "I am not a poor-spirited person, and should like to hear of an explanation. Meanwhile I have given up the house."

Learning of these facts, the learned and very circumspect English Society for Psychical Research instituted an enquiry by a special commission, which endorsed the authenticity of the story without, however, clearing up the mystery. Let us add that in this case nothing indicates the presence of the organic cause (a girl or a boy) which we mentioned above.

That haunted house made much stir in England. Mr. Phillips himself told in several interviews the strange things which happened in his dwelling. All went well while he occupied the house, but when he left, the owner of the house, Mr. Arthur Barrett, found no more tenants. Nobody wanted to live with invisible spirits who opened and shut doors, knocked on the walls and furniture, and so on. Mr. Barrett then brought an action against the *Daily Mail,* one of the papers which had concerned itself with the house at Egham, and against *Light,* which had reproduced the reports.

The *Daily Mail* was condemned to pay the plaintiff £90 and *Light* was to pay £10.

The *Daily Mail* appealed against this judgment, as making the position of the Press very difficult in these matters, and the higher court decided in favour of the paper, in consideration of the fact that the house was commonly held to be haunted before the publication of the story; and that the Press had a right to collect facts of this kind if it did so in good faith, and without any intention of damaging anybody.

Such incidents are not as exceptional as many think. It is the people who deny them who astonish me. A long time ago[8] Lombroso wrote that 150 houses in England had been given up on account of haunting. Let us also sample the following story.

The excellent Italian review, *Luce e Ombra,* published in 1905, over the signature of Sgr. V. Cavalli,

---

[8] *Hypnotism and Spiritism,* p. 237.

an article entitled, "A Radical Means of Expelling Ghosts from Haunted Houses," which is worth reading. Here is a translation:

It is a means difficult to accept, but apparently the only means possible in certain desperate cases, when, for instance, the house is apparently "phantomogenic"—*i.e.*, contains all the psychic conditions as yet unknown, but necessary in this provisionally transcendental physical science for producing turbulent manifestations of occult entities. That means consists in *the entire demolition of the haunted building down to the ground.*

This practice, like many others, goes back to antiquity. Here is a quite respectable instance which goes back to the sixteenth century:

Ferdinand of Aragon, King of Naples, offered to his secretary, the celebrated Giovani Pontano, among other things, a very high square tower, since called *Pontaniana.* This tower, according to what Capaccio says in his *Historia Neapolitana,* vol. i, p. 61, has had to be demolished, as it was infested by low evil spirits, *cacodœmona incoli.*

It is logical to assume that, before deciding to destroy an edifice of such importance on account of its antiquity and historical value, it must have been clear that no method but this very radical one can have been found for eliminating the haunting.

Another example of more recent date is furnished by Mrs. Grove in her book, *The Night Side of Nature,* where we are told that Frederick the Great of Prussia had a haunted house in the village of Quercey pulled down and another constructed at some distance from it.

We cannot believe that the Voltairean king made this decision lightly, seeing that he first sent officers of the guard to investigate the manifestations talked about. The representatives of the king on approaching the house were preceded and accompanied by a military march, without being able to discover the musicians. A captain who called out, "This is the work of the devil!" had his ears boxed by an invisible hand.

Here is another still more recent case:

Mrs. Ida Pfeiffer, the famous traveller, an intelligent woman of a rather masculine character, has noted in her *Voyage round the World* (p. 340) the story of a tragic haunting *(infestazione)* which happened in 1853 in a small house belonging to the Residency of Chéribon (Java). The population had been so excited about it that the Dutch Government confidentially charged a superior officer with an investigation of the facts. This witness, stupefied by the phenomena, used every means of discovering their cause, and had at length to give it up. Finally the Government put an end to it by *demolishing the house.*

Thus experience shows that this radical remedy has been employed in order to destroy the dynamic focus of the haunting, which then disappears. It is remembered in connection with sorcery that not only the witches were burnt, but also incriminated objects.

Does the principle *Sublata causa tollitur effectus* apply here also? Was the cause suppressed, or only the conditions necessary for its operation? *Cum hoc* is not logically equivalent to *propter hoc.* The cause may be of a psychic, intelligent nature, and the condition, on the other hand, material.

This subject of *loci infesti,* less rare than one thinks, is one of the most obscure of transcendental psychology: spiritism, mediumism, odic force, what is at the bottom of it? For centuries this obscure field has been explored in all directions, and hardly anything has been found. There is much digging, but we do not find the source. More even than in medicine we can say with Hippocrates: *Ars longa, vita brevis.*

From the *Luce e Ombra* report we may conclude that the subject has been universally discussed.

The trial in connection with the haunted house

of Egham mentioned above raised certain half-legal, half-humorous discussions of these quotations in the British Press. Mr. Andrew Lang, the well-known anthropologist, wrote for the *Morning Post* an article, in which he recalled the similar trials to which disturbing spirits had given rise at all times, and the legislation which was finally made on this subject.

Alfenus, the author of the *Digest,* is the principal authority for those who maintain that the tenant of a haunted house is bound to prove something beyond a common fear to obtain a legal cancellation of a lease.

Arnault Ferton, in his *Mœurs de Bourgogne,* is of the same opinion as Mr. Lang. He maintains that "phantoms which disturb the repose of people and make the night sinister" are a sufficient ground for the rupture of a tenancy contract. The Parliament of Granada adopted this point of view on several occasions.

In the Middle Ages Le Loyer quotes, in connection with the discussion of the manifestations in Parliament, cases of houses where "spirits appear or make noises of all sorts, and disturb the tenants at night." He speaks of Daniel and Nicolas Macquereau, who rented a house on a lease, "and they passed no time when they did not hear noise and clatter of invisible spirits, who allowed them no sleep or rest. The Parliament broke the lease, thus admitting that there could be places haunted by supernatural beings.

Now M. Maxwell, Advocate-General of the Court of Appeal at Bordeaux, has quoted decisions of several parliaments which, in the eighteenth century, cancelled leases on account of haunting.[9]

---

[9] See *Les Phénomènes Psychiques,* p. 260.

Jurisprudence knows more recent cases. The *Journal des Débats* of April 18, 1912, reports the following:

Mr. J. Denterlander owns a house in Chicago, 3375 South Oakley Avenue. The rates commission assessed that important property on the basis of a rent of 12,000 dollars. Mr. Denterlander protested. Instead of benefiting him, his house had been nothing but an annoyance. He had all the trouble in the world to let it because it was haunted. A young woman had died there under mysterious circumstances—probably murdered—and since then every new tenant had been awakened by moans and cries. The tenants had been discouraged. One after another had given notice. For that reason Mr. Denterlander asked for an abatement. After discussion the commission agreed, and lowered the basis from 12,000 to 8,000 dollars. Thus at the same time they officially recognised the existence of ghosts.

The story of haunted houses is not a fantastic romance.

Much has been written about the cancelling of leases and the diminution of the rent value of dwellings on account of haunting. I need only recall the remarkable thesis upheld at Naples by the advocate Zingaropoli in defence of the Duchess of Castelpoto against the Baroness Laura Englen, asking "whether the tenant of a house infested by spirits can demand the cancellation of a tenancy contract." Here is a summary of it: [10]

There is a vast juridical and doctrinal literature on this question.

The most ancient law, which marks the point of departure of the dispute and on which other discussions have been founded, is that of the advocate Alfenus, reported in Book XIX. of the *Digeste* (Tit. II, Law 27).

---

[10] See *Annales des Sciences Psychiques*, November, 1907.

"Iterum interrogatus si quis timoris causa emigrasset, deberet mercedem, nec ne? Respondit: si causa fuisset cur periculum timeret, quamvis periculum vere non fuisset, tamen non debere mercedem; sed si causa timoris justa non fuisset, nihilominus debere."

This fragment is commented upon by Gotofred (transl. Vignali, *Digeste,* vol. iii, p. 133; Naples, 1857).

The fear must be *imminent,* and the tenant has the right to quit a dwelling in consequence of a justified fear. I remember that when I was a young man, Ludovic Santonio, a very eloquent barrister of Paris, who was also my trustee and brother-in-law, obtained the cancelling of the lease of a certain client who complained that he had not been able to enjoy the house rented on account of spectres and ghosts which haunted it, affirming that a tenancy was similar to a sale, and that it must transfer to the tenant the risks attached to the thing rented. He quoted witnesses, above all contest, bringing in the Holy Scriptures, and quoting Matthew viii, Mark v, Luke xiii, also the passage in Pliny the Younger, Book XXVII, Letter 7. He recalled the story of the shade of Samuel which appeared to Saul, and the striking passage of St. Augustine in his treatise, *De Cura pro Mortuis Gerenda.*

The commentaries and quotations of Gotofred show the importance attached to the question. In the Middle Ages it was magnified and exaggerated by the preponderance of demonological literature. These mysterious manifestations, these disturbances and troubles inflicted upon the inhabitants of a house, overwhelmed them beyond measure on account of the rooted conviction that it meant a satanic intervention. One must go through the best-known demonological books, the *Malleus* of Sprenger, the *Formicarius* of Nider, the *Disquisitiones Magicæ* of Fr. Martin del Rio, and also those of the Protestant theologians of that epoch, beginning with Martin Luther, to see how far the Devil's power was thought capable of extending. It is *everywhere,* and any event, even the simplest, can be caused by a malign influence. It is also omniscient, and knows the past, the present, and the future.

Numerous quotations of ancient and modern authors are reported by l'Espagnol del Rio in his *Disquisitiones*.

Grimaldi Ginesio, in his *Istoria delle Leggi e Magistrati del Regno di Napoli* (vol. ix, p. 4) in the Pragmatic Commentary, *De Locato et Conducto,* published by Count de Miranda on December 24, 1587, writes as follows. "If it happens that in a rented house the tenant, driven by panic terror, believes he is assailed by those malignant spirits called in Naples the *Monacelli,* he is allowed to leave without a payment in compensation."

All the best-known French legal commentaries deal with this question at length, mentioning the jurisprudence of the ancient parliaments of Paris and Bordeaux.

Troplong, treating *De la Permutation et de la Location* (Article 1702 of the Code Civil of Napoléon, which corresponds to 1577 of the Italian Code, par. 197), mentions, "*ce vice rédhibitoire,* apparition of ghosts and phantoms in rented houses."

A certain person having rented a house, says Charondas *(Responsi,* Book VII, 232), he had hardly entered when he heard very loud and fearful noises of ghosts which appeared in the house, and gave insupportable annoyance to himself and his family. During the night several visions presented themselves to his sons and tormented them. The tenant on that account demanded of the proprietor the cancellation and annulment of his contract, since the owner, before completing the lease, knew that these phantoms and spectres appeared in the house, having known it from previous tenants who had abandoned the house for the same reason. "The fact having been amply proved, the law alone was in question." The court did not wish to decide the question of spirits *because that question appertained to religion.* It judged, nevertheless, that it had jurisdiction with regard to the observance of agreements and contracts between persons, and found nothing in Roman or French law to show that fear of apparitions or ghosts was held to be sufficient to cancel or annul the lease of a house, and judgment was delivered accordingly.

See also Dalloz *(Jurisprudence général: Répertoire de*

jurisprudence, Paris, 1853, vol. xxx, p. 313, par. 190); Duvergnier, No. 528; Troplong, No. 197, etc.

Such is the thesis sustained by the Italian advocate.

We see that the lawyers are in accord with general opinion. I only point out these facts in order to establish first of all the following fact:

Haunted houses have been recognised for several centuries by European jurisprudence.

To deny the reality of haunted houses is an error such as is committed by ignorance very often in such matters.

Haunting has always existed. Theologians have often commented on these facts, for, during centuries, civilisation has consisted in discussing *words,* instead of studying *realities* by observation or experiment. They explained everything by demons. But in our days one hardly believes in demons. We require an explanation more accessible to verification.

This first survey has shown us a certain number of very varied examples—queer, inexplicable, puerile, childish, of a rather irritating triviality, but real, observed, and verified—experienced by unimpeachable witnesses, who suffered to the point of abandoning their dwellings where they had existed very comfortably, and of asking for the cancellation of important leases. What can be the meaning of these incomprehensible doings whose triviality repels us? They reveal intentional acts, confused ideas, an inferior mentality. On our planet we have no example of thought without a brain. Yet certain effects of lightning are so singular as to give the impression of a hidden intention, as in the case of the lady who was discussed at the *Académie des Sciences* (*Autour de la Mort,* p. 311).

On the other hand, the laws which govern the world system do not come from a brain. There is spirit in nature.

What is that "instinct" of a fowl which sits on her eggs for twenty days to hatch chickens? What is the perpetual renewal of myriads of living beings? The singular facts we wish to study here indicate fantastic manifestations of this unknown spirit, which is probably unknowable to us.

It is only, as we say, a first survey. A general excursion among haunted houses will be presented later.

We have a large number of facts for careful examination. They are so numerous that before entering this forest we must first stop to consider some examples which have been precisely observed. We shall start with one of the most typical and complete.

The true but hardly credible story which follows will bring us straight to the part of this very mysterious domain of haunted houses.

CHAPTER III

STRANGE PHENOMENA IN A CALVADOS CASTLE

HERE, as I have just said, we penetrate to the heart of our subject. The following account of the strange phenomena observed in 1875 in a Norman castle was drawn up by M. J. Morice, doctor of laws, on the report of the owner and witnesses, and was published in the *Annales des Sciences Psychiques* of 1893. "The honesty and intelligence of the owner of this castle," so writes my learned friend, Dr. Dariex, the editor of the *Annales,* "cannot be questioned by anyone. He is an energetic and intelligent man. He himself noted down every day all the extraordinary facts which he and the inhabitants of the castle witnessed, just as they occurred. These persons attested in turn the reality of the facts. But the owner has asked the narrator to see that *no names are printed.*" (We may regret this restriction.) Here follows the account, abridged where possible, for the observations were numerous, and lasted a long time:[1]

About the year 1835 there existed in that parish an old castle belonging to the B. family.

The place was in such a state of decay that a restoration was considered out of the question. It was replaced by another, built 150 yards to the north of the old castle.

M. de X. inherited it in 1867, and took up his residence there.

In the month of October of that year there was a series

[1] See *Annales des sciences psychiques,* 1893, p. 65.

of extraordinary incidents, nocturnal noises and blows, which, after ceasing for some years, says M. de X. in his diary of 1875, commenced afresh at that time.

The Châteaux du T. had always passed for a scene of fantastic phenomena, and the haunt of more or less evil ghosts. The X. family knew nothing of these noises when it took possession.

Here are some extracts from the diary in question. These detailed relations are very long, but of intense interest. They form, indeed, a documentary procès-verbal.

This is October, 1875 [writes the owner]. I propose to note down and record every day what happened during the night before. I must point out that when the noises occurred while the ground was covered with snow, there was no trace of footsteps round the castle. I drew threads across all openings, secretly. They were never found broken.

At present our household consists of the following: M. and Mme. de X. and their son; the Abbé Y., tutor to the son; Émile, coachman; Auguste, gardener; Amélina, housemaid; Célina, cook. All the domestics sleep in the house, and are entirely trustworthy.

Wednesday, October 13, 1875.—The Abbé Y. having told us that his armchair changed its place, my wife and I accompanied him to his room, and we minutely observed the place of every object. We attached gummed paper to the foot of the armchair, and so fixed it to the floor. We left him then, asking him to call me should anything extraordinary happen. At a quarter to ten the Abbé heard on the wall of his room a series of slight raps, which, however, were loud enough to be also heard by Amélina, who slept in the opposite room. He then heard in a corner of the room a noise as of the winding of a big clock. Then a candlestick on his mantelpiece was moved with a grating noise, and finally he heard and thought he saw his armchair move. As he durst not get up, he rang the bell, and I went up. On entering the room

I found the armchair had moved over a yard and was turned towards the fireplace. An extinguisher placed on the base of the candlestick was put on the candle; the other candlestick had been moved into a position where it overhung the mantelpiece by about an inch. A statuette placed against the mirror had been advanced 8 inches. I retired after twenty minutes. We heard two violent blows from the Abbé's direction, who rang the bell and assured me that the blows had been struck on the door of his wardrobe, at the foot of his bed.

There is a promising beginning. But let us continue the diary:

Thursday, October 14.—Violent blows are heard. We arm ourselves and go over the castle, but discover nothing.

Friday, October 15.—About 10 p.m. the Abbé and Amélina clearly heard steps imitating my wife's and mine, as well as our conversation. It sounded to them as if we were going along the passage into our room. Amélina maintains that she recognised both our voices. Then she heard the opening of my wife's door, but was not frightened because she thought it was ourselves. We were asleep and heard nothing. But at a quarter past eleven everybody was awakened by a series of very loud blows in the green room. Auguste and I made a general tour of inspection, and while in the drawing-room we heard blows near the linen-press. We went there, but found nothing, and came down. Madame and Amélina heard a piece of furniture being dragged on the floor above, where nobody was. It then seemed to fall heavily.

Saturday, October 16.—Everybody is awakened by a series of heavy blows, about half an hour after midnight. An armed tour of inspection yields no result.

Monday, October 18.—The number of witnesses is increased. The curate of the parish has kindly come to sleep in the castle since Saturday. He has heard the noises quite clearly, and will continue to pass the nights here. He will therefore be a witness of anything else which may be heard. To-night Marcel de X. will arrive. He will sleep on the second floor, and leave his door open so as to estimate the nature and direction of the noises. Auguste sleeps in the passage near his door. About eleven o'clock everybody was awakened by the noise of a large and heavy ball descending from the second floor to the first, and jumping from step to step. After half a minute there was a very loud single blow, and then nine or ten muffled ones.

Tuesday, October 19.—The parish priest of M. has come at our request to sleep here. He clearly heard a heavy tread slowly descending the stairs, and then, as the night before, half a minute afterwards, a single heavy blow from about the middle of the staircase which leads down to the ground floor. He has no doubt this is supernatural. Marcel returns home with the same conviction.

Why supernatural? Do we know all the forces of nature? But let us continue this fantastic story:

The sounds ceased completely until Saturday, October 30, when everybody was awakened by a series of loud blows.

Sunday, October 31.—A very disturbed night. It sounded as if someone went up the stairs with superhuman speed from the ground floor, stamping his feet. Arrived on the landing, he gave five heavy blows, so strong that objects suspended on the wall rattled in their places. Then it seemed as if a heavy anvil or a big log has been thrown on to the wall, so as to shake the house. Nobody could say whence came these blows. Everybody got up and assembled in the passage of the first floor. We made a minute inspection but found nothing. We went to bed, but more noises obliged us to get up again. We could only go to rest at about three o'clock.

Wednesday, November 3.—At 10.20 p.m. everybody was awakened by resounding steps, which quickly ascended the stairs. A series of blows shook the walls. We immediately got up. Shortly afterwards we heard the noise of a heavy elastic body rolling down the stairs from the second to the first floor, and bouncing from step to step. Arriving on the landing, it continued on its course along the passage, stopping at the balusters. Then came two loud thumps, followed by a formidable blow as with a carpenter's mallet swung at arm's length upon the door of the green room. Then a series of tripping and repeated raps sounding like the steps of animals.

Thursday, November 4.—When we were going to bed Auguste asked me to come and hear a long series of taps he heard on the second floor, where he sleeps now. When I got there I heard nothing. I minutely inspected the granary and the red room, leaving the door of the latter open. Auguste and Armand, Amélina's brother, were with me, and we carried a light. At the end of three minutes, five very distinct blows were heard in the red room, which nobody could enter without being seen or heard, nor, I must add, without coming within range of my revolver, which never leaves me, as everybody knows. Hardly had I gone downstairs when five more blows were heard, distinctly by Auguste, and feebly by me, as I was on the floor below.

Friday, November 5.—At 2 a.m. some being rushed at top speed up the stairs from the entrance hall to the first floor, along the passage, and up to the second floor, with a loud noise of tread which had nothing human about it. Everybody heard it. It was like two legs deprived of their feet and walking on the stumps. Then we heard numerous loud blows on the stairs and the door of the green room.

Wednesday, November 10.—At 1 a.m. there was a rushing gallop in the hall and on the stairs. A big blow was heard on the landing, followed by another violent one on the door of the green room. This took two minutes. A storm of wind, thunder, and lightning came and made the night hideous. At 1.20 the door of the green room was unlatched. Then there were two loud knocks on the door, three inside the room, three more on the door, and finally a prolonged rapping on the second floor, forty raps at least. This lasted 2½ minutes. At that moment everybody heard something like a cry, or a long-drawn trumpet call, audible above the storm. It seemed to me to come from outside. A little while afterwards everybody heard a long shriek, and then another, as of a woman outside calling for help. At 1.45 we suddenly heard three or four loud cries in the hall, and then on the staircase. We all got up and went round inspecting carefully. At 3.20 there was a galloping in the passage. We heard two fainter cries, but these were in the house.

Friday, November 12.—Several blows were heard, then shrill and loud cries as if there were several people. More plaintive cries in the hall. At 11.45 these stifled cries seemed to come from the cellar, then other louder ones on the staircase. At midnight everybody got up, for cries were heard in the cellar, then inside the green home, and finally sobs and cries of a woman in horrible suffering.

Saturday, November 13.—Not only are we troubled by night, but to-day even in the daytime: at 3 p.m., blows in the dining-room; inspection without result. At 3.15, noises in the green room: we go there and find an easy-chair moved and placed against the door so as to prevent its opening. We put it back. At 3.40, steps in Madame's room, and easy-chair was moved. We paid a second visit to the green room, and found the easy-chair placed against the door again. Madame and Amélina went with the Abbé to his room, and before their eyes the window of the cabinet, which was closed, opened. The wind was southerly and that window was to the north. In Madame's room an easy-chair changed place again. In the Abbé's room, the window, which was closed, was opened again.

Saturday, November 13, *at night.*—Galloping as on preceding nights. Thirteen raps on the landing, eight violent ones on the door of the green room. The door opens and is banged violently. At 12.15 a.m., two loud cries on the landing. It is no longer the cry of a weeping woman, but shrill, furious, despairing cries, the cries "of demons or the damned." For another hour violent blows are heard.

Sunday, November 14.—The Abbé's windows, though well closed, were opened during Mass. He had locked his door and taken the key with him. Nobody could get into his room. During Vespers another of his windows opened.

Tuesday, November 23.—About two o'clock I was awakened from profound sleep by knocks in the passage and other noises in my room, but the sudden and painful awakening did not allow me time to find out their true nature. Next morning the Abbé told us he had heard at the same hour similar noises coming from the same direction. My wife, on getting up, found a general upset on her dressing-table.

Sunday, December 19.—During Vespers Émile, who stayed in the house, heard the shovels and fire tongs in the kitchen fall on the floor. On returning from Vespers, Mme. de X. heard walking up and down. It was the noise of heavy steps in the Abbé's room, where there was nobody.

Monday, December 20.—At a quarter past twelve Mme. de X. found on entering her room two chairs placed upside down on two arm-chairs. I went into the other rooms. In the blue room I found a chair placed on the side table.

Friday, December 24.—At midday, when all the domestic servants were at table, we found, in the Abbé's room, the bed turned on its side and the table pushed under it. In the evening, at six o'clock, we opened the door of the same room, which was locked, and found the table placed on the middle of the bed.

Saturday, December 25.—At noon, when all the servants were at table, knocks were heard in the Abbé's room, though his door was locked. We inspected it and found an arm-chair placed on Maurice's desk. On returning from Vespers we found in the Abbé's room the couch upside down, the alarum on the glass case of the clock, and a chair on the table. In the evening, at 9 p.m., we heard the broom moving about the passage of the second floor. On going up we found that it had changed its place.

Sunday, December 26.—Coming home from High Mass, we went with the Abbé up to his locked room. The cushions of the couch had disappeared. We found them placed on end, one beside the other, on the outer window-sill of his toilet cabinet. Before I put in a second window I had stopped up this window by a piece of wood securely nailed to the inner frame. That piece of wood had been torn out without the trace of any tool and placed beside the cushions. The window was closed again.

1 p.m.: Twice we heard knocks in the house. Mme. de X. went on a round and found the Abbé's room open, though he had locked it. A few minutes afterwards the drawing-room couch moved forward in two noisy rushes. Further noises upstairs, and another inspection. The Abbé's door, which had been locked, had opened.

5 p.m.: After vespers we found a candlestick on the top of the Abbé's lamp, and the water-bottle placed on the base of the glass, which had been reversed. In his cabinet two shoes had been disposed fanwise on the window and others on the plate by the night-light.

Sunday, December 26 *to Monday, December* 27.—In the evening, at nine o'clock, I went with Auguste to stay in the linen-room, leaving the door open. We heard a series of knocks like those of a stick walking and knocking on the floor of the passage facing us. We had lighted a light. Shortly afterwards Amélina heard steps descending to the kitchen, and the noise of pieces of wood being broken, though none were in the kitchen. Nobody was visible.

Monday, December 27.—In the afternoon we all went to V——. The cook, who remained alone with a daily helper, told us that all was quiet. We went into the Abbé's room, which had been locked, and found all his books, at least a hundred, strewn over the floor. Only three volumes remained up, each on its shelf. These were books of the Holy Scriptures. Devotional books had also been thrown on the floor from the mantelpiece, and the broom had been placed over them.

This account is very lengthy, of course, but it is evidently very varied. I abridge it as much as is possible while preserving its intrinsic value. Here is the sequel:

Night of Tuesday, December 28 *to Wednesday, December* 29.—Three loud muffled blows on the second floor, followed immediately by numerous knocks along the second-floor passage. Then three series of three knocks each delivered sharply on the Abbé's door, then two isolated knocks followed by the noise of ironware. Two more sets of three knocks, sharp and impatient, and finally a big blow on the door of the green room. Total duration, three minutes.

Wednesday, December 29.—One of my music books is placed inside the piano. Mme. de X., hearing a noise in the Abbé's room, goes up there, followed by the latter. She heard a movement in the room, and put out her right hand to open the latch of the door. Before she could touch it she saw the key turn quickly in the lock and detach itself, hitting her left hand. The Abbé witnessed this. The blow was so strong that the place was sensitive and visible two days afterwards. In the evening we found in the blue room a coverlet thrown into the middle of the room and a night-table taken into the cabinet and resting on a pillow. The ewer had changed places with a crystal bottle.

Night of Wednesday, December 29, *to Thursday, December* 30.—At 12.30 a.m. we were suddenly awakened by four thunderous blows on the door of Mme. de X.'s room. To acquire some idea of their violence, one must imagine a wall collapsing, or a horse or four cannon-balls thrown against a door. It would be no exaggeration. The noise suddenly changed over to the other end of the passage and a violent blow was heard on the door of the green room. Several loud muffled knocks were heard upstairs, which shook the house. They moved about, growing in loudness.

12.40 a.m.: Two noises of ironware at the end of the passage. A loud knock on the door of the green room.

12.50 a.m.: A prolonged walking with great strides on the second floor. A witness counted thirty-two paces. Forty blows on the Abbé's door, five on the green room, ten on the flooring, two on the door, and five muffled blows which made the walls and furniture tremble on every floor. Total duration, four minutes.

Thursday, December 30.—After lunch, when all the servants were at table, we found in the Abbé's room a footstool placed on my son's desk and covered with an antimacassar. At 2 p.m. I went up with the Abbé to his room, and we found the arm-chair on the table. On its seat the antimacassar was spread out, and a lamp was placed on the antimacassar. A cross and some blest medals, which had been attached to the door, had disappeared.

Night of Thursday, December 30.—At 12.40 a.m. three blows were struck slowly on the door of the green room; eight muffled blows upstairs, shaking the house. Three noisy blows on the first-floor landing. Many steps were heard along the whole second-floor passage, sometimes quick, sometimes slow. These steps were quite unlike human steps. No animal could walk like that; it was more like a stick jumping on one of its ends.

6 a.m.: More raps on the second floor, witnessed by the parish priest of Saint P——, who slept here. Some things happened in his room. He heard something like the noise of an animal with boards under its feet, coming to the room adjoining his own, climbing on to the side table, crossing over to his pillow, entering his bed and stopping at the level of his left elbow. The priest had a light and was wide awake, but saw nothing. At 6 a.m., having gone into the green room, he heard something like the noise of rubbed straw, first on the couch, then in the window corner, on the curtain rod, and finally on the bed. The priest said there was no straw or anything like it in the room. Martial, our farm-manager, slept with us that night. He was followed by noises heard under his feet in the gardener's presence.

New Year's Eve, 1876.—At 12.40 we were all awakened by a series of terrible blows on the door of the green room. After these came others inside the room, and then a single blow, followed by quick running along passages and stairs. Nine strong blows inside the green room. Prolonged rappings in the second-floor passage, and finally four muffled blows. Total duration, seven minutes.

Night of Saturday, January 1, *to Sunday, January* 2.—At 1.5 a.m. loud blows were struck on the door of the green room, and we all awoke. A stampede along the passage of the first floor and then of the second floor.

Afterwards we heard thirteen irregular knocks, in pairs, inside the green room. Then various steps coming from above. A violent blow fell on the door of the green room, and three more inside. Eight muffled blows seemed to come from the second floor. The taper beside me shook at each blow.

6.30 a.m.: Several blows in the passage resembling those of the night. It is notable that for the last three mornings those who come downstairs from their rooms are followed step by step down to the ground floor by raps which stop and start with them. The parish curate has been followed in this way, but saw nothing.

Monday, January 3.—In the evening I was alone in the drawing-room about 5.15 p.m. I had a light and heard six well-marked raps on the small table standing two yards away from me. I turned round, but saw nothing.

Night of Monday, January 3, *to Tuesday, January* 4.—At 3 a.m. a dozen blows were struck in pairs on the door of Mme. de X's room. The nearest window shook at every blow. There was a light in the room. We were wide awake and quite cool, but saw nothing. Five minutes afterwards we heard a stampede, something like a stick jumping on one of its ends, in the first-floor and then in the second-floor passage; then some dull and feeble knocks. Dr. L., who has slept here, heard the noise of the running in the passage, but nothing else. The parish priest of La B—— slept in the red room, and heard during the greater part of the night a series of feeble but very extraordinary noises in his passage. He did not venture to go to bed. He is convinced that this can only be supernatural.

Wednesday, January 5.—The Rev. Fr. H. L., a Premonstrant Canon, has been sent here by the Bishop to judge the facts and help us. About 5 p.m., a few moments before his arrival, Mme. de X. heard in the drawing-room with her son the sound of the door shaken violently and saw the handle turn quickly. Maurice was frightened, and Mme. de X. began to sing loudly to prevent him hearing it.

Presence of the Rev. Fr. H. L.—From the moment the Rev. Father arrived a sudden and absolute calm set in. Nothing happened either by day or by night. On January 15 he made a religious ceremony. From that day we heard some isolated and unusual noises in the night, but always from places too far away from Fr. H. L. for him to hear. He left us on Monday, the 17th, and his departure was immediately followed by a new set of phenomena as intense and serious as those which preceded his coming.

Night of January 17 *to* 18.—At 11 p.m. there was a noise as of a body falling in the first-floor passage, followed by that of a rolling ball giving a violent blow on the door of the green room. Prolonged stampede on the second floor, followed by twenty dull knocks in the same place and eighteen inside the green room. At 11.35 p.m. there were five great blows on the door of the green room, and fifteen dull ones on the second-floor staircase, two kicks on the landing, and ten dull knocks on the second-floor staircase, making everything round us shake.

Night of January 19 *to* 20.—At 11.15 p.m. we were wakened by a stampede upstairs, followed by fifteen violent blows on the door of the green room and fifty-five more inside. Shortly afterwards five blows as with a carpenter's mallet on the first-floor stairs. Prolonged stampede. Five dull blows, drumming inside the green room, three blows on the door of the room, twenty-seven on the window of my room, the last two of which made the windows of Mme. de X. shake. Duration, ten minutes.

At 1.45 a.m. eleven blows in my room.

M. de X., having left for a few days on a visit to his brother, requested his wife to take notes in his absence. Here are these notes:

Night of January 20 *to* 21.—1.8 a.m.: Five ordinary raps, followed by nineteen blows in the passage; two on the door of the linen-room, followed by six more; nine on the door of the green room, and eleven on the second floor, followed by a number of rhythmic raps on the second floor. Duration, seven minutes. Twelve dull knocks on the second floor, and eight raps seeming to pass from door to door.

1.25 a.m.: Everybody hears four loud cries like bellowings, outside but at the level of the window, then something like strokes with a wand on the stairs. Shortly afterwards ten stronger blows, followed by drumming on the second floor.

1.30 a.m.: Two heavy blows on the second floor, shaking mirrors and other objects in the rooms.

2.5 a.m.: Numerous raps on the stairs, one on the door of the linen-room, several on the door of the green room, one of them a resounding one; five strong dull blows on the second floor, which shake all the furniture. Five feebler blows on the stairs, four on the second floor. Bellowing in the north outside the house at the level of the first-floor windows.

5.45 a.m.: A blow sounds in the passage. Running is heard, then the door of the green room, which opens and shuts violently. It is locked and the handle is torn off. Finally a sort of ball seems to roll along the same passage and to deliver a blow near the top of the stairs. The same night Mme. de X. heard a voluminous body falling heavily from her table to the ground. She looked, but could see nothing.

Night of January 21 *to* 22.—At 3 a.m. we are awakened by fifteen knocks on the second floor.

Night of January 22 *to* 23.—At 3 a.m. we are awakened by a set of twenty dull blows on the second floor.

The following notes are by M. de X.:

Night of January 23 *to* 24.—At 9 p.m. a stampede was heard in our passage, followed by a series of feebler raps. The night was calm. This morning at 6 a.m. and then at 7 a.m. we heard a series of raps also in our passage. To-day I leave for P——. My wife will note what takes place in my absence.

January 25.—At 4.30 p.m. much noise upstairs. Madame goes up with Amélina and finds the beds of Auguste and Émile turned over, and, strangely enough, in an absolutely identical manner. After observing this disorder, Madame goes to the red room; the door resists, being obstructed by a heavy arm-chair. She puts it back and continues her inspection. As she goes to my study a frame placed inside against the door falls against her legs, and she finds everything in disorder—prints thrown on the ground, the arm-chair upside down and heaped with papers, maps, etc.

5.10 p.m.: The Abbé was reading his breviary. Although for three days there had been beautiful weather, a mass of water fell through the chimney on to the fire, extinguishing it and scattering the ashes. The Abbé was blinded and had his face covered with ashes.

Night of January 25 to 26.—At 12.20 a.m. two blows in the hall. At 1 a.m. twelve blows, followed by long drumming, then thirty rapid blows of a peculiar character, or, rather, a shaking of the whole house. Beds all over the house shaken. Afterwards nine blows in succession, five on the door of the green room, then a long stampede. The total duration was only five minutes. A minute afterwards the entire house was shaken from top to bottom. Then there were ten terrible blows on the door of the green room, a dozen cries outside, three bellowings, then furious shouts. A very loud drumming in the hall, apparently in rhythm. Fifty blows quite close to my room. Several knocks at the door of my son Maurice.

1.30 a.m.: The house was shaken twenty times, seven blows on the door of the green room, followed by blows so rapid that they could not be counted; two on the door of the green room, twelve near Maurice's room, thirteen which made everything tremble, then in succession five, ten, and eighteen blows, shaking walls and furniture. There was hardly time to note them down. Nine terrible blows on the door of the green room, a drumming interspersed with loud blows, seven which shake everything, one very resounding, then a series of ten blows in pairs. At this moment a sound was heard like a bull roaring, then other inhuman furious cries in the passage near my wife's room, who got up and rang to waken all the servants. When everybody was up and assembled in the Abbé's room, we heard two bellowings and a shout.

At 4.20 everybody went back to bed. Mme. de X. heard a rather loud blow on the organ in her room, two yards from her bed. It was followed by three more blows whose direction she could not make out. The noises were heard clearly on the farm.

Night of January 26 *to* 27.—Two further witnesses: the parish priest of Saint M—— came to pass the night, and Mlle. de L. came for several days.

At 12.15 a.m. everybody was awakened by a very violent noise such as would be caused by a board falling on the floor of the first-floor passage. It was followed by a cry. At 12.45, a stampede and heavy blows. After a short pause they began again and seemed accompanied by the shifting of heavy boxes. Maurice's door was shaken. Finally there were four blows on the door of the green room.

Night of January 28 *to* 29.—At 11.15 p.m., a piercing cry on the stairs, raucous and sharp. Seven blows in the green room; six very loud ones on the door of the room.

At 11.45, nineteen very dull blows on one of the doors in the passage.

At 12.55 a.m. we heard something like the voice of a man in the first-floor passage. It seemed to cry twice "Ha! Ha!" Immediately there were ten resounding blows, shaking everything all round. One blow on the door of the green room. Then the sound of coughing in the first-floor passage. We rose quickly, saw nothing, and found at my wife's door a large earthenware plate broken into ten pieces.

We have had a Novena of Masses said at Lourdes. The Reverend Father has made the exorcisms and everything has stopped. (See below p. 128).

I must admit that every worldly reader who has never heard of the phenomena of haunting might attribute the preceding descriptions to the brains of lunatics or persons under hallucination. Yet these facts are true. The idea of the supernatural is evidently dominant in this family and their surroundings. We have to appreciate these things in a purely scientific manner. Out of numerous attestations collected by Dr. Dariex I shall quote some documents as complementary declarations, which will replace details suppressed in the preceding descriptions to avoid undue prolixity.

A letter from the Abbé D., late tutor of the son of Madame de X., and now parish priest in Normandy, to M. Morice.

I have been a witness of all the things which happened at the Castle of T—— from October 12, 1875, to January 30, 1876. I can testify that the things related in the preceding MS. cannot be the work of a man. All these noises were not only heard by one person but by a large number of witnesses, and the blows were so loud that they could be heard at a distance of 500 yards. I shall not give a new account of the facts, because you know them. Occurrences of this nature also took place in the older castle. During all these troubles M. de X. took every imaginable precaution. How could a man have got into my room and changed the places of all the objects without my seeing him? How could he have got on the chimney-piece and poured water on my fire so as to cover me with ashes? And this in the daytime, and at a time of drought? My pupil was a witness of the occurrence, and I can still see him running. How was it that M. de X.'s dog, a well-trained animal, showed no astonishment amidst the greatest noises? How explain the opening of a well-closed window before our eyes? The cries we heard were not the cries of human beings. Often the walls of the castle were so much shaken that I was afraid of the ceiling falling on my head. Where could we find a man who could do all that? I, for one, can only think of the Devil.

Letter from M. Morice to M. Dariex.

M——,
January 12, 1893.

Dear Doctor,

M. de X., as we see by the last sentence of his MS., attributed the cessation of the phenomena to the ceremony of exorcism and to the prayers he had said after the ceremony. When he wrote it—*i.e., on January* 29—M. de X. certainly had some reason; but circumstances soon disillusioned him.

By itself, the ceremony of exorcism yielded no result at all. It was performed on January 14 or 15, and we know by the account given by M. de X. himself what happened from that date until January 29. We must admit that after the prayers prescribed by the exorcising priest peace seemed to return at the end of January. But at the end of August and especially in September the castle of T—— again became the scene of events as strange as those which we know already.

I have applied to one of the witnesses who spent the whole year 1876 at the castle of T—— as tutor to M. de X.'s son, and this is his answer:

Letter from the Abbé M. to M. G. Morice.

B——,
January 20, 1893.

Sir,

After the exorcisms a great calm set in. One almost incredible thing took place, which gave us much hope for the future. Here it is: You have seen from the diary that medals of St. Bénoit, indulgenced crosses, and Lourdes medals had been placed on all the doors. These medals and crosses amounted to a good-sized package. You have also seen that on the following night a tremendous noise occurred and that next day medals and crosses had disappeared so that nothing could be found, though they and the doors were very numerous. Now the exorcisms had ceased and were succeeded by several days of peace. You may imagine how agreeable these days were. But two or three days afterwards Madame was writing some lines on her knees by a little desk when suddenly an immense packet of medals and crosses fell in front of her on the desk. It might have been about 10.30 a.m. Whence came these medals? They were all the medals placed on the doors except those of Lourdes.

The good priest of T——, to whom the story was told, and who, like myself, knew the sincerity and honesty of the castle people and wished to keep them in his parish, said to them: "Have courage, the Devil surrenders his arms, everything is finished I may assure you. You will be left in peace." But to me the good man said: "I am still afraid, much afraid, because Lourdes has not come back."

Towards the end of August the small noises came back more frequently and clearly. One night several persons, including myself, heard quick and fairly loud knocks in the linen-room. They were just like those produced the previous year when the phenomena commenced.

One Saturday night before the third Sunday in September a great noise occurred in the drawing-room and continued for a part of the night. In the morning, M. de X., who had the key of the drawing-room in his pocket, went down in some anxiety. He opened the door and found the couch and arm-chairs moved far from their places. All was arranged as for a council meeting, horseshoe-fashion, with the couch in the centre.

Well, the Devil had held council and was about to begin again. M. de X. opened his harmonium and played for a long time. As he closed the instrument, some of the airs he had been playing were repeated in the opposite corner of the drawing-room for a considerable time.

Some days afterwards M. de X. was away for three days. During that time Madame kept a lamp and two candles alight in her room. As she was particularly afraid of ghosts, she bolted the door of her toilet cabinet and said to herself, "Now I shall only have the entrance door to keep in view." At midnight we all heard a terrible blow, which awakened us, and Madame heard something like the noise of a package of linen which had fallen into her room. At that moment the lamp and candles went out and Madame heard the click of the bolt being withdrawn. And *it had been drawn.*

The next day Madame heard a note of a small organ in her room sound for some time. The next day after that I heard about 2.30 p.m. the same organ playing several airs. Madame and a lady friend were away. I expected M. de X. back, but he only came in at 6 p.m. I told him what had happened, and he said: "I have the key of the organ in my pocket." It was true, *and the organ had been locked.*

Another time, in my own room, a cupboard heavily laden with books and linen *rose* 20 inches from the ground and remained up for some time. My young pupil pointed it out to me. I pressed on the cupboard, but it did not yield. It resumed its place of itself afterwards. It may have been 3 o'clock in the afternoon.

One evening the windows of my room opened several times. There was no wind.

(Sg.) X
(Parish Priest of B——).

There is only one thing to be added, viz., that the authors of the above letters are priests whose perfect good faith cannot be doubted for a moment.

(Sg.) G. Morice.

Here, to clinch the matter, is an extract from a letter of Mme. Le N. de V. to Dr. Dariex:

The Castle came into the possession of M. de X., I believe, by inheritance. The former owner is said to have died in final impenitence, and was supposed to revisit her castle.

When the first noises occurred, M. de X. thought he had to do with living people wishing to frighten him sufficiently to make him abandon the castle, which would in such circumstances have been sold for a song with its surrounding land. He therefore instituted a close examination and sounded the walls and cellars to find the forgotten passages by which one could enter. In spite of the most careful vigilance no origin of these noises could be found, and they increased in spite of all precautions.

He bought two formidable watch dogs, which were released every night, but to no purpose.

One day the animals started barking in the direction of

one of the thickets of the garden with such persistence that M. de X. thought the miscreants had hidden themselves there. He armed himself and his servants, surrounded the thicket and released the dogs. They rushed in with fury, but hardly had they got in when their barks changed into plaintive whines, like those of dogs being chastised. They ran away with their tails between their legs and could not be prevailed upon to go back. The men then went in and searched in every direction, but found absolutely nothing.

The Abbé's room was always the place where the greatest devilries took place. He never went out without double-locking it and putting the key in his pocket. It made no difference. His window, carefully closed, was found open. His furniture had been moved and upset. The window was screwed up. It was opened all the same, and the screws were found on the floor. One day, as the Abbé descended, he heard in his room a noise so loud that he immediately went up again. His library was upset and his books thrown to the other end of the room, not pell-mell as out of a piece of furniture which fell, but in regular files, just as they had been on the shelves.

The state of fear became so great that the Abbé and his pupil went to stay with the parish priest.

Another thing: A friend or cousin, an officer, wanted to spend a night in the particularly haunted room where nobody slept as a rule. He had his revolver and was determined to shoot at anyone who would disturb his sleep. He kept a light burning. He was awakened by the *frou-frou* of a silken robe. He felt that the coverlet over his feet was drawn away. He addressed the nocturnal visitor without eliciting a reply and lighted his candle, which went out again at once. Three times he lighted it, and three times it went out. And still the *frou-frou* and the interference with the coverlet continued. He decided to shoot at the point indicated by the displacement of the bedclothes as the probable position of the intruder and thought to hit that being point-blank. He fired without any result. Yet the balls had not been withdrawn from the cartridges, for they were found in the wall next morning.

Here is another supplementary letter:

Letter from Fr. F., Parish Priest, to M. Morice

MONSIEUR LE DOCTEUR,

I can testify that I heard the strange noises reported in the diary of M. de X. I have read that diary and find it perfectly accurate.

I have no doubt concerning the nature of the occurrences at the castle of T——. To me they are *diabolically supernatural.* You might consult Rev. Fr. H., who is acting as parish priest of M——. He passed a fortnight or three weeks at the castle. He had been sent by the Bishop to make the (secret) exorcisms if he judged it appropriate.

(Sg.) J. A.
Parish Priest of S—— D——.

The letter of the Reverend Father has also been published. But, indeed, any further documents would be superfluous. The reality of these amazing phenomena is beyond doubt.

As a consequence of this intolerable state of things, the despairing owner sold the castle, and went to live elsewhere.

Dr. Dariex terminates this important account of the incomprehensible occurrences in the following lines:

I have recently had a visit from Prince H. who will try, with M. Morice, to extend, if possible, this enquiry already so rich in documents and testimony from witnesses of undoubted honesty and credibility.

The castle of T—— is by far the most remarkable case of haunting we have come across which rests upon such rigorous documents and testimony.

We can cast no doubt upon these numerous observations. They are very remarkable in many ways, and the good faith of those who report the phenomena is undoubted.

(Sg.) XAVIER DARIEX.

This whole story is most extraordinary, no doubt. But its authenticity is as certain as that of the German war of 1914-1918, which, with its terrible crimes, was still more mad and stupid. It is one of the best-established cases within our knowledge, and on that account it is here given at the beginning of our treatise, with its principal details, and not summarised. I shall not stop to consider the matter of the "diabolically supernatural." That discussion must be reserved. Let us continue our investigations without any preconceived ideas. Explanatory researches can only come logically when we have all the observations before us.

Yet it seems to me that we cannot but feel authorised to conclude from all this that *there are invisible beings.*

I shall now bring to the notice of my readers another typical case of a haunted house, which will give us quite as much personal instruction.

CHAPTER IV

THE HAUNTED HOUSE OF LA CONSTANTINIE (CORRÈZE)

MY learned and much-lamented friend, Albert de Rochas, administrator of the École Polytechnique, whose psychical researches are so universally appreciated, always spoke to me with special interest about the observations made on this property in the Département of La Corrèze (district of Objat), and particularly about the special enquiry made by M. Maxwell, *locum tenens* of the Procurator-General, whose competence in these questions is equally known to all. Colonel de Rochas published this enquiry in his book on the externalisation of motricity (Paris, 1896) in the following manner, accompanied by a plan of the house:

La Constantinie is quite a considerable property. The dwelling-house, built on the slope of a hillock, is composed of structures in the form of a square. That portion of the house which contains the front doors is on a ground floor raised some steps above the ground. It contains a large kitchen comprising the whole width of the building. To the right of the kitchen are a drawing-room and a bedroom.

On the left of the kitchen is a wing of the house, forming two sides of a square, and consisting of a ground floor and a granary with a window. The ground floor of this part of the house is higher than the floor of the kitchen and the two other rooms.

There are four rooms in this wing: a large double-bedded room, lighted by two front windows; an ante-chamber or passage; a second smaller room, "Mme. Faure's room"; and a four-windowed room looking out on the yard surrounded by servants' quarters and containing two beds.

The personnel of La Constantinie comprised a certain number of farm servants, Mme. Faure, her mother-in-law, aged eighty-five, and a young servant of seventeen, Marie Pascarel.

Mme. Faure is a well-educated woman of culture. She is intelligent and energetic, and directs the administration. She comes of an honourable family.

Her aged mother-in-law appears to have preserved all her faculties, though heavily burdened by her age.

The young Marie Pascarel is intelligent and self-confident, with easy manners, though no reproach can be directed against her respectability. Physically she is rather thin, and appears delicate. At the time of the occurrences described below she had not arrived at a state of puberty. She has a sleep-walking sister, and her family are considered rather extraordinary people.

The numerous servants of La Constantinie take their meals in the kitchen, on a solid wooden table 3 feet wide and 9 feet long. The kitchen contains an oven, an immense fireplace with a little bench on the left and two chairs on the right, and some cupboards and shelves.

The phenomena started in the second fortnight of May, 1895, with knocks apparently made on the wall separating the dining-room from the bedroom of the elder Mme. Faure. On May 21, about 9 a.m., Mme. Faure told her daughter-in-law that her bed seemed to strike the partition. Mme. Faure, jun., did not attach much importance to this remark, which she put down to a mistake. Next day at the same hour the sound came again in the same place. Mme. Faure, jun., heard it distinctly. On May 23 nothing remarkable occurred. On Friday morning, the 24th, the noise started afresh in the same room with greater force. The noise was as if the bed hit the partition.

An hour afterwards Mme. Faure, jun., entered her room and found the quilt, the blankets, the sheets, and the pillow thrown on the floor. Other disorders occurred in the house. Three empty casks were displaced in the cellar. In another room the bed was disturbed, the bedclothes being strewn on the floor; a statuette of the Virgin and a coffee-pot filled to the brim had been transported from the cupboard to the middle of the room. They were on the floor, besides a crucifix which had been taken down from the wall.

These things appeared inexplicable to Mme. Faure and they frightened her. She asked her mother-in-law to sleep with her during the night from Friday to Saturday, and Marie Pascarel slept in the same room. The night was, as usual, calm and undisturbed.

On the Saturday morning three great blows were struck on the door of the attic. The stairs leading up to it are closed by a door opening on the hall.

The Faure ladies and their servants immediately went to the room. The bed was in disorder and the coverings again on the floor. The coffee-pot was broken. On leaving this room they went to the kitchen, but they had barely got there when they heard "a frightful commotion." They found three sugar-bowls, a dozen cups, photograph frames and engravings broken on the floor. The three women were very much frightened, for at the moment when all this damage was done in the room the farm servants were in the fields and nobody was in the house except the two ladies and their servant, and all together. They were convinced that supernatural things were happening. Visits from their neighbours reassured them a little, but soon the manifestations took place in the presence of the visitors, who also were frightened.

Amélie Bayle (Mrs. Madrias), an intelligent and reasonable woman of thirty, went to the Faures' at 7.30 a.m. to see the damage. In her presence the cover of a soup-dish standing in front of the fire was thrown violently into the middle of the kitchen. Mrs. Madrias was at that moment sitting in front of the fireplace, with her back to the fire. Mme. Faure, Marie Pascarel, and a young lad were in the room. Mme. Madrias was between the soup-dish and the others.

This phenomenon scared her. She at once left the house with the two young servants.

They returned at about 11.30 a.m. Marie Pascarel was busy in the kitchen picking up the broken crockery which littered the floor. For, according to the witnesses, pots, plates, glasses, and dishes were taken down from the shelves by invisible hands and thrown on the floor, where they broke. Mme. Madrias saw a wooden bottle jump from a shelf and crash at her feet.

Disorders were found in the room where the Faure ladies slept. Mme. Faure's bed was upset. A mirror was taken down. Papers from a shelf were strewn on the floor. Later one of the papers was opened and two drops of blood, still moist, were found on it. Five minutes afterwards Marie Pascarel returned to the room. She then found six drops of blood on the paper.

A number of objects were broken that day, notably an iron saucepan. A plate was torn from the servant's hands.

From Sunday, May 26, to Wednesday, May 29, inclusive no phenomena took place. On Thursday, the 30th, they started afresh with increasing force. Saucepans hanging from pothooks in the kitchen chimney were violently thrown to the ground. About 6 p.m. old Mme. Faure saw her bed move along by itself in her room. The chair on which she was sitting was drawn back. She got up at once and the chair was upset. Marie Pascarel was with her in the room. About 7 or 8 p.m., at supper-time, pieces of wood in the kitchen fell of themselves on the Faure ladies.

Everybody was so much frightened that the Faure ladies and Marie Pascarel went to stay with neighbours.

On Friday, May 31, they sent for the Mayor of Objat, the syndic of bailiffs of the arrondissement of Brive, a ministerial officer of high respectability. M. Delmas wanted to make sure of what was happening and to find the cause of the occurrences. He hesitated to believe that material objects could be thrown and moved without apparent contact. He went into the kitchen and placed some plates on the table, where there was already a stove-brush. M. Delmas sat down in front of the fireplace, with Mme. Faure on his left. The young servant worked at her duties. Under the eyes of M. Delmas, the brush was violently thrown into the fireplace. The servant was at some distance from the table where the brush had been lying.

The ideas of the honourable Mayor of Objat underwent a complete modification. He had come with the conviction that the occurrences described were due to evil-doers. He found that the movements of objects under his eyes were spontaneous. His surprise gave way to uneasiness when he saw a pair of kitchen bellows which lay on a bench in the fireplace slide along the bench, avoid the projections due to the legs of the bench, and throw itself with a great clatter into the middle of the kitchen.

He immediately had the house cleared. Just as she was leaving with the Mayor and the Faure ladies the young Marie Pascarel was hit on the back by a stick 16 inches long thrown with considerable force.

Hardly had he returned to Objat when he was called back. Fire had broken out at La Constantinie. Marie Pascarel had observed that a thick smoke issued from Mme. Faure's room. On entering the room it was found that it came out of the bed of Mme. Faure, jun. There were no flames and no brazier (*sic*). Mme. Faure even used this singular expression in her account of the episode: "The fire went back into the bed." A phenomenon of this kind had already been observed. Marie Pascarel and the elder of the two ladies had sometimes noticed a thick smoke which seemed to issue from the old lady's skirts.

Two days afterwards Marie Pascarel left the service of the Faure ladies without giving notice. They went home, and since then the peace of their house has not been troubled.

These occurrences were told me by M. de N., an official of the Bank of Limoges, whose family possesses estates at Objat. I immediately asked one of my friends, M. B., a Justice of the Peace at D——, and a friend of the Mayor of Objat, to give me details of these events, which had been seized upon by the Press, "The Haunted House of Objat" constituting an attractive title. M. B.'s communications seemed to me sufficiently serious to justify a visit. I went to Objat with this magistrate, and interviewed Marie Pascarel, as well as her brother and guardian.

Accompanied by the Mayor of Objat we went to Mme. Faure, who at first made some difficulty about receiving her former servant.

I then explained that the object of my researches was purely scientific; that the phenomena she had observed interested certain savants with whom I had the honour of communicating, and that the precision and number of testimonies confirming the observations made it desirable to have a detailed account of the events of which her house had been the scene to submit to the scrutiny of these savants. With a very good grace Mme. Faure consented to allow me to collect all the particulars on the spot, and to make any useful experiments. I went over the house, gathered all the details, and made a rough plan of the rooms. The results have been given above.

I have had to confine myself to the principal facts, for on several days movements of objects, without apparent contact, were produced at La Constantinie almost every moment. Even the house cat was one day thrown at the elder Mme. Faure. On another occasion, the latter was slightly injured in the head by an iron hook of the saucepan rack.

Does the strangeness of the phenomena narrated to me by the inhabitants of La Constantinie and their neighbours suffice for rejecting them? Persons who contest *a priori* the possibility of these spontaneous movements of material objects will, of course, not be convinced. But it may be questioned whether it is prudent thus to deny on principle every inexplicable thing. Such a negation is not, in my opinion, in conformity with the true scientific spirit. We know the natural forces we have learnt to utilise, but only very imperfectly. Can we maintain that other quite unknown forces do not exist? I am inclined to think that the contrary is more certain, and that the future will reveal many things. Nature is infinite and we hardly know it.

From this point of view, the study of the phenomena of La Constantinie presents a considerable interest. It has seemed useful to me to describe them to you. It is not less useful to discuss their reality. This discussion can be reduced to the examination of two hypotheses: Was there fraud? And was there much error of observation among the witnesses? The second hypothesis is inadmissible. The material proofs are irrefutable. Numerous movable objects were broken under the very eyes of witnesses. The noise of the fall of these objects, the existence of fragments, gathered at the places where the objects were seen to break, give clear objective confirmations of the testimony. These circumstances also rule out the possibility of hallucination.

There remains the hypothesis of fraud. It naturally occurs to one's mind. It may explain some of the phenomena, but it would seem to require many improbable accessory hypotheses to explain all the facts collected.

If a fraud was committed, by whom was it done? Only three persons can be suspected—the Faure ladies and their servant, Marie Pascarel. Most of the phenomena took place in the presence of those three persons.

The movement of objects without contact was observed in many cases when the other inhabitants of La Constantinie were absent, and could not, therefore, occasion them. Among these cases are the phenomena observed by the Mayor of Objat, and the raps, damages and disorder of the beds in the various rooms of the house when the Faure ladies and their servant were alone.

The Faure ladies can also be eliminated. Without even considering their respectability, the manifest terror in which they lived, and the damage which they suffered, it should weigh with us that no link between them and the phenomena was ever discovered. The latter ceased completely with the departure of Marie Pascarel; on the other hand, certain things occurred when that girl was alone with one or other of the Faure ladies. Finally, the state of physical infirmity of the elder of the Faure ladies precludes her participation in any fraud.

On the other hand, a connection was observed between the presence of Marie Pascarel and the movement of objects without apparent contact. She was always present when the phenomena occurred. Some took place when she was alone, such as the shifting of the casks in the cellar and the fire in the bed. It was she who was the apparent cause of these strange happenings. She was suspected by everybody. Her departure brought about their cessation.

We cannot, therefore, attribute fraud to anyone except Marie Pascarel. Yet even in her case the hypothesis is difficult to admit. Some circumstances seem to make it possible; others tend to eliminate it. The former can be briefly summarised as follows:

She was always at La Constantinie when an inexplicable phenomenon occurred. Her character had its faults. She was not always polite to Mme. Faure. She was intelligent and bold, and meddled in what did not concern her. But her honesty was never doubted. It was she who announced the fire.

If the occurrences were due to fraud, we may conclude that it was she who devised them and who cleverly deceived all the witnesses. Yet the circumstances which tend to exclude fraud are more numerous and weighty than the opposite ones:

(1) Absence of an intelligible motive. Marie Pascarel was in a good situation, and given the country customs in Limousin, she could not easily find another place at that time of the year. It was not, therefore, in her interest to expose herself to a dismissal, or to leave her employment of her own accord. We should remember that at her age, and in her station, she could have no occupation but that of a servant. Her business was to get a job.

These considerations render the hypothesis of a fraud inspired by ill-will very improbable. Yet I admit it is not impossible. But then we should have to attribute to Marie Pascarel a singular audacity. That young girl must, then, have cleverly broken the crockery of her mistresses and upset everything to harm and frighten them. Yet nothing reveals such evil intention in her, though it must have been powerful in order to prevail upon Marie Pascarel to expose herself to all the perils of a discovery. On the other hand, the fire becomes inexplicable on that motive. If she wished to occasion damage, why give the alarm? Indeed, we must credit this young girl with a great deal of daring to believe that she set fire to Mme. Faure's bed at a moment when everybody's attention was excited and her direct or indirect participation began to be suspected.

We must add that the phenomena only occurred in full daylight. A person animated by evil intentions, or simply by an intention of mystification, would surely have chosen the night for the action. She would have found more security, and would have more surely frightened her victims, for night and darkness predispose to fear and credulity. On the contrary, if Marie Pascarel tricked, she chose broad daylight and the presence of many witnesses to carry out her projects of mystification.

Was she impelled by a desire for mystification? Or did she wish to convey the impression that she had a supernatural power? I think not.

In the former case, her mystifications resulted immediately in a considerable increase of work for her, for she had to pick up the fragments and dispose of them. She had to make the beds afresh and repair the disorder in the rooms. She exposed herself to being found out and dismissed under conditions which would have damaged her reputation and rendered her employment by others difficult.

In the other case, she would have passed for a witch. It suffices to know the opinion of the peasants of Limousin concerning witches to realise how undesirable such a reputation would be for a girl. The unfortunate Marie Pascarel did, in fact, not escape this danger, and I felt the undeserved repulsion which she inspired.

(2) Necessity for an unusual cleverness.

This circumstance is indispensable to make fraud possible. For during several days, at any moment, movements of objects without apparent contact were produced in the presence of numerous witnesses. A gross fraud would have been detected at once, especially when some witnesses, such as the Mayor, were on the look-out for evil intentions.

The testimony of this magistrate, that of the Faure ladies, of Mme. Madrias, and of the man-servant, are conclusive. The Mayor placed some objects on the table. A stove-brush lay beside them. The brush was forcibly thrown into the fireplace. Could Marie Pascarel have thrown it herself when she was under supervision? Could she have thrown the glass which stood on a shelf of the cupboard she was opening while the Mayor watched her movements? How could she throw the bellows which left the fireplace to alight in the middle of the kitchen?

In this last case the Mayor was between her and the bellows, while she was several yards away. Could she have pulled it with a string? The string would have been seen. How could the girl have arranged all those strings without anyone noticing them? Should we not have to assume the complicity of all the respectable people who recounted their impressions? It is very unlikely that a young peasant girl of sixteen should, in broad daylight, in a kitchen frequented by a large staff, in the presence of several persons, have accomplished conjuring tricks which an expert could not perform thrice without having his procedure discovered.

An examination of the circumstances in which the phenomena reported by Mme. Madrias occurred confirms this view.

At the general supper in the kitchen on May 30 a series of extraordinary phenomena occurred. Marie Pascarel held in her hand a plate of soup. At the moment when she started to eat the plate was roughly torn out of her hands and thrown into the middle of the kitchen. Everything on the heavy table round which the Faure ladies and their servants were seated was upset. A basket full of wooden logs placed in the chimney corner was overturned. The logs of wood flew about the room, fell on the Faure ladies and their servants, and slightly hurt M. Bosche on the head. Can this have been a "trick"?

Without going into further detail, the witnesses must have really seen what they narrate, fraud must be ruled out, and, if we admit human testimony at all, we must take the phenomena at La Constantinie as having actually occurred. The declarations of witnesses so numerous, so truthful, so respectable for the most part, would certainly convince in a matter of capital importance a jury and a court of assize.

Such is the report of the famous magistrate Maxwell. This haunted house certainly differs from that of Calvados. But it is not the less interesting: Raps without apparent cause, overturning of beds and furniture, shifting of objects, movements without contact, breaking of objects, drops of blood, fire; but no sound of footsteps or wailing, no symptoms which indicated acts of the dead. Among all the known physical forces we are tempted to think of electricity in its protean forms. But the blood-stains? The observations are certain, but the cause is undecipherable for the narrator, M. Maxwell, for the special student, M. de Rochas, and for me, another student, who know nothing.

I have sufficient experience of these phenomena to deny with certainty that the servant was the responsible agent. The ancient adage, *Cum hoc, ergo propter hoc,* is here, as elsewhere, inapplicable.

A deduction to make, on the other hand, from the Calvados case, as well as the Corrèze case of haunting is that invisible beings exist.

To assume the unconscious duplication of personality of the servant in a waking state, endowed with fantastic faculties, is more daring than to admit the existence of invisible beings. We must explain these intelligent displacements of objects (p. 139), the crucifix taken down, the mirror unhooked, the stove-brush thrown under the observant eyes of the Mayor—all these exercises which have no connection with the effects of somnambulism.

All these observations are considerable by their number alone. I know well that it is not because Victor Hugo wrote 127,934 verses that he is a great poet. But quantity does not in itself depreciate quality.

CHAPTER V

HAUNTINGS: ANCIENT AND MODERN

A disturbed house in Auvergne—A psychic incident in Monaco—Physical phenomena and deaths—Death and clocks.

IT is not in one volume that the authentic examples of haunted houses could be collected. It is rather in ten or twenty volumes. Without counting the innumerable direct narratives I have received for so many years from witnesses who have kindly written to me, the observations published by competent authors are often so characteristic that I am tempted to bring them before my readers in the first instance for their independent instruction. And they go back very far.

One of the most ancient cases is that of Pausanias, general of the Lacedæmonians at Platæa, condemned to die of hunger in the temple of Minerva, 477 B. C., whose spirit, they say, manifested itself for a long time afterwards by cries and terrible noises. Be they legends or memories, ancient history is full of these stories of posthumous manifestations.

In a work read even now by all educated people, Pliny the Younger reports the almost classical episode of the Athenian ghost, where the philosopher Athenodorus had bought a house very cheaply on account of haunting. During the first night, while he was reading and writing as usual, he suddenly heard what seemed to be the dragging of chains on the floor. On looking up he saw an old man of sorrowful appearance, loaded with irons, who came nearer, beckoned him to follow him, and led him to a place in the yard, where he disappeared. The philosopher recounted the story to the judges, and digging revealed a chained skeleton. Honourable burial was given to it, and all the phenomena ceased.[1]

It is by the hundred that I could bring before my readers these stories reported for thousands of years from all sorts of sources, stories which we must not indeed take literally, but the majority of which cannot be attributed to invention; among others, the story told by Pliny, who has always [2] been considered worthy of credence. From the most ancient times these descriptions have continuously followed each other. The more recent ones are, as a rule, finished with more documentary evidence. These are in considerable number, and we have almost a superfluity of choice, even while limiting ourselves to observations made by a large number of witnesses.

M. Georges de Dubor, the learned author of the *Mystères de l'Hypnose,* (1920), gives the following description of a haunted house, obtained from absolutely intelligent and respectable people, whose truthfulness is above suspicion. The head of the family, M. Boussoulade, holds an important appointment at the Ministry of Finance. He is a serious and settled person, esteemed by everybody. Here are the facts according to a statement written by Mme. Boussoulade, and certified as correct by the other members of the family, who witnessed the phenomena: [3]

On July 1, 1914, I left Paris for the village of Vodable, in Auvergne, with one of my cousins, her children, and my two little girls aged nine and twelve respectively. We

---

[1] *Letters of Pliny the Younger,* Book VII., Letter 27, to Sura. Athenodorus, a stoical philosopher, born at Tarsus, was tutor to Augustus.

[2] I omit the amusing diatribes of Lucian of Samosata.

[3] See also the *Revue Métapsychique* of November, 1921, for supplementary details.

had rented a property in a beautiful situation, dominating a rich valley. The house, built upon the remains of a feudal castle, had a ground floor with thick walls and solidly built vaults. Inhabited for a long time by the same family, it was full of old furniture and portraits. It was arranged as follows: ground floor—library, drawing-room, and dining-room; first floor—an ante-room, furnished and hung with portraits, three bedrooms, one of them papered red, with a much larger one adjoining it, and a smaller one with a single mahogany bed, Empire style; second floor—my two rooms and two others occupied by servants.

The month of July passed by undisturbed. August brought the anxieties of the war, and on the 1st of September my sister arrived from threatened Paris, accompanied by her son aged nineteen, a tall and strong lad.

They had barely recovered from the fatigue of their long and comfortless journey when the phenomena commenced which are the subject of this letter. On September 7, about 8.30 p.m., as we were assembled in the red room of the first floor, inhabited by my sister, we heard the bell ring in the ante-room. Nobody had pulled the cord of that bell, which was under our eyes.

On September 8 more ringing, repeated several times at the same hour. Then a portrait fell on my nephew's head in the ante-room. We put the nail and the picture back in their places.

Next morning, September 9, a sword from a panoply fixed in the library wall on the ground floor was found on the floor without its scabbard, while the nails which held it on the wall were intact. In the evening the bell on the first floor started ringing again and the picture fell at the same hour as before.

Nothing on the 10th. On the 11th, frequent ringing between 9 and 9.30. Much annoyed we put paper into the bell. The paper fell out and the ringing recommenced. I then asked my nephew to pull down the intolerable bell. He did so with some difficulty. A moment afterwards one of the portraits in the ante-room was violently agitated and pendulated to and fro.

On the 12th the pictures in the dining-room were found

awry. At 7 p.m. a copper flower-pot placed on a staircase window-sill came downstairs on its base step by step and only stopped on the ground floor. Put back in its place, it descended again.

On the 13th, as I was going to enter my room on the second floor, about 7 p.m., I found to my consternation that the door was double-locked from within, the key being inside. It was the same with the door of the passage admitting to the second room. I could therefore not get in. The locks were afterwards picked and the rooms opened.

That same evening, as we were all in the library with two visitors, we saw a portrait detach itself from the wall and fall into the middle of the room. The nail remained in the wall and the cord was unbroken. We went up to see our rooms. Behind us a trunk fell from the top of a chest and a door was locked. The key, which had been hidden by my sister in a drawer only known to herself, had disappeared.

On the 14th a big fire was spontaneously lighted in the fireplace of the drawing-room. A picture in the ante-room was thrown over the head of the chambermaid. Its nail was in the wall and its cord intact. As we sat down to table in the evening we saw the cord of the dining-room bell move downwards and the bell started ringing. In the library, under our eyes, a picture fell, torn down from the wall with the nails which held it.

On the morning of the 15th my cousin was locked into her room as in a prison. The keys of the door had disappeared and we looked for them in vain. The locksmith came and the keys so laboriously sought were found in a very obvious place. From this day on, our keys always remain in our possession and we lock our rooms on going away to avoid any new tricks, and yet every evening my cousin, my sister, and my nephew find in their beds on retiring some object —turnips, pincers, plates, thistles, and even a bust of the former owner of the house.

On the 16th the copper flower-pot went up to the first floor. The sword fell to the ground, outside its scabbard.

On the 17th a plate hidden in my nephew's bed and then placed on a piece of furniture was violently thrown on the ground. From another piece of furniture opposite a candlestick was thrown.

On the 19th I left with my children for Bordeaux, where my husband was, glad to leave that inhospitable house; but my departure did not stop the course of those pleasantries, which continued in my absence.

On the 20th my nephew, when about to go to sleep, felt himself lifted with his heavy mahogany bed almost vertically upwards by an invisible force. My sister and cousin, who came on hearing him shout, witnessed the occurrence.

In the face of these phenomena, as strange as they were troublesome, our departure for Paris was decided upon. Then the phenomena multiplied. The bust of the former owner was found in the bed of the red room, its head on the pillow and the bedclothes tucked in round his chin. Afterwards it was found in my nephew's bed. A copper flowerpot, placed in the ante-room, made a prodigious bound and fell back in the middle of the stairs. Replaced on the window-sill it went down the steps as it did before, under the eyes of those present. An earthenware pot bounded across the stable-yard and broke in pieces on the dining-room table, passing through the open window.

On the 24th, the day of departure, the fallen pictures were replaced. They fell again. The furniture of the drawing-room, where nothing had happened yet, was upset. It was picked up, but fell again. The same thing happened in the second-floor room. The case of the clock on the mantlepiece opened of its own accord. None of the chairs remained standing. Sitting round the dining-room table for the last meal, they all saw the table shake, rise up, and move in the direction of my sister.

On returning to Paris my sister, cousin, and nephew recovered the peace which I myself enjoyed at Bordeaux, and we forgot the fantastic events which I had witnessed.

In the course of December I returned to Paris with my husband and my children. On the 17th of that month we were assembled at my cousin's for a family dinner on the eve of my nephew's departure for the army. We were hardly seated round the table when it began to move and rise up. The wood gave continual raps. We questioned the table—one rap, yes; two raps, no—but the replies were ridiculous and incoherent. We finished our meal with difficulty. During the evening three electric bells sounded of their own accord.

Next morning there was another meeting in my house for lunch. The table simply bounded as soon as we sat down, and was even more agitated than the night before, so that it required all our forces to keep it down. In the drawing-room, after the meal, a bronze flower-pot left its support under our eyes and threw itself three times into the middle of the room. An arm-chair was also thrown on the ground three times. On leaving the guests had to look a long time for their hats, which were eventually found on the beds or behind the furniture.

My cousin left, and peace reigned once more. On her return an hour afterwards the table moved again and objects were thrown across the room. Everything ceased on her departure.

Under these circumstances my nephew left for the army (he was killed in May, 1915), and since then we have had no phenomena of the kind to record.

This narrative of Mme. Boussoulade shows that the departure of the young man brought about the cessation of the phenomena. Yet they only took place in the assembled family, as if other forces beside his were necessary to produce them.

The narrative is confirmed by her husband and other witnesses.

All these physical actions appear to us incoherent and purposeless. Yet we have here real facts interesting to verify a study.

Two incidents strike us in this very remarkable story: the bell sounding without assignable cause and the strange and repeated fall of the picture. I know several dozen falls of pictures without a known cause, which coincided with deaths, and more than a hundred equally unexplained bell-ringings. We shall return to this later.

It is not uncommon for a portrait to fall at the hour of death of the person it represents. We have in vol. iii of *Death and Its Mystery* the story by Alexandre Dumas of the fall of a fine pastel coinciding with a death, and also of a painting in similar circumstances, etc. Quite recently an analogous incident occurred close to myself. In the course of the winter 1920-21, while I was at Monte Carlo, I heard that a similar incident had occurred at the Bishopry of Monaco. I was able to institute a personal enquiry on the spot, and to gather all the details from the witnesses themselves, who kindly communicated them to me. Here is this curious history:

Monsignor Béguinot, Bishop of Nîmes, died on February 3, 1921, at 6 a.m. He had been in close friendship with Mgr. de Curel, Bishop of Monaco, who died on June 5, 1915, and had given him his portrait as a mark of friendship. It was a beautiful framed engraving, which the Bishop of Monaco had placed in the great hall of the Bishopry, facing his own portrait. After the decease of M. de Curel, the Bishopry of Monaco was occupied by Mgr. Vié (August 16, 1916, to July 10, 1918). On February 3, 1921, the episcopal palace was vacant and was in charge of Canon Perruchot, then alone at the Bishopry. In passing through the great hall on the morning of that day, he saw the portrait on the ground, with the glass broken, and immediately had the impression that this inexplicable fall (the cord and nail had nothing to do with it) might correspond to a misfortune. The same day, M. l'Abbé Foccart, almoner of the hospital, passing by, gathered up the fragments of the frame, put the picture together and put it back in its place.

(The new Bishop of Monaco has since removed it, and substituted his own.)

It was learnt on the same day that the Bishop of Nîmes had died that day.

Mgr. Béguinot had often come to see his friend Mgr. de

Curel, being a close friend, and had even made him his general legatee.

These incidents were personally vouched for by Mgr. Perruchot and the Abbé Foccart, for which I thank them. (This Abbé is the brother of the learned traveller, to whom we owe a picturesque account of the Flammarion Lake in Guadeloupe.)

We may ask how the soul at the moment of death can produce physical effects of this kind. Whatever be the explanation we know that there was a sympathetic link between the two bishoprics. The distance between Nîmes and Monaco is 145 miles, but we know that in telepathy space does not count. The spirit of the deceased could be in Monaco just as well as Nîmes.

I may remark in passing that my collection of documents contains several correspondences of the same kind. The following case of a frame reversed after a death was communicated to me textually as follows:

Mérignac (Gironde),
November 10, 1922.

Honoured Master,

I take the liberty of announcing to you a strange occurrence which unexpectedly took place at my house on October 5.

Mme. Lafargue, a healing medium, of the Rue de Lescure, Bordeaux, died on 14th of October, at eleven p.m. Next morning, between nine and ten, one of her people came to tell us of her death. My wife received the messenger and took her for a few minutes into our room, where she showed her at a distance the full-length portrait of our only son, who died for France in September, 1918. Then she saw her out, after shutting the door of the room.

I ought to tell you that to the right and left of that portrait there are, also in frames on the wall, the various academic honours of our son, his medical doctor's diploma on one side and on the other his Baccalaureate and his P. C. N.

Each of the frames is fixed on the wall by a double brass wire attached to a hook and nail.

A few minutes after the departure of the visitor my wife returned to her room, to which nobody had access during her short absence. On entering the room she experienced an ardent wish to gaze once more upon the image of our beloved son. To her extreme surprise she found that the frame of the doctorate diploma was turned right round to the wall. I may say that on making the experiment that this rotation could only be accomplished by slightly raising the metallic suspension under the nail. Without this precaution the frame could only do a half-turn, which would put it at right angles to the wall. Any force would tear out the nail.

This, honoured Master, is the strange fact of which I wish to tell you. You will, no doubt, draw a conclusion consistent with your humanitarian aim of discovering the manifold faculties of the human soul.

Yours, etc.,

(Sg.) F. MONLINET

(*Retired Primary Teacher, Officier de l'Instruction Publique.*)

P.S.—The late Mme. Lafargue, knowing the great affliction of my wife, sincerely deplored her incredulity as regards human survival. Could she, ten or eleven hours after her death, have wished to give her a tangible proof by such a manifestation? I am rather disposed to think so.

I know a number of happenings quite as suggestive (and as authentic) as that which I have just told.

These phenomena, we see, are found in all countries and in every stratum of society. Of course, we do not understand them. They are usually regarded as coincidences, and despised as such, but they deserve better treatment.

That physical effects, like falls of pictures, the breaking of portraits, the stopping or starting of clocks, are produced in correspondence with certain deaths has been observed too often not to be admitted, and we may eliminate the idea of accidental coincidence. Let us follow the precept of Laplace (see p. 44).

On p. 351 of my book *Autour de la Mort* I wrote that in 1913, at the hour of death of an old relative, her watch, which hung in her room, stopped, that nobody could get it to go, and that it started again several years afterwards on the day her son died.

Pasteur Luc Mathey, of the Bernese Jura, told me of the stoppage of an alarm clock at the moment of a death, which he had specially verified (Letter 4,833, February 21, 1922). We appeal to chance, but these examples are rather frequent, and clocks do not generally stop in the middle of their going.

M. Duquesne, of Orsay, related to me on June 25, 1922, an incident of the stopping of a clock on the death of a person whom he had placed in the Salpêtrière, and who had made him a present of this clock.

M. Lucien Jacquin, in Paris, told me (letter dated October 1, 1922) that on the day of the death of his grandfather, his grandfather's clock had stopped, to the great astonishment of the whole family.

I think that these singular manifestations are not so raro as one imagines.

Having recently conversed on this subject with my friend, the celebrated historian, Arthur Lévy, author of *Napoléon Intime*, of *Napoléon et la Paix*, and of other valued historical works, I received the following letter from him dated June 11, 1923:

My Dear Old Friend,

Here is a little contribution to your enquiry on psychic phenomena, which awakens in the whole world some more or less long-forgotten memories. My narrative relates to facts which I cannot now date exactly, but they certainly fell between 1856 and 1860.

It was in my parents' house at Épinal. There was a clock on the mantelpiece, under a shade. The whole family was at table, under the light of a hanging lamp. My father and mother were playing bezique. The children were doing their school tasks. Only the tick-tock of the clock broke the silence which reigned in the semi-darkness of the room. One evening, about nine o'clock, a short rolling noise was heard in the clock, and all eyes went up. "There," said my father, "the clock is going queer." But nothing more happened, and the clock went on. We decided to send for the clockmaker in the morning. He found nothing wrong and the mechanism was quite in order. He found no explanation of the strange noise.

Next day—it was not a question of telegraphing in those days—we heard of the death of my maternal grandfather who had died on that evening, perhaps at the very hour when that sinister rolling was heard. A curious coincidence which was talked about, but without attaching much importance to it.

Next winter, however, there was a repetition of the same noise. My parents were startled. Would there be another death? There was. An uncle of mine died at the time when the clock made the noise. That clock was thenceforward an object of anxiety in the family. At the least indistinct murmur frightened eyes turned to the clock.

These, my dear old friend, are the things observed in a *milieu* where psychic problems received scant attention. A numerous family was concerned with more material speculations.

I guarantee the absolute accuracy of what I have told. My memory is very clear. And I must ask you to believe that I should consider it a sacrilege to associate the memory of my parents with a story concerning which there was the slightest uncertainty.

(Sg.) Arthur Lévy.

Not only do clocks stop at the moment of a death, but others, stopped for a long time, set themselves going. Here is, for instance, a rusty clock, which began to go without anyone touching it. The following letter was sent to me from Paris on January 5, 1923:

DEAR MASTER,

Being a student in Paris, I have the honour to solicit your kind judgment on an occurrence which interests me profoundly.

On December 19 last I had the great sorrow of losing my mother at the age of forty-nine.

In the night which followed her death, while there were three of us in a room adjoining the death chamber, an old clock which had been silent for many years started going and its striking mechanism struck in the clearest notes the hour of midnight, though the hands were at rest on 11.20.

What mysterious force set that clock in motion with its rusty mechanism?

To you, dear Master, who have analysed the human soul, I put this disturbing question, assuring you of my gratitude for the honour of an answer.

(Sg.) E. IMBERT.

23, RUE SAINT-ANDRÉ-DES-ARTS,
PARIS.

The only answer to give in the present state of science is that we have a great number of similar examples, which prove their reality and eliminate chance. They can only be explained by a comparative study. Was the soul of the deceased not in action in this case?

Can we try to interpret these "coincidences" as symbolic?

What is a clock or a watch? It is an instrument for measuring *time*. Now time is the essential element of life, and leads to death.

In the universal psychic force which governs all things there is an unknown intelligent principle associated with all events, both great and small—the evolution of a world, the instinct of a bird or that of an insect.

Would not the stoppage of an instrument measuring time correspond to the stoppage of a life? And would it not thus have a sense, a significance, instead of being a casual effect of an unknown cause?

These physical effects associated with the dead are surely incomprehensible. A stopped clock which starts going; an object which falls. Chance, placed at the service of the calculus of probabilities, does not explain these coincidences. A long time ago (*L'Inconnu,* p. 175), I published a story telling of the fall, with a great clatter, of a coffee service, coinciding with the hour at which the son of the house died in Africa. In that letter, dated May 4, 1899, there was another incident, which I did not publish. Here it is:

My grandparents had left the country and gone to live at La Rochelle.

A new coffee service had been put on the mantelpiece as before. Six years afterwards, in 1841, my grandparents heard the same noise in the parlour. They ran up. Door and windows were shut, so there was no draught in this case either.

On entering the room, my grandparents were amazed to see the same phenomena as that which had occurred at the death of their son. The service lay in a heap of fragments.

A great fear oppressed them: what new bereavement would they hear of? Some days afterward they heard of the death of their son-in-law, carried off by an epidemic on the very morning on which the service was broken for the second time.

My grandfather, who is not inclined to superstition but rather sceptical of imaginary things, told these facts to my father and then to my mother. I have it from them. The seriousness and strictly honourable character of the persons in question admits no doubt concerning their truthfulness.

(Mlle.) Meyer.

Niort (Deux-Sèvres). (*Letter* 549.)

Let me say again that we *do not understand* these queer things in the least. But the strictest honesty obliges me to announce them.

The reflections inspired by these trivialities are those which have puzzled me for years and years. In this connection M. Castex-Degrange, the learned Director of the École Nationale des Beaux Arts of Lyon, wrote to me on April 17, 1900, after reading my work *L'Inconnu,* as follows:

I have had occasion, dear Master, to commence the reading of the different cases of manifestations of the dead related in your work. May I make a remark?

I am struck by the childishness of these manifestations: unusual noises, windows closed, upsetting a gentleman's coffee, etc.

As regards this last, which is what happened to my father-in-law, it always astonished me. The case is indeed absolutely authentic. But it seems to me that whatever brought it about might have found something else to do. My father-in-law's brother went through the Normale. He was a Doctor of Literature. He knew Hebrew and Sanskrit. He was a real Brain. It seems to me it would have been more agreeable to his own and his brother's dignity to find something rather less—culinary. And these things always fail in that direction.

According to what Dr. Dariex told you, everything in his cabinet was upset. A force capable of displacing a light object was therefore available. Why, therefore, not take up a pen and put something intelligent on paper? Pen and paper are always found on a doctor's table.

This has always worried me. You are right a hundred times over. We must search with care, not admit or regret anything without serious cause.

(Sg.) CASTEX-DEGRANGE.

PALAIS-DES-ARTS, LYON. *(Letter 899.)*

The rational interpretation of these posthumous manifestations would be that it is not the intelligent and conscious soul which produces them, but a force inherent in that soul, acting physically, like electric induction, a vibration in the ether, an automatic act. Our blind ignorance of the psychic world is appalling. No hypothesis is satisfying. We cannot maintain that it all comes from us.

I could add a large number of further observations (see also Blavatsky, *Isis Unveiled,* vol. iii, p. 25), but shall not try the readers' patience, who are personally familiar with many.

But since we are dealing with physical effects probably attributable to deceased persons, I shall mention the following. It is our duty to analyse coolly and eliminate every cause of illusion. This is what I do, with due regard to the scientific weight of the testimony. We have seen the episode of the Bishopry of Monaco, the Gironde case, that of Epinal, those of Paris, etc. If the following story had been sent to me by just anybody, I should not have attached much importance to it, because illusion is possible. But the observation was made with care, and the narrator had no analogous sensation in his life. This is the story:

At the beginning of 1893, being in garrison at Mont-Valérien, I broke my right leg on the ice, and was taken to Versailles military hospital for treatment. It was on January 23.

My wife, who was then very ill, had been in bed since the previous December.

On February 17, I heard of her death. I could only leave the hospital in April to return to my quarters in Mont-Valérien.

That evening I went to bed about ten o'clock. Before going to sleep I thought over all that had happened in the three months.

At one moment, in the dark, I felt a strong breath on my face, as if a fan had been waved in front of it.

Thinking of my wife I called out loudly: "Is it you, my dear wife, who thus show your presence?" Immediately, another breath passed over my face for several seconds. That was all.

What can we conclude? I was and am sure that it was the soul of my wife which wafted me a last and final good-bye on the day when I had returned to our dwelling.

I am anxious to send you this observation as an argument for the survival of the human soul, to be used at your discretion.

(Sg.) DEFLANDRE
(Retired Colonel),
(Letter 4473.)

4, RUE DORIAN,
PARIS.

As I remarked before, the value of the observations depends very much upon the value of the observers. An illusion can hardly be admitted here. We shall have other cases where illusion is altogether impossible.

CHAPTER VI

MYSTERIOUS NOISES AT A PARSONAGE. THE TEACHER'S HOUSE. AN INVISIBLE COMPANION

IF the haunted castle of Calvados struck us particularly by its indisputable authenticity, the parsonage in the next story will give absolutely the same impression.

In the report on Phantasms, published by the Psychical Research Society, and translated in the *Annales des Sciences Psychiques,* the celebrated naturalist, Russel Wallace, tells a remarkable story of a haunted house, due to a dignitary of the Anglican Church, who lived in the house for twelve months, and in which he particularly observed the behaviour of the dogs. During an attempted burglary at the parsonage the dogs gave the alarm, and the clergyman got up on hearing their ferocious barking; but during the noises of haunting they did not bark at all, though the noises were louder and more disturbing. They were found in a corner in a state of abject terror. But let us read the account itself,[1] which is worthy of attention.

It is the observer himself who speaks, a learned clergyman, and an upright and reasonable man, in the enjoyment of all his intellectual faculties:

About eighteen years ago, having completed the probationary period of two years from my ordination as deacon, I was in search of a curacy. Amongst others which

---

[1] *Proceedings of the S. P. R.,* vol. ii., p. 144; *Annales,* vol. i., 1891, p. 242.

came under my notice was one in the southwest of the county of S——. The parish was extensive and the situation very retired. It was a sole charge, and a commodious house was at the disposal of the curate. The curacy was accepted, and in due time my wife and I proceeded to take possession of our new home. We reached it on the afternoon of a dull February day.

The vicarage we were to occupy was a square spacious building, surrounded by lawns and shrubberies, garden and orchard. The house was detached, situated a short distance from the village, and separated by a road from two or three cottages, which were the nearest dwellings. Our rooms were large and sufficiently lofty, everything was in good repair, and we congratulated ourselves on having secured a comfortable home.

It was, I remember, a Friday afternoon on which we arrived, and we worked with a will, and had two or three rooms fit for occupancy by Saturday evening.

Night fell, shutters were fastened, bolts shot, and keys turned, and my wife and I retired to bed on that Saturday not reluctantly, for we had worked for a couple of days as hard as porters in a warehouse.

We had not as yet engaged a servant, and had, therefore, availed ourselves of the help of an honest country woman who lived hard by. When I made all fast on the Saturday night, that honest country woman, my wife, and myself were—to the best of my knowledge and belief—the only three living beings within the four walls of the vicarage. Long before twelve we were all in the land of dreams, and probably some way beyond it—in that realm of sleep to which no "extravagant and erring" dream ever finds its way. Suddenly, however, there broke on our drowsy ears a sound which murdered sleep. In a moment, almost before consciousness had come, I was out of bed and on my feet, and even then it seemed as if that strange noise was only just passing into the accustomed silence of deep night. My wife was as abruptly and completely roused as myself, and together we listened for some repetition of what had disturbed us, or for some further token to guide us to the discovery of its cause. But nothing came. It was obviously my business to make an investigation without delay, for the natural solution of the mystery was that some one or more persons had made their way into the house.

Accordingly I hurried on a few articles of dress and set out on an exploring expedition. Before doing so, however, I looked at my watch, and found that it was just 2.5 a.m. I wish to call particular attention to this fact. I made a thorough search over the whole house. I examined the fastenings of the doors, the shutters of the windows. All was safe, all was quiet, everything was in its place. There was nothing left for me to do but to return to my room, go to bed, and think no more of the disturbance. This last was not so easy. Neither my wife nor I could persuade ourselves that it was a mistake. The sound was so palpable, broke on our sleep with so peremptory a summons, pealed on our half-awakened senses with so prolonged a crash, that neither could its reality be doubted nor its impression thrown off.

It struck me then and afterwards as being like the crash of iron bars falling suddenly to the ground. Certainly there was a sharp metallic ring about it. Moreover, it was prolonged, and instead of coming from some fixed point it seemed to traverse the house like a succession of rattling echoes treading hard on one another's heels.

I speak of it not specially as it impressed me on the particular occasion to which I am referring, but from my general estimate of its character, for I may as well say at once that my acquaintance with it was not limited to the experiences of that one early Sunday morning. Of course, on my return to my room, when we talked the matter over, it occurred to us to ascertain whether the good woman from the village had also been roused by the din. However, as she had not herself given any signs of alarm, we resolved to wait to see whether she had any tale to tell in the morning.

Well, the remaining hours of darkness passed away quietly enough, and when morning came we found that the third member of our household had been a sharer with ourselves in the mysterious visitation. She, like us, had been rudely awakened, and had long lain awake in a state of considerable disquietude and alarm.

To her, however, the thing was not quite so strange and unlooked for as to us. "Oh dear!" she said, "I've heard tell of it afore; but never till last night did I hear it, and don't want to again!"

She had heard tell of it before. But there was not much more to be got out of her, and she seemed unwilling to discuss the subject. "It was a conceit," she said, and that was all she chose to say about it. On one point, however, she was clear enough, and that was the necessity of going home that evening to look after her house and children. She would give us her services during the day, but she could not well be spared from home at nights. To this effect, therefore, an accommodation was made with her, and my wife and I stood committed for the coming night to be the sole garrison of the vicarage, whether it was to be assailed by tangible force or impalpable sounds. The Sunday duties were duly discharged. I met my parishioners in their church for the first time; looked round with satisfaction on a large and attentive, though not perhaps especially intelligent, congregation, and could not help wondering whether any of those stolid young farmers and peasants, whose faces were turned so impassively towards the pulpit, had been indulging in a grim practical joke at my expense.

In due time my wife and I found ourselves alone in the vicarage, the darkness of a winter night without, a snug wainscoted parlour, a bright fire, and sundry creature comforts visible. Thus we sat till about eight o'clock. It then occurred to us to make an examination of the house, though we had taken care, as soon as it became dark and our handmaid had left us, to make everything as far as possible secure. We rose, then, and set off together, and, passing out of our sitting-room, found ourselves in the square entrance hall, the door of which opened into the garden. Scarcely were we there before we heard a noise which made us pause and listen. The sound came from the long passage upstairs into which all the bedrooms opened, and was simply the sound of human footsteps walking slowly but firmly along the passage. There was no mistake about it. Bold, distinct, and strong, each footfall reached our ears. At once, candle in hand, I dashed upstairs, three steps at a time, and in a moment was on the landing and in full view of the passage. But there was nothing to be seen. My wife, of course, followed me, for she was becoming nervous. Together, therefore, we entered and searched the bedrooms. But our search was fruitless. If anybody had been there he had contrived by some way inexplicable to us to make his escape. A more complete and anxious examination of the house was the necessary consequence of this adventure, and we pretty well satisfied ourselves that, whatever might have caused the sounds we had heard, we were not the involuntary entertainers of any unbidden guest of flesh and blood. To make assurance doubly sure, I unbarred the yard door and took a survey of the outside premises. From this work, however, I was rather hastily recalled by my wife, who announced that the inexplicable footsteps were again in motion; and though on my return they had ceased, yet once more that night they did us the favour of letting us hear them before we went to bed. Now at this point I am bound in honesty to say that when we returned to our parlour fire, which had a very encouraging and comforting look about it, my wife and I, in discussing the matter, did hint at the possibility of our having fallen in with "a haunted house." And it is only fair to add that we neither of us were so settled in all unbelief of the supernatural as without further consideration to scout the notion as absurd. But assuredly we did not jump at once to any such conclusion, and were content with simply passing a resolution to the effect that the disturbances were somewhat extraordinary and rather disagreeable than otherwise.

That night we experienced no further annoyance, and indeed for a week or two there is nothing of any particular significance to record. In the meantime we found ourselves fairly settled. One strong and willing female servant did all that we needed to have done indoors, and a lad of about fourteen years of age was engaged to look after a couple of ponies and to do the sundry odd jobs. This boy, it must be observed, did not sleep in the house, so that unless we had a visitor, which did not often happen, the number of the inmates was only three. Our female servant was a stranger from a village at some distance, and had not, as far as we knew, any acquaintances in the place.

For some little time, as I have intimated, we were not much disturbed. The unexplained sound of footsteps we occasionally heard, but we troubled ourselves as little as possible about it, believing that whatever it might be it was at all events very inoffensive and not likely to interfere much with our comforts or prerogatives.

However, in due time we were favoured with a new development, and that, too, of a kind which was sufficiently distinct and obtrusive. There was, it must be understood, a range of attics at the top of the house reaching over the full extent of it. We found them empty and in good repair, and we converted them into storerooms for our boxes, packing-cases, etc. They were reached by a small staircase opening off the main passage upstairs; and having deposited in them everything that we wished to put out of the way we secured the staircase door.

We had gone to bed one night as usual, and were about quietly to drop asleep, when all at once there commenced a tumult overhead, which very soon made us as wide-awake as we had ever been in our lives. The noise was, confessedly, of the most vulgar, commonplace, and substantial kind. It was—or rather I should say it seemed to be—the result of the tossing about over the attic floors of all the boxes, cases, and bundles stored there. It was loud, boisterous, and persistent. There was a bump, and a rattle, and a roll, and a crash. Of course, an investigation was an obvious necessity, but an investigation discovered nothing. All was quiet. Everything was apparently undisturbed and as much in order as it ever had been, or, in such a place, could be expected to be. We were confessedly perplexed, and moreover, as far as that as well as the other occurrences went, we were condemned to the humiliation of remaining in a state of unrelieved perplexity.

But, besides, some supplementary entertainments were

provided for our benefit. From time to time a succession of distinctly audible knocks would greet our ears. These knocks varied in their type. At one time they were hurried, eager, impatient; at another, slow and hesitating. But, however, in one style or another we were treated to them, I should say on the average, four nights a week during our sojourn at C——. These were, of all the phenomena, the commonest. I am bound, in justice to the unknown cause of them, to say that we were seldom disappointed in our expectation of hearing them. They were not very alarming, certainly, and after a little familiarity had bred the requisite measure of contempt, they were not particularly disturbing.

One feature about them, however, deserves to be noticed. Sometimes, while lying awake, an involuntary listener to their tattoo, I was provoked to the use of a little sarcasm or what schoolboys would call "chaff." I would, for instance, address the hypothetical agent and bid it "be quiet, and not disturb honest people in their beds," or I would challenge it, if it had any request to make or any complaint to lay, "to come out and do it in a manly, straightforward way." Somehow or other these remonstrances were not well received. They always led to louder, more hurried, and, if we may use such a term, more passionate knocking. The reader may smile at the notion of any connection between any wild words and the intensified rappings, and I do not wish to assert that there must necessarily have been any connection. I simply state the fact that, coincidently with my challenge, the rappings intensified. I do not theorise, I tell a sound, unvarnished tale. Possibly it was a coincidence and nothing more.

Did we—it may be asked—say anything to our neighbours about what we were so frequently experiencing? For a considerable time we did not. We had determined to hold our tongues for several reasons. In the first place, if we talked about what had so much of the mysterious about it, we might give rise to exaggerations, and excite alarms which would make it a difficult matter to keep a servant or to get one. Moreover, we knew little of the characters of the people amongst whom we had come, and we thought that if it was the result of a trick we should, by saying nothing about it, be more likely to discover it, or to tire out the performers by assumed indifference. Hence, though our servant, who was a stout-hearted country wench, sometimes dropped hints of nocturnal disturbances, we always put aside the subject and discouraged her attempt to talk about it. So far I have strictly confined myself to what came under my own observation—to what I heard with my own ears. And I think that the experience of my wife and myself does not reach beyond the rappings, the confused noises in the attics, the well-defined pacing of footsteps about the house, and that grand satanic crash. On these the changes were from time to time rung.

They began soon after our arrival, they were kept up with tolerable activity during our stay, and for anything I know we left them behind us when we departed. The great noise which greeted us on the first Sunday morning, as it was the most startling of all the phenomena, so it was the least frequent. Weeks sometimes passed without our hearing it at all. But whenever we did hear it—if we took the trouble to ascertain—we always found that it occurred at *two o'clock on a Sunday morning.*

In the course of time, we had incontrovertible evidence that it might manifest itself to some person in the house, without my wife or myself being conscious of it. Knowing how overwhelming the sound always appeared to me when I did hear it, I cannot but consider this fact one of the most wonderful things in the whole business. I will show, however, that it was so.

As the winter passed away, and our country became more attractive, we had a few visitors; amongst the earlier comers was a young lady, a very near relative of my wife. We agreed to say nothing to her about our own experiences, partly because we did not want her to be frightened by anticipation, and partly because we wished for a little independent, unprejudiced, and spontaneous testimony. We very soon got it; our friend had not been many nights with us before she began to put questions as to why we had made such a stir in the house after everybody, as she supposed, had retired to rest. Our answers to these enquiries were, as might be expected, a little vague and unsatisfactory. Once or twice she asked whether there was to be a funeral, for she had heard under her window what she concluded to be the sexton digging a grave, and she expressed a little surprise that he should choose to ply his melancholy trade during the hours of darkness. She was, of course, assured, as was indeed the case, that no funeral was about to take place, and, moreover, that whatever she heard under her window, it was at all events not the process of grave-digging, for the churchyard lay on the other side of the house. This was conclusive enough, no doubt, against her theory, but she did not the less persist in asserting that on several occasions she had heard a noise beneath her window, and that that noise was, in her judgment, the result of some form or other of spade-husbandry. I have no doubt of the reality of the impression made on her mind, but I never myself heard the sounds which she described.

I was not, however, particularly surprised when, on another occasion, she told us that someone had walked along the passage, and knocked at her door, but that in answer to her call of "Who's there?" no reply had been vouchsafed, and no attempt at entrance into her room had been made.

At length Sunday morning arrived, and we met at the breakfast table.

"Whatever was the matter last night?" was our kinswoman's earliest greeting. "What a clatter somebody made! I was so thoroughly awakened, that I got up and should have come out of my room to see what had happened had it not been that I was afraid of encountering your dogs! However, I was so much disturbed that I could not easily compose myself again to rest, and as I stood at my window, peering into the darkness, *I heard the church clock strike two.*" Hereupon my wife and I exchanged very significant looks. Our friend had heard that night—though we had not—what we had begun to call "The Great Sabbath Alarum." We then told her something of our own experience, and her impression of the sound harmonised with our own. I shall only mention one more incident collateral to what we ourselves observed, for it is on our *personal* experience that I rest the value and the interest of my story.

We were absent from home for a week or two during the autumn, and on our return our servant reported the following occurrences:

One evening she had gone out into the village to do some business and had left the servant boy in sole charge of the house. He was seated by the kitchen fire, when he heard someone, as it seemed, tramping about the passages. He went to ascertain who it was, and what might be his business, but finding no one, he returned to the kitchen and tried to fancy that he was mistaken. Presently he again heard the apparent and palpable sound of human feet, and again he ventured to explore the premises, though with nerves a little more unsteady, and a glance more hurried and retrospective. Again he made a bootless quest. But when from his quiet seat in the chimney-corner he heard for a third time the same mysterious echoes, it was too much for boyish flesh and blood. He rushed out of the house, hurried down to the village, and never stopped till he told his breathless tale to the gaping inmates of his father's cottage. I have already mentioned that for some time I said nothing to any of my parishioners on the subject of these nocturnal disturbances.

Ultimately, however, I introduced the subject in a conversation with a very excellent Christian woman, a long and patient sufferer from a bodily infirmity, which altogether confined her to her bed. She had seen better days, was a Churchwoman of a good old type, full of a calm and sober religious spirit. Her cottage was just opposite to the vicarage, and the window of the little room in which she lay commanded a full view of it.

I told her what from time to time we had heard and asked her if any reports of such matters had ever reached her ears. She at once said that there had often been talk of such disturbances, and that some, at least, of my predecessors in the curacy had been a good deal annoyed by them. Moreover, she added what I am sure she would not have said if she had not thoroughly believed it—that she had herself at times seen flickering and intermittent light at the attic windows. Now it must be borne in mind that, during my occupancy of the house, these attics were not used, that I never myself entered them at night but on the occasions when I sought to discover the cause of the noise heard there, that there was but one possible entrance to the whole suite, and that we had made that secure, and as far as we could judge, had the means of admission exclusively in our own power.

My informant further told me of certain transactions which had taken place in the house in the last century, and of which she had heard from her elders, which, if they could be verified, and could be fairly connected with the disturbances in the relation of cause and effect, would certainly assist in enabling one to arrive at a theory as to the nature of the disturbances themselves.

But it is not my object to theorise, but simply to relate phenomena and leave them to be judged on their merits. For the facts related, I again say I can honestly vouch; for their cause I am almost as much thrown on conjecture as my readers, for with all the pains I took, I never could make any discovery. The explanations which will probably suggest themselves to many did not fail to suggest themselves to us. There was first of all the possibility of a practical joke. But supposing that with the care I took, and the watch I kept any persons could have gained admission to the house, they must have been the most patient and dreary jokers that ever gave their unrequited and unappreciated services to the genius of mischief. To say nothing of former years, only fancy anyone troubling himself to keep up for twelve months at all hours of the night (and *occasionally in the daytime*) a succession of incoherent and inarticulate noises. Methinks a performer of average ability would have tried the experiment once or twice in way of a *visible* manifestation.

Then, again, there is the resource in such cases of *rats*. Well! I have a great respect for the capabilities of rats in the way of nocturnal clamour. If, however, they really achieved all that came under my own observation, then

I must say that their abilities are wonderful. How, for instance, did they accomplish—and how did they so exactly time—the Great Sunday Crash? There is a circumstance that deserves to be considered by anyone who may care to suggest an explanation of what I have related. I have always been something of a dog-fancier, and I had at that time two Skye terriers of pure breed, excellent house-dogs, uncompromising foes to vermin, ready for any fun, with no delicacy as to letting their sweet voices be heard, if they saw good reason for speaking out. Once during our sojourn at C—— they did speak out to good purpose. The winter was a rough one, times were not good, and there were several robberies of houses in the neighbourhood. An attempt was made on the vicarage. My trusty dogs, however, gave prompt alarm. I was roused by their fierce barking, reached a window in time to see more than one dark figure on the lawn below, and was able to address such a remonstrance to them as led to a retreat, expedited in some measure by the discharge of a few shots from a pistol. I mention this incident simply to contrast the behaviour of the dogs on that occasion with their conduct in the presence of the mysterious noises. Against these they never once by bark or otherwise made any demonstration. Perhaps they did not hear them. It would seem otherwise, however, for when at such times, in making search about the house, I came where they were, I always found them cowering in a state of pitiable terror. Of this I am quite sure—that they were more perturbed than any other members of the establishment. If not shut up below they would make their way to our bedroom door and lie there, crouching and whining, as long as we would allow them.

Our experience of the phenomena, which I have described, extended over a period of twelve months. At the end of that time I was appointed to a benefice in another part of England, and consequently resigned my curacy. We turned our backs on the vicarage, not sorry, it must be confessed, to be done with our nocturnal alarms, but disappointed at not having been able to discover the cause of them.

I have never visited the place since, and never had the opportunity of learning whether the attentions paid by those secret and invisible agents to us have ever been renewed in favour of our successors.

This haunting cannot leave our minds in any doubt any more than those of Calvados or Corrèze.

Here is another example, which deserves being placed beside that of the parsonage just described. My friend, Dr. Dariex, received the description in 1895, and published it in that year in his *Annales des Sciences Psychiques* (p. 76). It is an observation scientifically made and minutely described:

For twenty years I have kept the secret of strange and unexampled occurrences, but now I shall give you a precise and rigorous description of them.

In the first days of 1867 I was a national school teacher at Labastide-Paumès (Haute-Garonne).

I was then twenty years of age.

My dwelling, standing forty yards from the parish church, was an ancient presbytery placed entirely at my disposal. In bad repair in 1865, it was repaired at the beginning of 1866 for my convenience. When I arrived it looked as good as new.

The ground floor, too low to be habitable, served as a cellar and a wood-store. It communicated with the first floor by means of a wide oak staircase. At the foot of the stairs were two doors, one leading out of doors, while the other led to the ground floor, which had no other interior entrance.

I never used the attics.

I exclusively inhabited the first floor in the company of my brother, Vital, now a professor of mathematics at the Belfort *lycée,* and of my sister, Françoise. The dwelling consisted of four very spacious rooms, designated in the annexed plan by the letters A, B, C, D. A was the kitchen and dining-room combined, B my bedroom, C my brother's room, and D my sister's. E indicates the landing of the staircase on the first floor.

The schoolroom did not form part of the presbytery, but joined it back to back. It dated from 1865.

In the evening we went to bed generally about nine o'clock, and got up at 6 a.m. Before going to bed I care-

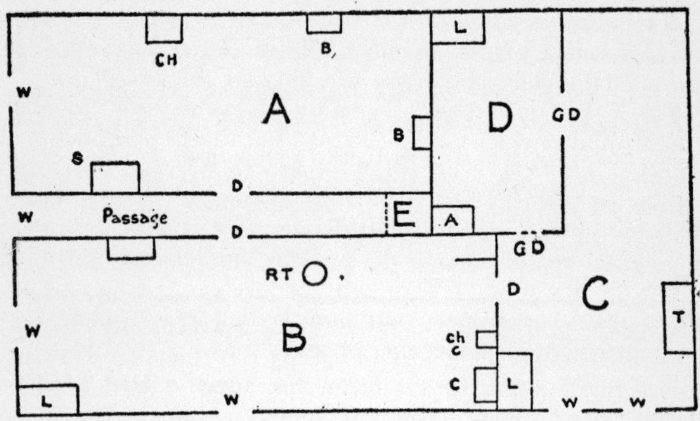

THE HAUNTED HOUSE OF LABASTIDÈ-PAUMES.

Abbreviations: W., Window; D, door; CH, fireplace; C, chest of drawers; B, sideboard; L, bed; T, table; RT, round table; A, wardrobe; Ch c, closed chimney; S, sink; Gd, glass door.

fully closed the openings leading out of doors and the only door which led from the first floor to the ground floor.

I had no cat, nor dog, nor caged bird. Since the house was repaired animals from the neighbourhood could not have got in.

I must say, before proceeding, that I am not supposed to belong to a fanciful family. Besides, I give my name and address in full, and my mental state can be investigated.

Well, on a night of April, 1867, towards 11 p.m., I was suddenly awakened by a peculiar noise. Loud sharp raps were heard on the table and sideboard in the kitchen as with a stick swung vertically down. I listened. Bang!

bang! bang! And a few minutes afterwards again. Bang! bang! bang!

Curiously enough, I was not afraid. With a turn of the hand I lighted the candle, jumped out of bed, and went through the passage into the kitchen. I found nothing out of place and heard not the slightest noise. I went downstairs. The two doors mentioned before were locked and bolted. No human being could have escaped that way, for how could he, either outside or in the cellar, lock the doors in this way and leave the keys in the locks?

Yet I had not been dreaming. I went back to the kitchen and opened the sideboard—nothing! I lighted up the chimney. The tiles placed there to prevent the rain falling on the fire while allowing the smoke to pass were in their places.

I passed again through the kitchen, the passage, and my bedroom, also into the rooms of my brother and my sister. They slept profoundly. "Of course," I said to myself, "I must have been dreaming." So I lay down again. Hardly had I put out my candle when the noise started afresh. Bang! bang! bang! Then some plates moved in the sink, spoons and forks jumped in a drawer, and chairs danced in the kitchen.

This lasted until about 3 a.m., and was repeated every night for two weeks.

Yet on getting up every morning I found the glasses and plates, which ought to have been reduced to fragments by their furious escapades, arranged just as they were when I went to bed.

Only once I found a chair upset, and a napkin which had been on the back of it the previous night was thrown about two feet away. Then I shuddered. For the first time since the commencement of the phenomena I was shaken by an absurd and unreasoned fear. Why not confess it?

One evening before going to bed I had drunk some sugared water. The coffee-spoon which had served to stir the sugar was left in the glass. I had written a note and left it under the glass, saying: "If spirits make the noise, will they please keep quiet and allow us to sleep."

For fully two hours the spoon turned in the glass, only

stopping occasionally for barely a minute. Once at least, possibly twice, the glass seemed to roll on the table without falling on the flags of the kitchen, where it would have been broken to pieces.

On getting up I found the glass, the note, and the spoon placed absolutely as they were the previous evening!

One night three raps sounded on the wood of my bed with a sound as of a stick falling vertically on the panel.

This time a friend (T. L.) had consented to pass the night in my company. He addressed me politely: "I believe that you have some infernal power, and that you are making the hubbub without meaning to do so." An attestation written by him is found below.

Another night it was a friend of my youth who came to me. His attestation is also appended, as well as a declaration by the Abbé Ruffat, who even last year, in spite of his eighty-six years, administered the parish of Labastide-Paumès. The testimony of my brother Vital will be read as well. All these witnesses are still alive.

One night I heard steps in the kitchen. They were heavy, ponderous steps of a man or woman. I went in, and only found complete silence and a total absence of visible beings.

Another time I had been away and only returned very late. For an hour at least my brother had heard steps in my bedroom. Thinking that I had come home, he had called to me several times from his bed. As I came in he cried in a temper: "*Will* you let us sleep at last? You have kept us awake for more than an hour!" "But I have only just come in," I said with some feeling. "I can understand your temper, because as I came up I heard the witches' dance in the kitchen." It was true.

This inexplicable noise began to alarm me, and I decided one morning to speak to the venerable curate of the district, Abbé Ruffat. The worthy man received my declaration with more apparent indifference than astonishment. He said: "All this is of slight importance. The house is old. It probably has not been blessed for a long time past. If the noise comes again I shall go there and bless it; and since a prayer to God is often heard, perhaps you will hear nothing more." From that day the noise ceased entirely. This coincidence is very singular, and is perhaps the most astonishing fact among the strange facts which I have told.

(Sg.) J. SALIÈRES
(Professor of Mathematics at the Lycée of Pontivy).

ATTESTATIONS.

I.

I certify that all the facts related by my brother as having happened in 1867 at Labastide-Paumès, canton of L'Isle-en-Dodon (Haute-Garonne), in the house placed at the disposal of the teacher by the parish, are exactly correct.

(Sg.) VITAL SALIERES
(Professor of Mathematics at the Lycée of Belfort).

BELFORT,
June 25, 1891.

II.

In 1867 M. J. Salières, teacher at Labastide-Paumès asked me to spend a night with him and to witness some extraordinary phenomena, and the following occurred:

About 11 p.m. some rather violent blows were struck, as with a stick held horizontally, on the table and sideboard of the room which served as a kitchen. At the same time chairs danced, plates moved without breaking, and glasses knocked against each other, being found intact afterwards.

About 1 a.m. three distinct blows, rather loud, were struck in our own room on the wood of M. Salières's bed.

The whole house is occupied by M. Salières, one of his brothers, and one of his sisters. The latter could not be the author of the noises, which only happened on the first floor.

All the openings to the outside, as also the sole door

which led from the first floor to the ground floor, were carefully closed.

No human being could have entered from outside into the house through any of these openings. Nothing unusual was noticed on searching the rooms.

I consider it impossible that these phenomena could have been produced by terrestrial living beings.

(Sg.) T. L.[2]

LABASTIDE-PAUMÈS,
June 26, 1891.

III.

At the time when M. Salières, now Professor of Mathematics at Pontivy Lycée, was teacher at Labastide-Paumès in 1867, he asked me to spend a night with him to certify certain facts.

About 11 p.m., when the outside doors and windows were solidly shut, and the house had been carefully inspected by himself and me, we heard heavy blows on the kitchen table. Bang! bang! bang! They went on until at least 3 a.m. There were knocks on a door and a sideboard also. The latter was in the kitchen, to which the door gave access.

A candle being lighted, a minute inspection was made of the room. While our inspection lasted nothing was heard, but on putting out the candle the noise recommenced.

As I cannot admit that beings of flesh and bone could get into the house through keyholes and out invisibly, I must admit that these facts are as inexplicable as they are incontestable.

(Sg.) L. N.

LABASTIDE-PAUMÈS,
February 19, 1891.

What do these observations prove?

They prove, like the preceding ones, that there

---

[2] At M. Salière's request only initials are given.

are haunted houses, and that those who deny their existence either do not know the facts or act in bad faith. We cannot take all the observers for hallucinated persons.

I do not discuss explanations; I state facts. Statement is simpler than explanation.

The rarity of authentic observations has no bearing upon their reality, whatever certain queer disputants may say.

What are the witnesses consulted by the law? Those who have seen, naturally.

What should we think of the following sentence:

"Whereas ten persons saw the accused commit his crime and forty million did not, the accused is acquitted."

Would the forty million inhabitants of France who had not seen it have the slightest negative weight?

Yet this is the sort of reasoning advanced by our adversaries against these sincere researches.

In an excellent article on haunted houses, Professor (Sir) William Barrett summarises his views as follows:

1. Fraud and hallucination do not suffice to explain all the phenomena.

2. The noises, movements of objects, and other physical phenomena seem to have some relation with an invisible intelligence which, in spite of its imperfection, has some resemblance to our human intelligence.

3. These phenomena are usually associated with a person or a locality, so that a *point d'appui* seems necessary to their production.

4. These phenomena are sporadic and temporary, lasting some days or months, appearing and disappearing suddenly without a known cause.[3]

---

3 "Poltergeists, Old and New," *Proceedings S.P.R.*, 25, 1911, p. 377.

I think with Barrett and Richet that the testimonies are too precise to be denied.

Very numerous cases, severely examined, that there are movements of objects without contact, and noises, of which no ordinary mechanical explanation can be given.

It is absurd to suppose that for weeks and months several individuals, masters of themselves, conscientious, responsible, scrupulously observant in a dwelling said to be haunted, should have seen nonexistent things, and heard loud threatening noises which did not occur. If it were a single case or a single person one could respect the hypothesis of illusions or hallucinations. But that explanation is childish. We say "hallucination" to get rid, by means of a convenient word, of an unusual fact which troubles our peace. This procedure is that of a simpleton.

But let us not stop to make useless discussions, but continue our study. In any case, we may conclude from what happened at the teacher's house, as we did from the happenings at Calvados, Corrèze, etc., that *there are invisible beings.*

Phenomena of haunting take all sorts of forms. Some show an unintelligent triviality, which is rather disconcerting. Others show some association with the dead. Others appear quite independent of deceased persons, whether known or unknown. Others, again, give evidence of intelligence without any association with a person who was formerly alive. We are in an invisible and unknown world. We must analyse these amazing occurrences all the more carefully.

I shall here quote a recent letter of 1900 (Letter 898 in my list) from Mme. Manoel de Granford, my colleague of the Société des Gens de Lettres, reporting a personal observation of a singular character and incontestable authenticity:

PARIS,
RUE DU PRINTEMPS,
February, 1900.

You know, dear Master and Friend, that I am incapable of deceiving you, as you accuse some correspondents of doing whom you do not know from Adam or Eve. Your scientific method may be severe, but you cannot doubt me.

Without wasting your time, I take the liberty of sending you this personal narrative, being sure that it will interest you because it is rigorously exact and because it happened to myself.

When I was very young I was extremely delicate, and one icy winter I was ordered to go south and stay there for at least a year. I left for a large town of Languedoc where my mother and grandmother lived, and, not far from them, I rented a quiet house in a quiet street, consisting of a single storey with a basement, built between front and back gardens, and surrounded by very high walls. There was no access to it except by a gate which was kept shut, even in the day, and by a flight of seven or eight steps leading to the front of the house and a large hall.

These details are necessary in order to explain that I was well guarded and well shielded from any temptation to break out. I had a man-servant given me by Khalil Pasha with a high recommendation for devotion. This good fellow "made the handle of the breadbasket dance" to an extraordinary extent, but apart from that he was an excellent servant who would have got himself killed to defend me from any danger. Besides him, I had brought my chambermaid from Paris, and had engaged a cook in the country to complete my staff

Imagine me, then, established with my young children in a house lighted by the sun from dawn till eve, perfumed by those large double violets which seem pale with the trembling intensity of the perfume they give off. No neighbours, male or female. No noise around me. A nameless peace descended from the great azure sky which stretched its silken veil over us. I thought myself in Paradise—but it was a mistake.

The first night passed at No. 9, Rue de la Croix, was peaceful. But on the second I was suddenly awakened by a noise similar to that made by a badly trained footman at his morning's work. I supposed, with my eyes still closed, that my wakeful Antoine was already at work, when the clock striking midnight told me that I was mistaken. I arose at once and called my servant, who appeared very sleepy; I told him what I had heard and asked him to inspect the house. He did. Nothing unusual appeared. But as he saw that I was very much frightened, he asked for a book (I believe I gave him *Monte Cristo*) and watched the whole night in the dining-room, reading Dumas's masterpiece.

That was the beginning of manifestations which for a whole year have occurred in the house of the Rue de la Croix: noises, books flung on the ground, scratching at doors and in the curtains, firearms going off, smell of powder, bursts of laughter—we were spared nothing—but the most curious thing was as follows:

Every evening—please note, every evening—between 10 p.m. and midnight, a great hammer blow was struck on the front door leading to the steps. Remember that in order to get there it was necessary to climb a high gate, traverse a court and mount the steps of the little terrace. As soon as the blow was struck Antoine rushed to open the door, and never a person did he find. Disappointed several times, and much humiliated at being tricked by one of those provincials whom he heartily despised, he determined to watch by the door itself, standing with one hand on the latch and in the other a thorn stick with which to chastise the nocturnal joker. On the blow falling, he was ready to rush forth and fling himself on the intruder. But in vain did he leave the comfort of his arm-chair and the society of my blonde chambermaid whom he greatly admired. Never did the hammer shake the door with its strident noise but at the moment when Antoine, overcome by sleep, left the door, took up his lamp and descended the inner staircase. Furious at being thus played with, my servant ran up at lightning speed, his stick in the air, threw himself on the door, opened it, crossed the court, and flung himself at the gate—but nothing met his eye. The silence and peace of the street were not disturbed by any steps or flight. All was asleep, even the dogs and cocks, in the peaceful Rue de la Croix where I have gone for rest.

Once, when my brother chaffed me about the mysterious though noisy spirit, I wanted him to make sure and asked him to stay with me. He consented, with many sarcasms at my poor spirit. I let him sleep in my dressing-room, separated from my room by a small salon. Although on that night I had heard nothing myself, I was awakened in the morning by my brother with a scared face, no longer mocking, who declared he would leave at once, without breakfast, as he had been unable to close his eyes a minute.

"You know," he said at the gate, "you might offer me 100,000 francs for passing another night here, and I should refuse."

What had he heard? I do not know. My brother never wanted to speak about it, he always got so angry; but I suppose that "Coco," as we irreverently called our too-familiar spirit, played him some of its tricks, as it did one evening to my mother, by striking such a thunderous blow beside her that she nearly fainted. I had to have her taken home by the valiant Antoine.

You may ask how I dared stay in the house with such a host. Well, it is very strange, because I am naturally very timid, but I was not at all afraid of "Coco." I talked to him, scolded him, asked him for services. I remember one evening, as I was dressing for the theatre, I told my maid that I was expecting an important letter, and, if it would arrive that evening by the last post, "Coco" would oblige me by rapping twice on the mirror in front of me. Immediately the two raps sounded. My maid let fall the taper in her hand and fled howling with fright. The letter arrived as announced.

And then—well, that is all. At the end of a year I

left that town and returned to Paris. I hoped "Coco" would follow me, but he did not. I heard nothing more. I have lost the faculty of attracting the spirits in which, after all I have told you, I have but scant faith. I find it difficult to believe that if so many dear ones now dead remain invisible, unknown spirits should be allowed to manifest themselves to us. But I conclude nothing, because I know nothing. I only tell you a true story.

(Sg.) MANOEL DE GRANFORD.

What shall we call the cause of these manifestations? I have discussed with the narrator the hypothesis of an unconscious duplication of personality and the externalisation of her spirit, as proposed by our friend, A. de Rochas. But neither hypothesis seems fit to be taken seriously. The brother's observation especially is opposed to them. Was it a random spirit, an Audible Invisible? Or a soul of a deceased person? In any case, it is an anonymous spirit. And our interpretation is identical with the conclusion published on p. 133.

I have received observations from all ranks of society, from the highest to the lowest. They are available everywhere to those who take the trouble to investigate.

That which follows is not the least strange among them.

CHAPTER VII

THE FANTASTIC VILLA OF COMEADA, COÏMBRA (PORTUGAL)

AT Comeada, a suburb of Coïmbra, a town particularly celebrated for its secular University, certain fantastic phenomena occurred which had better be set down here:

At the beginning of October, 1919, Mr. Homem Christo, a first-year law student, expelled from the University for refusing to conform to a religious custom and for armed revolt, had rented at Comeada a house consisting of a ground floor and first floor, where he had installed himself with his young wife and two maids. This lady, from the first night, complained of hearing strange noises in the house. Eight days afterwards, one of their friends, Mr. Gomez Paredes, a second-year law student at the University, having had business in Comeada, came and asked them for a night's hospitality, which was granted to him readily. After they had passed the evening together, they each retired to their bedrooms about 1 a.m.

Hardly had he put out his candle, when Mr. Gomez Paredes heard knocks on his window panes. He got up, lighted his candle, and opened his window quite widely, but saw nobody. He lay down again, and put out his candle, but then he heard steps quite close to him, and doors opening and closing all over the building. He lighted up again and searched everywhere, under the bed, the furniture, and so on. Nothing, nobody. He put out the light, and the noises recommenced. He lighted up, and they stopped. Not wishing to derange anybody, he suffered the situation all night long, and in the morning he asked his friend, Mr. Homem Christo, whether he had heard anything unusual in the night. "I heard nothing at all," he replied. "It is natural, because I sleep like a dormouse. And what is there to hear? There are no thieves in the house, and all the noises are pure fancy." Knowing the positivist convictions of Mr. Christo, Mr. Paredes did not insist. He returned home to Coïmbra and told his father what had happened. The latter listened with attention and said: "That is very singular. Another tenant before your friend left that house on account of the noises, and a woman who now minds the meteorological observatory situated opposite the house, having passed a night there, declares she will never go there again, as the house is bewitched. I advise you to tell your friend all the details and ask him to sacrifice a night to find out what it can be."

Mr. Paredes took his father's advice and asked Mr. Christo to devote a night to personal observations. The latter laughed, and went to bed as usual. Yet that night he heard noises which interested him and prevailed upon him to watch the following night, and ask his friend to bear him company. It should be noted that everybody slept on the first floor, and nobody was on the ground floor.

That night Mr. Christo told the two maids to go to bed as usual about 11 p.m. Himself, his wife, and his friend watched for developments. While there was a light nothing abnormal occurred, but as soon as it was extinguished, big blows were heard on the ground-floor door in the garden. Mr. Christo quickly descended the stairs and stationed himself by the door. The blows started afresh. He opened suddenly, and saw nobody. He went out to ascertain whether anyone ran away down a neighbouring lane. Hardly was he out when the door banged behind him and was locked. Outside he saw nobody. To return home he had to knock, and his wife came down and opened the door. Mr. Christo, much interested, was convinced that somebody had played a practical joke. He took up his revolver. "We shall see," he said.

The doors went on being shaken, and in a little room next to their bedroom, which had no exit, the noises were even louder. All this passed in complete darkness, for as soon as a light was struck nothing more was heard.

Mr. Homem Christo, more and more anxious to discover the trickster, stood on the landing of the stairs leading to the ground floor, revolver in hand. Hardly had a match which he held in his fingers gone out when he heard, close to his face, a loud burst of laughter which echoed over the whole house. He saw a white cloud in front of him, and two wisps of whitish light issuing from his nostrils. It was too much! The observer felt his courage giving way. The phenomena continued more or less the same until 4 a.m.

Next day Mr. Christo, who did not know or admit the possibility of psychic phenomena, resolved to call in the aid of a policeman, so that he should be a witness the following night. He wanted to catch the trickster at any cost, and was afraid of losing his coolness and killing somebody. An officer and two constables were placed at his disposal. When night fell the officer took up a position outside in the garden commanding the front door, to see if anybody entered or left. The two constables remained inside with Mr. Christo, Mr. Gomes Paredes and another friend, Mr. Henrique Sotto Armas, who had come specially that night to witness whatever occurred. After searching and inspecting every corner of the house the lights were extinguished. Knocks on the front door were immediately heard downstairs. "Do you hear that?" said Mr. Christo to the constables. "Perfectly," they said. The knocks continued, and Mr. Christo suddenly opened the door, but, as on the previous evening, he saw nobody, except, indeed, the officer calmly walking a short way off. "Who knocked?" he asked the latter. "Nobody." "But did you not hear the knocks?" asked Mr. Christo. "I heard nothing at all," said the officer. "That is too much; go inside!" said Mr. Christo. "And you constables had better watch outside." The same thing happened. The officer heard the knocks, but the constables neither saw nor heard anything. "Ah, that's it," said Mr. Christo; "let us all go indoors. That is where we must investigate."

He sent one of the constables into the room where Mr. Paredes had slept, on the first floor. When the constable went to sit down on the bench, the bench was drawn away so suddenly that he fell to the ground. The two friends, Mr. Paredes and Mr. Sotto Armas, were stationed with the officer on the ground floor. The wife remained in her room, and the servants in theirs, all on the first floor. Mr. Christo, as on the previous night, remained on the landing of the stairs leading to the ground floor. As soon as the lights went out, the noises and blows set in, especially in the small room, where there was only a trunk, and which adjoined the bedroom. It looked like a defiance.

Suddenly, in the guest room there was a terrible noise, like a fierce struggle. Everybody rushed in, thinking the constable had caught the offender. Disappointment! There was only an infuriated constable hitting out with his sword right and left, running from all the crowd which rushed in, back into a little boudoir where there was a wardrobe with a mirror, which he broke in his fury. He had to be restrained by force, or he would have gone mad. After that, things calmed down again. Lights were put out once more. Mr. Christo took up his place again on the landing and received on his left cheek a formidable blow which made him scream, for it seemed to him that fangs hooked his flesh to tear it out. Lights were struck, and everybody could see four finger-marks on Mr. Homem Christo's left cheek, which was red, while his right cheek was ashen. It was midnight. Everybody—the wife, the maids, the friends, the constables, and the officer, together with Mr. Homem Christo—were so terrified that they did not want to remain another hour in the house. With his wife, his servants, and his friends, he went to the hotel to pass the rest of the night there. The stupefied police went home, swearing never again to enter such a place.

Mr. Homem Christo sublet the house, but after two days the new tenant went away, declaring that the house was uninhabitable.

This narrative was given by my friend Mme. Frondoni Lacombe, of Lisbon, and published in the

Annales des Sciences Psychiques of March, 1910. The observer, Mr. Homem Christo, has himself told the story in other terms and with more detail in the book, *Le Parc du Mystère,* published in collaboration with Mme. Rachilde in 1923. I have had the honour and pleasure of knowing the latter for thirty years, and know that she will not admit the reality of psychic phenomena at any price, for the respectable but disputable reason that her parents were the victims of mediums.

Mr. Homem Christo, on the other hand, has become more and more convinced of their authenticity and scientific value, and has made them the chief concern of his life. His own account will, therefore, be read with interest from the book quoted.

In the first place, the friend who first came to spend the night with him told him the following:

"Having gone off to sleep after smoking for a long time, and having no more matches, I was awakened by a sensation of brightness under the eyelids, resembling that felt when one's closed eyes are struck by the sudden ray of a lamp or a fire. I saw before seeing. It fell upon my eyelids with such intensity that at last I opened my eyes and perceived that the shutters, which I had carefully closed in accordance with your recommendation, since I was on the ground floor, had parted and that the moon's light fell directly upon my face. I was, or thought I was, sure I had closed them hermetically and had pushed the bolt into the sill as directed, but I might have made a mistake. Then, since I wanted to sleep, suspecting nothing, and since the moonlight bothered me, I went to the window, raised it, hung it to the spring provided to keep it up, and bent over to pull in the parted shutters. *They resisted.* Now there was no wind. On the ground floor it might have been somebody coming along the garden path. Suddenly remembering what you and your wife had told me, I murmured in a chiding tone, but not loud enough to awaken any of you: 'Hullo; if anybody is there, let him get out, or he'll catch it!'

"But almost instantly the spring which held up the window came undone and I got such a furious blow in the neck, my dear fellow, that I was nearly choked and had to struggle a long time to get free. I did not want to call you, as I feared the ridicule of my position. When I was out of the trap I closed the window again, and for greater safety I inspected the neighbourhood of the garden gate. There was nothing in the garden nor on the road, the night was calm, and a bright moon brought out the smallest detail of my window shutters as I had left them, and showed, of course, no obstacle in front of them.

"Such evidence has the effect of bringing one back to order and coolness. It was clear that I had been mistaken. The shutters had not been held by any hand. The falling of the window was a mere accident. I had been half awake, my movements had been badly co-ordinated, as sometimes happens when one wakes up suddenly. I closed my windows very methodically, put the window down and went to bed again. Only this time I did not succeed in getting to sleep again. In the first place the back of my neck hurt me very much, the blood beat in my arteries, I was restless and oppressed and could not settle down.

"It was then that I observed that horrible thing in front of me, with my eyes open to every possible reality: *The shutters opened again,* their bolt having risen quite of itself (and I recollected the trouble I had had to get into the hole deeply enough, without making a noise), and then I heard behind my bed another horrible grinding like a muffled laugh. Somebody was making a fool of me, but who? 'Where is the fellow?' I said, clenching my fist. A series of heavy blows replied, struck on the wall, on the floor, and on the furniture, blows which found a dull echo in myself, as if aimed at me alone. There was nothing in my room, neither a hidden animal, nor revolutionaries, nothing but myself, shivering in the cold moonlight. My word, Francis, I did not take the trouble to warn you, I did not take time to think, I just bolted into the garden like a lunatic and ran straight before me, without a hat, without even shutting a door. It did not take many minutes to get to my father's house, for I went like the wind!''

When my comrade had finished I was silent for a moment. I had vaguely heard our professors telling about ''collective hallucinations,'' but I could not explain to him so many things at the same time, and I was also struck by the circumstance that the actions or strange noises happened in relative darkness, light destroying the phantasmagoria. I just drew his attention to that. ''Yes,'' he replied, ''I had, in fact, used up my matches smoking last night, but I saw with my own eyes in the moonlight my shutters slowly opening, as if moved by two hands, and when I wanted to pull them in I felt the queer resistence. Whoever held them was stronger than I, I assure you! I should swear to that even though that guillotine window of yours should cut off my head again. And the noises I heard are the same noises as those described by your wife. She told you that *several* walked in the room, pulling burdens along and shaking all the furniture as if there was a removal. And yet you heard nothing, which is another mystery!''

As for me, it seemed clear to me that after the row of my scandal at the University some practical jokers wanted to exasperate me: another ''rag'' among the jolly students of Coïmbra! One had to forgive them the morbid taste of their pleasantry, for after all there was a young wife and a six-weeks-old baby in the case.

The following night had hardly fallen when I installed myself in the suspected room, after inspecting the house from cellar to attic and locking in the servants. Considering the artfulness of servants, it was always possible that they could be in league with the mischief-makers up to a certain point. I provided myself with matches, and thinking that a candle was easier to light than a lamp, I took one with a high candlestick, saying to myself that this would not be blown out under my very nose. My wife, trembling in all her limbs, though my friend's adventure was unknown to her, put the baby's cradle at the foot of her bed upstairs, taking every precaution for the watching of the cradle and of her bolted door. She knew that she could expect no concession from me to the "supernatural," and that the trickster or tricksters, if caught, would be brutally done to death. It was, in fact, war.

I had begun to forget completely why I was reading a law book, sitting in an easy-chair instead of lying in bed, about 1 a.m., when my candle began to wane. The wick fell in a little pool of wax and went out. I need hardly say that I had closed the shutters, pushed the bolt well in, and let my guillotine of a window slide exactly down into its grooves.

As I put out my arm to seize the matches, I saw (this happened automatically as soon as the light went out) I saw the shutters opening slowly, and the moon introduce into the opening the white cold blade of its sword of light.

With one bound I was at the guillotine and raised it, hooked it up, and stretched my arms forward without bending my head, warned by the first inexplicable accident. I pushed the shutters with all my force, but *they resisted.* These shutters seemed to be held by a crowd of people. They were both resistant and elastic to the touch, as if held by muscles working against my own. I was silent, fearing to disturb her who slept up there, but I felt bathed in perspiration. I underwent the baptism of fear, a first impression of fear which is a sort of nameless anger, an impotent rage which can only utter itself in blasphemies.

Like my friend, I let go everything and bounded to the door of the passage leading into the garden. I opened it suddenly. The whole movement took me only five seconds. I found there was no human being behind the wooden shutters, no branch of a tree to stop them, no string stretched, nothing but the pure night air. I ran round the house and came back to the window: *It had closed itself!* I was the plaything of an unknown force! I stood for an instant dumbfounded, grinding my teeth and swearing. Yet I had to get out of this terrible force, a farce well planned, but by whom? Then I called my wife in a voice as calm as I could make it. She came at once, fully dressed, to the upper window, thus showing that she had not intended to sleep. "Please open," I said to her, "like a fool I have got through my window and the shutters have got accidentally closed and *of course* the front door is locked. It is silly, but after this little night round I believe we can go to sleep on both ears!"

My teeth chattered as I spoke, although it was summer. She came quickly downstairs and opened, not as yet suspecting my anxiety. I went to get my revolver, which I had left at my bedside, and I said to my wife, whom I held against my side with my left hand: "I have no more candle. I shall go up with you to find one. If I shoot at random, do not be frightened. There is really nobody. Only, you know, if somebody were there, it would be a good warning." "No," she replied, very much frightened, even more by my tone than by my words, "I do not understand. Are you frightened also?" "There is no cause, I assure you," said I, trying to laugh. "I am going with you, you will give me another candle, for it is because the moon lights up so badly——" I went rambling on.

As we were going up the stairs, pressed against each other, I suddenly felt her getting heavy and pulling me back with the weight of two bodies. She started crying and struggling: "Francis, help! Somebody has got hold of my feet."

We had arrived on the small landing lighted by a window towards the garden at the back of the house.

Without turning round—so convinced was I that I should not see anybody—I passed my right hand over my left shoulder and fired in that direction. The shot rang out fearfully in that sonorous house, and my wife, leaning across my arm, seemed to be dead; but I had not killed the evil thing which pursued me, for I received a violent blow on the cheek as if with *five small sticks*.

Singularly enough, the blow on the cheek gave me back all my energy. Being struck means that one strikes out and reacts immediately. I bore my wife from the terrible grip which sought to take her away from me, and by the vague light of the window I saw once more that there was nobody behind her. We reached our room and I banged the door feverishly as if I were crushing something in the doorway. My wife, feeling herself saved, and thinking of a malefactor because I defended myself with a revolver, rushed to the cradle of her child: *the cradle was empty.* Then she fainted away.

Savagely watching the circle of feeble light which the lamp shed around me and the woman on the floor for a sign of the something which would no doubt appear there, I waited. It was useless to think of defence. Knife, revolver, all this became powerless against an enemy who could not be seized.

From afar the servants, having heard the firing, howled like dogs at the moon. I know of nothing more demoralising than the cries of women in the night. But the soft wailing of a baby which seemed to come from under the floor awoke me from my moral feebleness. It had to be found, the little mite, for I knew from my wife's fainting fit that it was not she who had put it away.

So I had the courage—it required some courage to go up and down stairs in that house—to search the whole ground floor, holding the lamp on high. I found the infant, quite naked, all its swaddling-clothes taken off, placed on its back in the middle of a marble table, like an object of no value abandoned by the redoubtable robber in his haste to escape in the light.

All night long I had to soothe the hysterics of my wife and the tears of my infant child. It was only at sunrise that everything returned to its natural order, and the mother went to sleep with the baby's lips on her breast.

I must say that this horrible adventure put me into such a state of breakdown that I could no longer face my invisible enemy or enemies. This last conjuring trick, this baby taken from one storey to another without our being able to guess how it passed the staircase—or the walls—it could not be explained, could not be tolerated.

My heart sank before a new fear, that of having to give way before having understood. When day broke, I decided not to yield without at least having informed the Portuguese police of what had occurred.

Here I must claim your attention, my dear Rachildes, for you have always heard that these mysterious events only happened to one or two persons, more or less trustworthy, and that as soon as the police begin to investigate they reduced themselves to nothing, as these haunted houses were not in the habit of yielding their secrets to the curiosity of the representatives of law and order.

Now in this case of a mad persecution or practical joke, which I sought to explain as one demonstrates a theorem on the blackboard (the board was black, indeed!), I found no other solution but to call upon the Coïmbra police to investigate these audacious burglars who tried to make us leave our house in the middle of the night in order the more easily to pillage it.

They were very incredulous at first, but the notice given by both our servants on the day after the events created a very impressive situation. They went away like two hens frightened by a motorcar, bawling and cackling in every key, and adding details which were the more circumstantial for their having seen nothing.

My friend, who had done the first watch under our roof, came back with several comrades, and a ghost *battue* was organised with enthusiasm. Among my political enemies (I had some already) it was hoped that everything would turn to my complete confusion. It was decided, at the first sign of danger, to place orderlies behind and in front of the doors which locked themselves, and the shutters which opened in spite of the most substantial bolts.

All the phenomena happened in exactly the same way as soon as the light was put out. When the lights went up, the traces of the criminal or criminals were found, but never the shadow of their arms.

A policeman, stationed in a boxroom with instructions to seize a malefactor who was heard to laugh aloud there, received such a terrible drubbing that he nearly killed himself fighting the walls, and he came out of that dark place declaring that he would sooner resign as a defender of the peace than start again on that kind of war.

Boxes of linen, yet unpacked because of our recent arrival, were found emptied on the floor by hands which could not be caught in the act. Blows sounded throughout the cursed dwelling in the ears of the protectors who had come to help us. Cries and jeers smote them without giving them any idea why they were persecuted.

There were no cellars in this specially haunted house where wires, good or bad conductors of electricity, could have been concealed, no thickets in the garden where clever disturbers of the peace could have concealed themselves. No. It was Mystery taking possession of a very modern scene and playing the Drama of Fear without accessories or scenery, addressing itself only to the mentality of incredulous man, perhaps in order to show him that, whatever the times, the unknown forces always remain formidable, and that the humble mortal destined to be their prey is particularly guilty if he does not seek instruction regarding his final destiny while he knows nothing, and wants to know nothing, of his origins.

To tell the truth, I was more angry than frightened. I could not admit any trickery, but it seemed humiliating to turn my back upon this cowardly and dishonest enemy who struck in the dark.

Yet we had to go and leave an uninhabitable spot in the night, because of the infant which cried and the mother who became more and more nervous.

Such is the story, such is the history lived through by the Portuguese writer, Homem Christo. This personal observation deserved on every account to be associated with the preceding ones. Perhaps it is even more amazing than the haunted castle of Calvados. What is the invisible world? Those who deny its existence can only follow one rule, and that is to call the narrators accomplished liars.

Here also we have *observed* facts.

CHAPTER VIII

CHERBOURG OBSERVATIONS. WHAT IS THE AURA OF A DWELLING?

Dr. Nichols and the fatal room—The maleficient ceiling of Oxford—The Cambridge obsession—Pierre Loti's mosque at Rochefort.

NOT all the manifestations of haunting present the same intensity or the same characteristics. The haunting which I am about to relate has the personal interest of being rather closely associated with myself. There is, however, no highly dramatic element in it, unless it is the anxiety inseparable from these sensations.

Does anything material remain in a dwelling after the death of the beings who have inhabited it? Certain observations would seem to indicate it. There, as everywhere, we find illusions, errors, misapprehensions, and also trickery. But there are some undeniable facts. The following one presents an authenticity which leaves no room for doubt, though the explanation is no easier than it is in the previous cases.

This little event happened in the night from April 26 to 27, 1918, and the next night, at No. 13, Rue de la Polle, Cherbourg. The house belongs to my friend, Dr. Bonnefoy, then chief medical officer of the Marine Hospital. I had stayed there in September, 1914, with my wife, my secretary, Mlle. Renaudot, and our youthful cook, at the invitation of Madame Bonnefoy, president of the Red Cross and of the *Femmes de France,* who had begged us to leave Paris on the approach of the barbarian armies. After returning to Paris in the following December we had gone back to Cherbourg in April, 1918, on a second invitation from Dr. Bonnefoy, in consequence of a new German offensive against Paris, and in order to avoid air raids and Berthas.

During this interval between December, 1914, and April, 1918, Mme. Bonnefoy died (October 25, 1916).

There had been a profound affection between us. She had placed in the house a marble plaque recalling my stay there in 1914.

Her husband had placed in a room which he regarded as a sort of oratory her death-bed, the old furniture she loved, her portraits, and her dearest mementoes.

At our return in 1918, this room happened to fall to Mlle. Renaudot.

It is in that room that the unexplained noises took place—commotions, movements, sounds of steps. The witnesses are two persons incapable of being influenced by any illusion, and both very sceptical although of different mentalities: Mlle. Renaudot, a lady of high scientific culture; and the cook, in conformity with her station, steady and prudent.

I asked them to write down their impressions at once, with the most scrupulous accuracy. They did so on May 7. Let them speak for themselves:

Narrative of Mlle. Renaudot

We arrived at Cherbourg, M. and Mme. Flammarion, myself, and the cook, on Thursday, April 25. Ever since Dr. Bonnefoy's invitation came I had been wondering how we should be lodged in that house, where we had shared the family life more than three years before with charming and most devoted hosts, where we should find ourselves in a very different atmosphere, seeing that the doctor had married again. I had not wished to be given the room and the bed of the departed lady, my old friend, who had shown me so much sympathy, and whom I mourned with a profound sorrow.

It turned out that though I did not get Mme. Suzanne Bonnefoy's room I at all events got her bed, taken from the ground floor, where she died, up to a first-floor room which had been her room as a girl. It was a great Breton bed, very old, of carved wood, and surmounted by a canopy hung with tapestry. The whole room was furnished with artistic old wooden furniture, bedside table, hat-rack, ecclesiastical desk. Opposite the bed was a portrait of Mme. Bonnefoy—a photographic enlargement of a striking likeness.

I was much impressed with it. The memory of the past came upon me constantly. I saw our friend again, as she seemed so happy in her active and harmonious life devoted entirely to good deeds, and I figured to myself how she must have been on this same bed, which for two days and three nights had been her death-bed.

The first night, April 25 to 26, I did not sleep, thinking of her in the past and the present state of her house. I was also rather indisposed.

Next day, April 26 to 27, I promised myself a good night. About 11 p.m. I went to sleep and put away my old memories.

At 4 a.m. on the 27th a loud noise awakened me. On the left of the bed terrible cracklings were heard in the wall, then went on to the table and round the room. Then there was a slighter sound, repeated several times, as of a person turning in a bed. The wood of my bed also creaked. Finally, I heard a noise of a light step gliding along to the left of the bed, passing round it and entering the drawing-room on the right, where Mme. Bonnefoy had been in the habit of listening to her husband playing the organ or the piano, he being an excellent musician

These sounds impressed me so much that my heart nearly choked me with its beating, and my jaw became stiff

In my emotion I got up, lighted a candle, and sat down on a basket standing on the landing outside the room.

There I tried to account for the noises. They continued with still greater force, but nothing was to be seen.

At 5 a.m., a prey to unreasoned terror and unable to hold out, I went up to the cook, Marie Thionnet, who slept on the third floor. She came down with me. After her arrival we heard nothing more. It may be useful to remark that the cook's character did not at all harmonise with that of Mme. Bonnefoy.

At 5.45 a.m. the doctor, on the second floor, got up and went into his dressing-room. The noises he made on getting up and walking about did not in the least resemble those I had heard an hour before.

In the course of the day I sought for an explanation of the phenomenon: cats, rats climing along the walls. I examined the wall to the left of the bed. It was very thick, covered outside with slates, smooth, and overlooking a yard. It was a bad run for cats or rats, as was the front wall on the Rue de la Polle. Besides, the noises were very different from those produced by animals.

On Saturday, April 27, I went to bed at 10.45 p.m., disturbed and nervous.

At 11 p.m. the noises started, as in the morning. I at once went upstairs to the cook, in my trepidation. She came down and lay on the bed beside me. We left our candles alight. For half an hour the noises continued, with loud cracks on the wall on the left. Raps sounded on Mme. Bonnefoy's portrait or behind it, and the raps were so loud that we feared it would fall. At the same time steps glided through the room. The cook heard all this, too, and was much impressed. She is twenty-six years of age.

At 11.30 p.m. the noises ceased. As these manifestations were very disagreeable, especially as being due to an unknown and incomprehensible cause, I composed myself in the course of the next day, and, supposing that the deceased might be associated with them, since it happened in her house, I begged her to spare me such painful emotion.

We remained in the house until Saturday, May 4. Having heard nothing more, and having calmed down, I then asked the deceased to manifest herself, and to let me know in some way what she might desire.

But I have not observed anything since then, in spite of my wish (mixed with nervousness) to test the phenomena and to obtain, if possible, an explanation of this strange manifestation.

(Sg.) GABRIELLE RENAUDOT.

CHERBOURG,
May 7, 1918.

THE COOK'S ACCOUNT

On Saturday morning, April 27, 1918, about five o'clock, Mlle. Renaudot came for me to witness noises in her room. I went down, but heard nothing.

The following night, April 27, a little after eleven, Mlle. Renaudot came again about the same noises, which had returned. I went down with her and heard noises behind the bedside table, as if somebody were scratching the wood. Then I heard as if somebody glided very quickly over the floor from the table to the drawing-room, and also as if somebody had struck sharp blows behind the portrait of Mme. Bonnefoy. These noises lasted about half an hour. I acknowledged that I was much afraid, so that my teeth rattled. There were two lighted candles in the room, and we were wide awake, talking about the noises aloud and localising them as they came.

The following night I went down again at Mlle. Renaudot's request, as she did not dare to remain alone in the room she was so disturbed, and I slept beside her. I heard some slight further noises, but was much less afraid. We slept very well, and then everything ceased.

It seemed as if my presence interfered with the noises, for they became feebler after I came and then stopped entirely.

Nevertheless, I heard them only too well. They were very impressive and extremely disagreeable to me.

I also slept in Mme. Bonnefoy's bed with Mlle. Renaudot on the nights of Monday, Tuesday, and Wednesday; but we heard nothing more, fortunately for me, for I should not like to pass again through the half-hour of April 27.

(Sg.) MARIE THIONNET.

CHERBOURG,
May 7, 1918.

It is useful to note that Mlle. Renaudot, a young astronomer of the Juvisy Observatory, a distinguished mathematician, at that time Secretary to the Council of the Astronomical Society of France, and editor of its monthly Bulletin during the war, a contributor to several scientific reviews, is accustomed to the exact sciences, not at all impressionable, very sceptical of psychic phenomena, and most unlikely to be the dupe of any illusion. She who never knew fear, who passed entire nights in the solitude of astronomical observations under the silent dome, who passes alone at midnight through the lonely avenues of a park and dark streets, did, for the first time in her life, know a terrible fear on that night.

What can be the explanation of this adventure? No normal cause can furnish it, neither neighbours, nor cats, nor rats, nor mice, nor anything imaginable.

That the deceased lady was in some way associated with it is extremely probable, if not certain, since these events happened in her house, in the room of her girlhood, where she lived for twenty years, in her personal *milieu,* near her death-bed; and since, in hundreds of cases (which I had collected and compared) the same coincidences are found. But we may agree that these noises signify nothing, and show a triviality unworthy of a cultured spirit such as we have known in Mme. Bonnefoy.

The essential feature of this manifestation is that it filled the two observers with a real sensation of horror and anguish. This also happens in corresponding cases, for those who experience them do not wish to see them again at any price. They remember a practical joke in bad taste, extremely disagreeable and incomprehensible.

This penetrating anguish had never been experienced before by either of the observers.

It was a vulgar and queer manifestation without any practical result.

It is right to say that its continuation would not have been desirable, and would have been very bad for the nervous systems of the two young women. Experience shows that the human being is not always strong enough to suffer with sanity these intrusions from another world, whatever their nature may be.

No explanatory hypothesis seems possible.

Could we not, without undue audacity, suppose that the living leave behind them a certain residuum of force, of vital fluid impregnating the dwelling, which, on effective contact with a sensitive can undergo a revitalisation capable of producing these strange phenomena?

> "Wherever we have passed,
> Something of us remains."

So we are assured by a doctrine proposed by Paracelsus and by Jacob Böhme.

A very cultured friend, M. Léon Morel, to whom I told this story in 1918, told me in his turn the following:

> I remember having myself experienced, seventeen or eighteen years ago, a similar sensation in my room at my father's house when I was a young man, a year or two after my mother's death. A terrible noise in a large mirrored wardrobe kept me awake for several nights. It was certainly not the noise of wood warping, but loud detonations of great violence, like firearms. Although I was at the time naïvely atheistic, yet I received a great shock. I naturally refrained from talking to my father about these noises, as he would only have chaffed me. The phenomenon never repeated itself, but I have since then always had an

insurmountable objection to sleeping in that room. My mother was very austere, rather prudish, and very pious. In her eyes I had the faults of a libertine, which, indeed, she did not forgive me even on her death-bed. I have often since then wondered whether these manifestations were not, according to your hypothesis, the revival of her displeasure which in her lifetime impregnated that room where I suffered in her presence, both physically and morally, for a long time. There we are in the midst of unknown and mysterious things.

There is nothing very daring in supposing that indefinite effluvia subsist after us. Everybody has observed that for many years perfumes remain attached to cut hair, to withered flowers, to articles of clothing. Let us also note that apparently slight causes can produce great effect. A cartridge can fire a formidable discharge of artillery, and the rubbing of a match an immense fire.

These pages were written a few months after the curious episode reported above, at Cherbourg itself, but in another house with a sea-view, in September, 1918. I often used to sit on the shore, just by the incoming waves. Every day the ebb and flow advance or withdraw the water before our eyes. To-day we know the hours of high water and low water, calculated by the moon's position, and we can even determine the weight of water raised by the attraction of our satellite, added to that of the sun. For the phenomenon of the tides is now completely explained. I ask myself, *à propos* of haunted houses, of which we have no explanatory scientific theory, what our ancestors can have thought of the tides before Newton's discovery of universal attraction.

Even two or three thousand years ago they had observed the connection between the tides and the lunar month, so that they necessarily associated the moon with them. Yet even Galileo laughed at

Kepler for teaching this association. But everything that could then be imagined concerning the nature of the moon's action was inevitably wrong. It would be the same as regards all we could now conceive towards an explanation of haunted houses.[1] And before it was found that the moon is the principal factor in tides, what fantastic hypotheses were current concerning the flow of the seas, each as erroneous as the others? Similarly, the phenomena which we discuss here are entirely beyond any explanation.

That effluvia, residual forces, and vital fluids remain impregnated in rooms around objects, and reveal themselves at the touch of some person who reanimates them in some way, is quite conceivable. The walls and furniture may preserve the imprint of events with which they were associated. Speak into a gramophone. So long as the record is preserved, the sound of your voice will be reproduced every time the gramophone is set in motion, whether you be alive or dead. The occult property of which I speak generally remains latent, and is only perceived by certain sensitives who, in some cases, describe the details of the associated circumstances. On the other hand, the deceased person may have been thinking of her earthly dwelling, of her memories, her friends, and may have animated the effluvia and produced the vibrations.

But, once more, our present science is not sufficiently advanced to allow us to build up a theory which could be considered definite. We must go on observing and recording facts.

To get back to our episode of Cherbourg, my readers remember, perhaps, that Mme. Bonnefoy was a convinced spiritualist, and that they met her

---

[1] See, among other things, the amusing talk of Caudebec's sailor, told in my *Astronomie Populaire,* in the chapter on tides.

name before.[2] According to what I knew of this friend, of her spiritualist and also anticlerical opinions, and of her attachment to her home, it was quite natural to presume that she might be the author of the manifestation with which we are dealing, and that no doubt she would have something to say. In order to elucidate the question, I communicated with the best spiritualist societies to ask for the evocation of her spirit. I regret to state that of ten so-called clairvoyant mediums questioned all gave replies which had no relation at all to either Mme. Bonnefoy, or her husband, or the situation. The spirits evoked appeared to be the creatures of some self-suggestion, though I had applied to the most important spiritualist organisations, who placed themselves absolutely at my disposal in this matter. Not only was no proof of identity given in the replies, but they were fantastically astray, as if the mediums had imagined whatever came into their heads in entire ignorance of the reality.

Dr. Bonnefoy assured me that he had ardently wished to receive even the slightest indication of the survival of his wife, but that he could never get anything, in spite of the prayers which he addressed to her during the first five months of his bereavement before a sort of tabernacle, where, though a convinced materialist, he had placed her portrait and her dearest souvenirs. He had brought in my name, thinking it would have more effect. Only one evening he seemed to see a gliding shadow, which gave him a feeling of fear never experienced before, but he at once attributed it to some play of the light.

According to the hypothesis just put forward, inanimate matter might have the property of registering and preserving in a potential state all sorts

---

[2] *Death and Its Mystery*,

of vibrations and physical, psychical, and vital emanations, just as the brain substance has the property of registering and preserving in a latent state the vibrations of thought. This would imply that the faculties of "telesthesia" possessed by the subconscious have the property of recovering and interpreting these vibrations and emanations, just as the memory-faculties of consciousness have the property of recovering and evoking the latent vibrations of thought. We may remark with Bozzano that the analogy is complete, and that no scientific consideration would stand in the way of inert matter possessing properties identical with those of living substance. In that case we should find, apart from the cerebral mechanism of memory, another sort of memory, related, but infinitely more extensive—cosmic memory. And the properties of investigating expansion special to the telesthetic faculty of the subconscious would be related to the cosmic memory in the same way as the property of investigating expansion possessed by normal psychic faculties is related to the cerebral memory. This implies no contradiction of known physical or psycho-physical laws.

Can certain phenomena of haunting be derived from dwellings? Can the walls and furniture of a house become impregnated with vibrations and present to the sensitives a special aura, as taught by "psychometry"? Dr. Luys assured me several times that that was possible when I attended his experiments at the Charité Hospital, and Professor d'Arsonval seems to me to admit the possibility. In his book, *Supramundane Facts in the Life of the Rev. J. B. Ferguson* (p. 168), Dr. Nichols reports the following occurrence from personal observation:[3]

[3] V. Bozzano, *Les Phénomènes de Hantise*, p. 174.

A lady of my acquaintance became suddenly very unhappy by the simple fact of having gone to live in a house which was really quite pleasant and convenient, and the feeling of moral depression which invaded her attained an excessive degree when she went into the best room of the house. If she persisted in remaining there she felt an irresistible impulse to throw herself out by the window. On the other hand, as soon as she went out and got into the street, the sentiment of depression with its sombre thoughts and impulses towards suicide disappeared entirely, to return at once when she went indoors. Under such an obsession the lady had to remove to another house.

I was informed of the fact, and, desirous of clearing up the mystery, I started an enquiry concerning the previous inhabitants of the dwelling. It was not long before I found that it had been occupied by a gentleman whose wife, afflicted with suicidal mania, had thrown herself head first from the window of the best room and was killed on the spot. Can one conclude from this that there was produced a kind of saturation of the aura, capable of being transmitted to the next person occupying the same room, even to the point of producing in her a repetition of the same sufferings and the same impulse towards suicide?

Now the new tenant was a stranger in the town and knew nothing of the people who had preceded him.

This account of Dr. Nicolas cannot fail to attract our attention, in conjunction with all the other similar observations.

Here is another case, related by Podmore, and which can be read in the *Proceedings of the Psychical Society* (iv, p. 154). Mrs. Ellen Wheeler, personally known to the writer, relates as follows:

During the summer of 1874 we moved into the dwelling which we still occupy (106 High Street, Oxford). We had rented the house several years before, but had sublet the rooms in question. We chose the room above the carriage entrance for our bedroom. The first night we slept in it, I awoke with a start at 12.45 a.m. (the quarter was striking from the clock of the church), under the most painful impression that something horrible was hidden by the ceiling of the room. I had no clear idea what this might be, but the obsession prevented my sleeping, so that after an hour's agitation I decided to awaken my husband and tell him of my state of mind. He thought he could dissipate my trouble by making me drink a small glass of liqueur, but I could not get rid of the strange impression and I could not go to sleep again. I felt that the aura of this room had become intolerable to me, and I went to the drawing-room and stayed there till eight o'clock. As soon as I was away from the room, every disagreeable impression disappeared.

The next night I woke up again exactly at 12.45, and for several weeks the same sensation came to me, with a persistent insomnia until 5 a.m., and the fixing obsession that something horrible was concealed by the ceiling.

As a consequence of this agitated state of mind and insomnia, my health was seriously shaken. This forced me to leave the house and go to my brother, who lived at Cambridge.

While I was there, I was informed that the ceiling of our room had fallen and the bed of the room above ours had fallen on our bed. I therefore found that the subjective impressions I had experienced were sufficiently justified, and thought no more about it. But several weeks later I was told that the fall of the ceiling had disclosed the mummified corpse of a baby, with its neck violently twisted. Evidently a new-born baby had been carefully concealed there.

Let us add to this tragic story that the husband of the lady who told it testifies to the authenticity of the whole narrative, and that Mr. Podmore found in the papers of that time a reference to the incident of the small corpse discovered in the ceiling. Outside that room the percipient felt nothing.

A certain number of observations lead us thus to establish some connection between dwellings and diverse phenomena of haunting. In her book, *Seen and Unseen,* Miss Katherine Bates reports a curious personal observation communicated by her to the English S.P.R., and published in its journal (vol. vii, p. 282). Here is the gist of it:

On May 18, 1896 [she writes], I had gone to Cambridge to live at No. 35, Trumpington Street. My friend Miss Wales was away, and I had remained alone for the night. When she came back next day I told her I had had a horrible night, haunted by persistently repeated dreams concerning a man whom I had not seen or heard of for many years, but who at one time had been long and intimately linked with my existence. In my dream I saw him beside me, reproaching me for not having married him and ironically alluding to the fact that, having refused him, I had found myself side-tracked in life. Several times I had awakened and slept again. But always the same man came into my dreams, and he always spoke the same words. During a sleepless interval I felt his presence with such force that I cried: "Go away; leave me alone. I have none but kindly feelings for you, but you persist in tormenting me, and you thus prove that I should have been unhappy had I married you. In the name of the Holy Trinity I command you to leave me in peace!" After that invocation it seemed as if the evil influence waned, and I got to sleep again, though I only slept restlessly and fitfully. So I felt a relief when the landlady's daughter brought me a cup of tea. Twice more, during the same week, I had the same dream, and it gave me such anguish that I said to Miss Wales: "This room seems haunted by that man, and I should like to know why. Should Peterhouse College be near by? I ask you this, because thirty years ago this man was educated at a college of that name." I got an answer in the affirmative, and Miss Wales added that the college was close by.

The last time I dreamed of him I thought: "I cannot think why he should haunt this room to such an extent; can he have lived here?" To enquire for traces of this after twenty-eight years seemed impossible, but I asked Miss Hardwick how long her mother had kept those lodgings.

"Seventeen years," she said. "And who had them before that?" "A couple who have left the town and are dead now, I believe." "And before them?" While asking this I explained that I wished to trace the movements of a man who had lived in the neighbourhood when he was a student at Peterhouse. Miss Hardwick replied that, before the couple in question, the lodgings belonged to a certain Mr. Peck, now a chemist in the next street.

I went to this chemist on the pretext of buying some boric acid, and asked him if, by any chance, he had lived at 35, Trumpington Street, thirty years ago. He answered in the affirmative. I then asked him if he recollected lodging a student of Peterhouse of such and such a name.

The chemist replied that he remembered him, and that the young man had inhabited his lodging for eighteen months. He had kept a clear recollection of it, and proved it by showing me a photograph of him taken with a big dog called Leo, whom I remembered well; and Mr. Peck also remembered that name. I then asked him what room the young man occupied, and he said: "The large room over the kitchen, adjoining the small sitting-room." Now I sleep in that very room, and use the same sitting-room.

I declare that before that time I had never set foot in Cambridge, and I had no idea of the quarters where the young student had passed his college years, or whether he was an external or internal student. I only knew that in 1867 and 1868 he had been at Peterhouse. At that time I knew him very slightly, and naturally I was not informed concerning his student life.

(Here follows the testimony of the chemist, Mr. Peck, and of the narrator's friend, Miss Wales.)

Thus the reality of the influence of the aura on the sensation of haunting seems established by independent and concordant observations.

We have the same impression in considering what happened in Pierre Loti's Turkish house at Rochefort, which to him appeared mysteriously haunted. I was never able to obtain anything really detailed on this matter, the sensitive poet having such a horror of death that one could not discuss it with him. I only knew the fact long afterwards, at a time when his faculties were already asleep in a sort of dream, and when those manifestations had already been going on for several years in his house, amid the Oriental souvenirs collected there.

Pierre Loti died on June 10, 1923. It was in the month of February, 1922, when speaking one day about these phenomena to the celebrated writer Courteline, then, like myself, at Monte Carlo, that he told me what he had heard from the author of the *Pêcheurs d'Islande*: "Several times Loti had been awakened during the night by raps on the door of the mosque built by him on the first floor of his house at Rochefort, and the same thing happened to several friends who had been guests in that house. Pierre Loti added that he had himself noticed repeatedly on the flooring of the mosque very clear traces of children's feet." In reporting this to me, Courteline assured me that there was no possibility of doubting the truth of this.

Is this the aura of objects? Or subtle emanations? Or the subconscious action of the Oriental traveller himself? Shades awakened? There is something, but what? It opens a way into quite an unknown world.

CHAPTER IX

A GENERAL EXCURSION AMONG HAUNTED HOUSES

MY first object has been to bring before my readers anxious to know the truth, certain characteristic types of haunted houses, and we have seen passing before us a few finished pictures of these strange manifestations. Such complete pictures are very rare. But less rich and more or less partial cases are, on the other hand, very frequent. I have collected these by the hundred for a long time in view of this work. We shall study a few of these, but there is not space enough for a large number.

Isocrates said to the Athenians, in the fifth century before our era, "Show on every occasion such a respect for truth that a simple word of yours carries more conviction than any number of oaths." Let us think and act like Isocrates.

How can we escape admitting the objective reality of certain phenomena of haunted houses after reading the preceding chapters and when observations like the preceding have been made with certainty? I shall here put in this observation, because I believe it is particularly remarkable. Had I known it sooner I should have published it in vol. iii of *Death and Its Mystery* with the corresponding cases. But it is in its place here, for it shows us that phenomena of haunting and material manifestations of invisible beings may commence at the very moment of death, which indeed we know from concordant observations.

What is space to a dead or dying person? A man is killed by accident, and seventeen miles away his mysterious presence is perceived. Among the numerous manifestations kindly communicated to me, the following is surely one of the most significant, all the more because it was scientifically observed and perceived by several witnesses as well as three dogs. This account was sent to me on July 6, 1922, by a learned observer, M. P. Legendre, Professor of Literature at the Lycée of Brest. Here it is:

I have just read your last work, and I consider it my duty to send you a *personal document.* It is what you prefer.

1. *The Witness.*—The undersigned is Professor of Literature at the Lycée of Brest, fifty-eight years of age, and in the full enjoyment of his physical and intellectual faculties. He once had the honour of making your acquaintance at the Mondays of Fouché [1] in the Rue Soufflot, in the company of Roujon, [2] Debled, Bernard, etc. He has even collaborated at the dictionary the publication of which you organised.

All this is to prove to you that you have not to do with a romancer.

I have cultivated science with coolness and philosophy with calm. I have never been passionately devoted to metaphysics, though I have dug into it. That is to prove that I do not bring to the critique of facts, of which I believe myself to be a sufficiently good observer, any preconceived opinion nor any school method. This is to show you the absolute independence of a testimony the interest of which is left to your own estimation.

2. *The Facts.*—It was in 1883. I was twenty years of age. I had just finished my studies at the Sorbonne and

---

1 Then astronomer at the Paris Observatory, founder with myself of the Société Astronomique de France; now *répétiteur* at the École Polytechnique and Vice-President of the Astronomical Society.

2 Then Secretary to the Minister of Public Instruction; since elected a Member of the Institute. Died as Perpetual Secretary of the Academy of Fine Arts.

terminated my first year of professorship. I had gone to spend my holidays on a quiet estate which my people owned near Rennes (commune of Chantepie). The hunting season was about to start. My father had invited to the opening three old friends of his (M. Richelot, retired tax-collector; M. Biancé, the same; and Dr. Cuisnier) and a young cousin of my own age or perhaps a year older. All these gentlemen had known each other very well for a long time.

On the Saturday, the day before the opening, we were all assembled, except my cousin Robert, at a very simple bourgeois dinner, round a table, or at least in the same room. We had regretted the lateness of my cousin and tried to explain it. The cook kept several dishes hot for him, because we thought that whatever caused his delay, he would arrive the same evening for the morrow's opening.

My father and his old friends talked "finance." Dr. Cuisnier and he were facing the glass door leading to the garden, the dark green shutters of the door being closed. Standing up, also facing that door, I was adjusting my gun. Suddenly the three dogs peacefully asleep under the table woke up, growled, and advanced towards the door. We concluded that there was some animal prowling about near the house, and we tried to soothe the dogs. A queer silence seemed to fall upon all of us. We remembered that singular silence afterwards.

A minute passed. The dogs, instead of being quiet, bounded furiously towards the door, while a very transparent bluish haze, about 5 feet 7 inches high, oscillated two or three times between the glass door and its closed shutters, remaining there for ten or twelve seconds and then dissolving and disappearing.

"A will-o'-the-wisp," said my father; "that fool of a Morel (the gardener) has left some dead carcase near the door" (this door was only rarely used; it often remained shut in the daytime, as it faced south-west, towards the farm belonging to the house, and only some fifty yards from its manure heaps).

I was sceptical, and knowing that Robert was fond of fun, I supposed that he had left his trap at the village, about a mile away, had got to the estate without making a noise, and had crept through some hole in the hedge; that he had then burnt some phosphorus or other chemical product previously introduced under the shutters.

I opened the door and the shutters, went into the garden and called out: "Don't be a fool, Robert; come and eat your soup, or Mama will . . . !" No reply! Not the slightest sound. The farm dog remained silent, and our own dogs still worried a little, but as if "after the battle."

We waited for Robert a good hour, talking of everything except apparitions; then, with considerable misgivings about him, we went to bed.

Next day at 11 a.m. an express messenger came to tell us that Robert had killed himself accidentally at 7.30 p.m. the previous evening.

I draw no conclusion, and leave it to you to comment on this fact: That Robert died at 7.30 p.m., and that the same evening, seventeen miles away, and in the place where he was due, the haze which I mentioned was clearly seen by three cool-headed people (and saluted by three dogs).

This manifestation produced such a deep impression upon the witnesses that for a long time afterwards they declared they had never experienced anything like it.

I only allow myself to insist upon this very special impression, of which I have a very clear recollection. I may define it like this: A sort of troubled *attraction* to the door which I obeyed automatically, with the certainty on the one hand that Robert was behind the door, and on the other hand that he could not be there, for even his hidden approach was for me almost impossible, knowing the locality and having at that time acute hearing.

I may add that next day it was verified that "this fool of a Morel" had consciously scraped his paths, and that no carcase was left lying near the door. Besides, the door and shutters presented no trace of the combustion of any chemical product whatever.

Those are the observed facts.

In remembrance of our scientific and literary discussions of long ago, I remain, etc.,

(Sg.) P. LEGENDRE.

This documentation is precise: A man who dies by accident manifests himself seventeen miles away to friends who are expecting him, and know nothing of his death. That is what we claim to be a reality and what we must explain. Evasion is no good.

How many deaths are thus announced by various physical manifestations we have seen by numerous examples in chapter ix of vol. ii and chapters iv and v of vol. iii, so we need not return to this definitely established subject. But I may recall, as a positive observation comparable with that of the Brest professor, the observation made by the famous Linné and his wife, of steps heard by them in the carefully closed museum of a friend of the naturalist, whom they recognised by his talk, and whom they heard with certainty at the very hour he died. Haunting phenomena may therefore commence at the very hour of death.

We have seen that unexplained luminosities accompanied the manifestation of Chantepie. I have received accounts of several incidents of the same kind, and among them the following, which has some analogy to the last.

A correspondent, who has begged me, in case I publish his letter, to give nothing but his initials (M. C. D., at Nîmes), wrote to me on March 27, 1899:

One night in 1868 my parents were awakened by a noise which they could not explain. At the same time my father saw a luminosity traversing the room. It was 12.30 a.m. The other people in the house had not heard anything, and the investigations made the next morning brought no explanation.

This strange phenomena made my grandmother say that we must have lost a member of our family, which seemed to us fanciful and imaginary. Next day a letter announced to us the death of a relative living thirty-seven miles away, the death having occurred at the moment when the noise was heard and the light seen.

Chance coincidence is always being invoked. But why these associations of ideas if chance alone is in question?

Among the manifestations of this kind which have been described to me I shall call the attention of my readers to the following, which I should have described as an hallucination if it had not been repeated under perfect test conditions. I take it from a letter sent to me on August 9, 1922:

After thanking you for all the good you are doing to humanity, I must tell you of a singular phenomenon I have witnessed.

We inhabit a feudal castle which is well preserved and full of memories. I occupy a large room in it. It has several times happened that I was awakened suddenly in the middle of the night by a mysterious *glow* which invaded the place, lighted up every object, lasted a few seconds, and suddenly disappeared, without my knowing what caused it. I have observed it on moonless nights, with hermetically closed shutters and without a light anywhere. I do not dream it, for I generally sit up in bed to observe the phenomenon and to see what happens.

My mother has also observed it in her room. What can be the explanation?

(Sg.) Fernande Boissier.

Château de Boissières,
Par Nages et Soloignes (Gard).

These observations, of which I only quote a specimen here, prove decisively that these unexplained phenomena are real, and present for our study the elements of a new science to annex to the so-called positive sciences, which have so far marked out the boundaries of scientific investigation.

What diversified observations we have to examine! The study of haunted houses is an immense mosaic.

We have just seen from the communication of the Brest professor that the manifestations of haunting can follow a death immediately. The following observation teaches us the same, for it was made at the hour of death, and constitutes an immediate haunting. Here is the letter of the observer whom it concerned:

February 24, 1911.

DEAR MASTER,

I have just read your book, *L'Inconnu et les Problèmes Psychiques,* which I had not heard of before.

I regret that I did not know of your enquiry, and was not able to contribute to your great study, which is particularly interesting to one who has been concerned with a manifestation of this kind. I should have confided my case to you. But it is my duty, even now, to submit it to you, if only to show the frequency of psychic communications.

I was married on July 4, 1888. My sister, aged fifteen, on the day of my wedding, as she was able to be present had been seriously ill, but was better, if not quite recovered, at all the festivities.

On July 6 my wife and I left for our honeymoon, and my sister saw us off.

We therefore went away happy, be it noted, and without any fear to trouble us during our journey.

The letters which we received from our relatives between July 6 and July 12 showed no sign whatever of any anxiety with regard to my sister. The 12th July (we were then in Paris) was, for me and my wife, a delightful day, up to ten o'clock at night. We spent the evening at the Châtelet Theatre. At ten o'clock I became preoccupied and filled with a great sadness. My young wife could not understand this sudden change in me; neither could I, for that matter. On leaving the theatre I hurried her back to the hotel where we were staying—Hôtel d'Espagne, cité Bergère.

Still gloomy, my wife having gone to bed, I went also. I put out the candle and remained in bed with my eyes open, silent, puzzled by my own condition. It must then have been about one o'clock.

Suddenly there was a crash, a terrible noise, in the room. My companion cried out, alarmed and frightened. I lit the candle. The door of the wardrobe was open. We had not touched it, and it was empty. I calmed my wife, shut the wardrobe door and got back to bed, quite myself again.

Next morning, on rising, we received a telegram recalling us to Marseillan (Hérault); my sister had died the day before at *ten o'clock*. She knew that we were at the Hôtel d'Espagne.

Had her last thought been for us, and had she transmitted it to us where we were? We could only receive it at the Hôtel d'Espagne.

There is no need for me to assure you of the absolute truth of this story.

I have since had other and very great troubles and everything has remained quiet. Those whom I loved and who are no more no longer communicate with me. Do they see my tears and my suffering? I could wish they did.

Believe me, etc.,

ETIENNE MIMARD.

This manifestation is very remarkable and worthy of attention. It is useless to invoke chance coincidences; such an explanation does not seem really satisfactory. There are unknown psychical and physical forces. Do not let us deny anything, do not let us shut our eyes; but let us observe, ascertain, discuss. Perhaps we shall find an explanation.

Why these strange noises accompanying the last hour? They seem to us absurd, but they exist none the less. Are they produced before the departure of the soul or at the very moment? One thinks of an electrical disturbance. What is electricity? Nobody knows.

We shall have before us a very great number of observations made in all classes of society.

The following communication was sent to me

from Rothau (Alsace) on March 30, 1899, with a request to give only the initials if I published it:

In the course of last year we had staying with us a young negress from South Africa.

About six weeks after she left us for her own country the whole family was in the dining-room when we heard footsteps ascending the staircase which led to the upper storey, enter the room above us without any sound of the opening of the door, walk and stop.

We went up immediately, for these apartments were unoccupied at the time; we visited all the rooms, but could not discover anything. We remarked to each other that if our negress had still been with us we should have thought it was she who went upstairs. It was exactly her heavy, slow and measured step.

About four weeks after we learnt of the death of this poor girl. The date of the death coincided exactly with the phenomenon related above. This young negress was very fond of us, and in her last moments she spoke only of her friends in Alsace.

Five or six persons have testified to this fact.

M. G.

ROTHAU (ALSACE).

That is a phenomenon of haunting following immediately upon a death, as in the first case described in this chapter.

Not a year passes without my receiving, from one country or another, accounts of similar observations. The one we have just read is dated 1899. Here is one, quite recent, dated 1923, which puts before us some singular psychical phenomena produced at the time of a death.

This manifestation took place at Frontignan on May 15, 1923, at 1.30 p.m., and was described to me by M. Al. Garnier, manager of an important petrol factory, and grandfather of the hero of the story. The latter had just died, at the age of twenty years and five months, of tubercular meningitis, which carried him off in five days.

This young man (Louis Garnier), who gave great promise of a life of intellectual activity, was then with his relatives at Sassenage, where his father and mother lived. His grandfather was at Frontignan, where also dwelt the family of his charming fiancée, who was very much attached to him whom she looked upon as her future husband. They had known each other since their earliest childhood. On Easter Sunday, April 1, there had been a reunion of the two families at a little party, "and we, the parents," writes M. Garnier, "looked smilingly at each other, thinking what a perfect couple these two would make soon."

Alas! six weeks after a sudden illness shattered everything. Louis died with the name of his fiancée on his lips. But let us listen to the narrator:

I was getting ready to depart for the funeral of my grandchild, when I was told that little Marie had just arrived, all in tears. "Louis died last night at half-past eleven," she cried, as soon as she saw me, and threw herself into my arms. "How do you know that, Marie?" "He came to tell us so himself." And between her sobs she told me a disjointed story which I could not at first understand, but which was told to me again later by her parents, and results in the curious event which forms the subject of this account.

Now on the preceding night, which was therefore the night of May 15 to 16, the S.[3] family, composed at this time of M. and Mme. S. and Mlle. Marie (a second daughter is postmistress at Corbie, Somme), went to bed about nine o'clock.

Mlle. Marie's room is next to that occupied by her parents. It contains two beds, each sister having her own. That of the couple S. possesses only one bed (S) which is

[3] I have the whole name before me, but am requested to give only the initials. Mr. S. is a factory inspector.

common to them both, and the head of this bed is against the partition which separates the two rooms. A free space of a little more than a yard is contrived between the outer edge and the wall, so that one can walk round three of its sides. Against the wall, with its end in a line with the foot of the bed, stands a little chest of drawers (E). On a small wooden pedestal on top of this piece of furniture stands a little ornamental clock (P) which is wound up regularly and keeps good time. Opposite the middle of

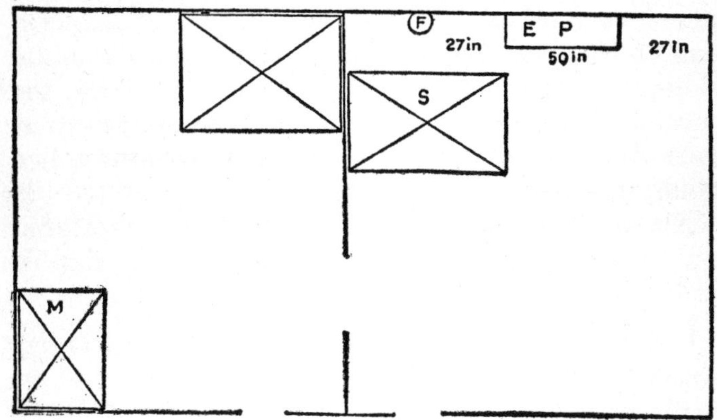

Plan of the Rooms at Frontignan.

the bed, against the same wall as the chest, stands an arm-chair (F), leaving an empty space of about 27 inches between it and the end of the chest of drawers.

This being stated for the better understanding of what follows later, we return to our three people in bed. Mlle. Marie did not sleep. Greatly distressed, she sobbed convulsively in her bed (M); her parents, after having tried to console her with gentle words, were growing drowsy, when all of a sudden a long, shrill, inarticulate cry, like someone being murdered, riveted everyone's attention. Mlle. Marie cried: "Father, Mother, did you hear?" At the same time there was heard the sound of a heavy body falling on padded springs which immediately deadened it. M. S. at once turned on the electric light switch at the head of his bed, and the room was flooded with light. The first object which caught the eyes of the couple was the clock, which the moment before had been ticking on its pedestal, and was now placed upside down on the seat of the armchair and had stopped, the hands pointing to 11.30. M. S. rose and minutely inspected the three other rooms of the dwelling without finding anything abnormal, neither dog nor cat, nor a living soul who could have uttered the cry heard simultaneously by the whole family.

Immediately after these psychic and normally inexplicable events, Mlle. Marie's sorrow was dispelled and she was filled with a certain sense of well-being. She concluded from this that her friend's sufferings had ceased at that hour.

To sum up, who uttered that mournful cry? Who threw the clock a distance of more than a yard? Who stopped it at the hour of the death of my grandchild? A mystery, all that. . . . We state simply the facts, but the causes are beyond us. It is for you, dear Master, to draw the conclusions which seem to you most reasonable.

Let us seek the conclusions together. We shall enquire into each occurrence. The psychic manifestation is incontestable, but how does it translate itself into material movements? "Elecricity," I hear someone say. Possibly. But by what process of transmission?

According to my regular method, I asked the S. family to describe to me personally the observations made by each member. M., Mme., and Mlle. S. kindly responded to my request in writing, and sent me their accounts, which are identical with that of M. Garnier. The cry was heard and the movement of the little clock was verified by the three witnesses.

It is our duty to place all sure and integral observations on record without renouncing our right of a thorough examination.

In November, 1913, a haunted house at Blois made a good deal of noise in the Press. There were noises, shouts, and knocks on the wall of a house inhabited by the Jarossay family, consisting of father, mother, and a girl of ten. An enquiry which I had set on foot showed that in all probability there was nothing serious in it (Letters 2,495 of February 18, 1914, and 2,510 of March 24). The noises ceased at the intervention of the authorities. The manifestations must have had the purpose of attracting public sympathy to the occupants. This happened in the Granges quarter, not far from the Rue des Gallières.

The following occurrence seems to me to deserve much more serious attention.

Some distance from Blois, at Fourgères-sur-Bièvre, a modest village of 700 inhabitants, priding itself on its old castle, which is classed among historical monuments, certain noises, more extraordinary than the last mentioned, and less suspicious, kept the whole population in an uproar from December 27, 1913, onwards. I received an account of them from M. Paul Gauthier, a manufacturer and former Mayor of Blois, and from M. Bon of Blois, who made a special enquiry, and sent me the accounts published in the papers. They may be summarised as follows:

The house is occupied by M. Huguet-Prousteau, a Master Surveyor, aged about sixty, who lives there with his wife, his son-in-law, and his young grandson aged about twelve.

The first occurrence dates from December 27. On that night M. Huguet-Prousteau suddenly remembered that he had forgotten an important item of correspondence the previous night. He therefore got up at 3.30 a.m., and lit the fire. Hardly had he entered his study when he heard his neighbour chopping wood, which, considering the hour, astonished him.

When the morning came he made some remark about it to his neighbour, M. Cellier. To the amazement of both, not only had M. Cellier not split any wood, but he had heard the same noise, which he attributed to M. Huguet-Prousteau, and he wanted to reproach him for disturbing his sleep.

From that day, every evening and every morning, knocks were heard in the parting wall, and the walls shook. Then the phenomenon grew and became an infernal row which was heard at 200 yards.

"If it is a 'chap' who does it," said M. Huguet-Prousteau, at first, "he is well-bred and lets us dine in peace. When we dine between six and seven, the noise only commences at eight o'clock. When I do not come home till 7.30, the noise only starts at nine."

The surveyor, though unable to explain what happened in his house, was not maddened by it, any more than his son-in-law or his little grandson. Only his wife was much concerned, and wished ardently to see the end of it.

Let us get to the facts, which I verified myself [writes a witness]. About 8 p.m., I was with M. Huguet-Prousteau. As, in listening to the story, I gave some slight indication of incredulity, the owner of the house said: "This is just the hour at which it takes place, as you will find yourself. I am quite prepared to think of electric phenomenon. In any case, the row was terrific last night, Sunday. The whole village is talking about it. The noise kept on from 8 to 10 in the evening and from 5.30 to 6 in the morning. So it should commence about now."

Such confidence impressed me, and I expected to witness the performance they announced. I was there with the whole family. My host filled the glasses and we drank.

Outside the house a murmur of voices indicated that the crowd was assembling. We opened the door and the corridor was quickly filled with sightseers. We took in as many as possible, so that they should hear better. [4]

Meanwhile, M. Baranger and I minutely inspected the garret and attics of the house, which is very old. I then went into the neighbour's attic, without discovering anything suspicious or suggestive of trickery.

---

[4] A mistake and imprudence, since control became difficult.

But what about it? Did I mean to frighten the spirit? Nine o'clock sounded, and nothing happened.

Outside the crowd passed the time in animated conversation of the sort one hears among the spectators at fireworks or a rustic merry-making. All the inhabitants of Fougères were there, as well as vintners from the neighbourhood. A mild evening favoured the long waiting.

I looked at the clock. It was 9.20 p.m. The Huguet-Prousteau family was surprised, and I began to chuckle to myself. But they persisted in saying, "It will come, without fail." The little boy was told to go to bed, and he consented, when suddenly several formidable blows shook the partition separating the passage from the room where we were. It was 9.25 p.m. I rushed into the passage and lighted up the wall with a candle. The blows succeeded each other with great force, falling anyhow, up and down, right and left, on the partition, which measures 6½ feet in height and 15 feet in length.

Then the blows ceased, and were followed by a terrible trembling, which shook the wall with a force which ten men could not equal. The scene lasted barely five minutes. M. Huguet-Prousteau stood there, smiling and phlegmatic. "I have known it stronger than that," he said; "that is nothing; you will see presently."

But it was finished for the day. I took leave of the surveyor, highly interested, but no longer sceptical.

The eyewitnesses had plenty to say in giving their impressions. In the garret, plaster and mortar had been torn from the wall in the presence of the little Huguet-Prousteau. I said to this brave youngster: "Then you are not afraid?" And he, who is only twelve, opened his eyes wide and said: "But, sir, I am with grandpapa!"

On the Sunday evening M. Lepage-Girault, a daily labourer of Fougères, struck a dozen blows on the wall. A dozen blows were struck in answer. Another man struck fourteen, which were repeated also.

Nothing is talked about in the countryside but these strange happenings. They wonder what causes them. At first they were laughed at, but now nobody knows what to think.

Quite naturally the little boy of twelve was suspected. But it was clear that he did not strike the blows himself, and they were often very formidable. Let us continue the description:

M. Prousteau's house is situated in a common court, and adjoins two other houses of the same appearance. Behind it is the garden of the presbytery. It is therefore easy to watch the house rigorously.

The noises commenced at the end of December, and continued until February. M. Prousteau and his family never breathed a word about them, but the neighbours whose houses touched M. Prousteau's, having become interested in the noises occurring at the same hours, told in the village what they had heard. It was like a powder-fuse. Every inhabitant wanted to see and hear. People came from neighbouring parishes, and the curious constantly surged about the house.

A decree by Baron de Fougères, Mayor of Fougères, put a stop to these incessant comings and goings by forbidding any person standing within a certain radius of the house.

One evening the noise was so great that it was heard distinctly not only in the neighbouring houses, but across the road, over 60 yards away. The house was shaken from top to bottom, the partitions vibrated violently, the doors and windows rattled with singular vehemence. It was found necessary to open them for fear of their glass being broken. According to reliable witnesses, the noises accompanying the vibrations of the house resembled the reverberations of distant thunder. On the other hand, the curtains of the bed were in constant agitation, as if moved by a strong draught, though everything was shut.[5]

Inside the house, several people unconnected with the family made some experiments. They struck a definite number of blows on the wall. Immediately a similar number would answer, but with peculiar sonorousness. The

---

[5] An analogous phenomenon was regularly observed in the experiments with Eusapia Paladino (see *Unknown Forces of Nature*).

noises were loud and muffled, and seemed to emanate from the whole house.

One night some determined men went up to the garret. They had hardly got there when the noise commenced and the house began to tremble. Their lights were nearly extinguished, and the men hurried down again.

These extraordinary manifestations, which everybody could verify [says M. Bon], made a vivid impression. The most ill-disposed are speechless. The presence of electric batteries in the walls had been suspected. The house was searched from top to bottom by electric fitters of the Montils factory, but nothing was found.

The grandson of M. Prousteau, whose bed was shaken while he slept in it, was sent to another house, and a child of the same age took his place. No manifestation occurred during young Prousteau's absence.

(Note.—Before coming to Fougères, the Prousteau family inhabited the parish of Sologne. It appears that at that time their house was the scene of similar phenomena.)

A judicial enquiry was made by the Public Prosecutor of Blois. He found the same facts and in the same conditions.

M. Bon added to his letter of February 18, 1914: I have known M. Prousteau for some fifteen years. The man has always seemed to me of a peaceful nature and incapable of indulging in eccentricities to amuse the public. He has a good reputation in the district, and his antecedents are excellent. I do not see, therefore, why he should place himself voluntarily into such a strange situation.

Here, as in most similar cases, the unknown cause producing the phenomena is associated with a young human organism. That is not an unusual condition.

We are entering a world more unknown than was America at the time of Christopher Columbus or Amerigo Vespucci, a world whose exploration is still more complicated than that of the natives of the New World, though we need not fear cannibals. We must endeavour to study it with all the rigour of the scientific method. Let us compare the observations. We have a plethora of choice even after eliminating doubtful and adulterated cases.

A charming lady reader, a woman of the world and an enlightened artist, sent me the following in February, 1920:

I must tell you, dear Master, that the occurrences happened on our property of Montmorency in October, 1912.

My father had been confined to his bed for six months with kidney disease and consequent uræmia. We had three devoted servants, a cook, a housemaid of twenty-eight, and a little help of fourteen years.

In August a violent storm produced a lightning stroke in the kitchen during the servants' dinner, and made a deep impression on the housemaid.

Our house, built on a height, has a ground floor erected on cellars, and two storeys. It is surrounded by a garden.

Well, towards October or November our little help, a degenerate child, daughter of alcoholic parents, and just undergoing physical development, became timid and nervous, and told us fantastic stories. Her face was contorted, and her eyes dark-rimmed, in an emaciated face. The housemaid, at the same time, seemed to be struggling with a thousand imaginary ideas. These two devoured cheap novels, telling the most absurd stories. Before long the house had a very strange reputation through the tongue of the girl. My mother, one of my aunts, and I wished to put a stop to this gossip, and especially not to draw the attention of our very sick patient to the disordered service which reigned in the house.

"The demon is knocking on the window, Miss; the demon is rapping loudly on such and such a room on the second floor," said the young girl. We could not take this nonsense seriously. But one Friday, when my mother and I had gone to Paris on business, we found, on returning, our good gardener (who is still with us) waiting for us in the kitchen, pale and frightened. The little maid had been sick several times and the housemaid too. My father's secretary, who had come for the signature of some documents, was also nonplussed.

What had happened?

1. As the secretary had gone to take his hat from the rack, regular knocks on the front door attracted his attention, but he had not been able to find anybody. That happened two or three times.

2. The drawers of the furniture opened of their own accord.

3. Terrible row in the kitchen, scales swinging, saucepans shifting about on the stove, and the coal drawer, containing a hundredweight of the precious fuel, being moved on its rollers.

4. Blows on the window-panes.

My mother and I were much annoyed at seeing our world upset. But we spoke with severity, and everything got into order again, which surprised ourselves.

But in the evening, after dinner, the two maids, green with fright, pretended they heard knocks. I did not hear them any more than the doctor who nursed my father. I took up a position for an hour in the garden to disconcert any manœuvre if there were any, but I discovered nothing. I thought it was the hallucination of the two female cowards. But when I came in again I also heard the raps very clearly.

Did my over-excited nerves put me into communication with "waves"? The doctor would say, "Take care, Madame, or you will be as mad as the others." Possibly, but I cannot deny hearing.

Next morning, about eight, the cook came to me in great alarm: "I can't get on with the work, Miss, there are knocks upstairs and on the veranda, and everything moves."

I went down to make up accounts in the dining-room, which has a bay opening on to the veranda, and watched the cook at work, while the housemaid was busy on the second floor, and I sent the little girl on errands.

I then saw a strange sight. On the pavement of the veranda, a chair began to turn on one foot, and the furniture made cracking noises. Preserving an imperturbable calm, I soothed the cook. Going up to the second floor

I heard two single raps in the room which the housemaid was cleaning.

Finding peace at home impossible, and suspecting a "subject" in the young girl, we asked her parents to take her back. This was not done without trouble, because my father was accused of being the origin of all the trouble. The housemaid was also dismissed, and as if by magic the house resumed its peacefulness.

I am quite convinced that the housemaid and the child acted unconsciously. I do not know what has become of the former. The latter grew up into womanhood and is now the mother of a family.

The poor invalid died on the following 12th of March, knowing nothing of the disturbances. We had done our best to hide them.

(Sg.) S. DE BELLECOUR.[6]

Such is the story told by the narrator. I have reproduced all the details for our personal instruction. These unexplained noises, these movements without apparent cause, are certain, and are associated with the presence of the housemaid of twenty-eight and especially the girl of fourteen. They do not do anything consciously. An unknown force acts and makes use of them. Did the dying man exert any sort of indeterminate activity?

Let us consider some other observations made with certainty. I offer to my readers those accounts by preference which have been sent to me at first hand by the witnesses themselves. The following narrative is one of the most extraordinary and incredible ones. Of several thousand reports I have received in a quarter of a century in response to enquiries instituted for the elucidation of problems usually considered insoluble, this is one of the first. Though the letter dates from 1899, it has never yet

---

[6] Name modified.

been published. It may amaze all who read these lines, as it amazed me. It is a case of strange sounds, of steps on a flight of stairs, and the forcible bursting in of a door, without a visible agent.

Two thousand years ago Ptolemy said: "There is nothing more ridiculous, more stupid, more laughable (πάνυ γελοιότατον) than the idiotic hypothesis of the movement of the earth." "What folly to suppose that lamps can burn and light up without oil and without wicks!" was said to the inventor of coal-gas, my fellow-countryman, Philippe Lebon, in 1804. "It is nonsense to suppose that vehicles could move without horses," they said to Stephenson a hundred years ago, before the first locomotive was built. "To make portraits without pencils, brushes, or paints is absurd," said the painters to Daguerre in 1838, and so on.

In the present work we have under our eyes certain unexplained and, at present, incomprehensible facts, whose apparent impossibility need no more stop us than the anti-scientific paradoxes preceding special fields of human knowledge. The following observation is as amazing as any which precede it. Let us hear the narrator.

The scene is at Strassburg, 5, Rue du Sanglier.

It was [says the witness] in February, 1855. I was fifteen years old. My widowed mother, my sister, and myself lived in that house in the centre of the city, an old two-storeyed house, the first floor occupied by a resident jeweller, an artist with a rare devotion to his work. This good man had seven daughters, the eldest being twelve at most. We occupied the lodgings on the second floor, and above us there were large common garrets, reached by a staircase closed by a door on our landing.

The first-floor jeweller had jewels of great value in his possession, and the only precaution he took was to say nothing about them to anybody. Nobody could have thought that that modest dwelling often harboured diamond necklaces representing a fortune.

One day the jeweller's wife told us confidentially that for some time she had seemed to hear steps on the stairs, going up and down in the night.

We laughed and told her that her senses were deceiving her. But she insisted and returned to the charge, assuring us that she did not sleep part of the night on account of her small children; that she was certain somebody passed on the stairs in the night; that she was afraid of thieves; that her husband, on her mentioning it, had only laughed, like ourselves; that he carefully shut his door—a fortified door—every evening, and slept soundly after doing so.

By constant repetition the good woman succeeded in interesting me. My mother had trained me from early youth to overcome all cowardice. I got up at various times in the night and searched the stairs from cellar to attic without finding anything at all. On the earnest representations of the jeweller's wife I, on several occasions, arranged glasses filled with water on the stairs, but found them intact in the morning. Then I thought of another expedient. I took a ball of black thread and in the night, without a light, I drew threads across the steps of the stairs at irregular intervals. *I found them all intact in the morning,*[7] while the woman assured me that she had heard more steps on the stairs.

I became interested and even alarmed. I feared thieves, an attempt on the jeweller, or what not. I then got a hatchet which I placed on my bed, within reach of my arm. I went to bed at ten as usual and sat reading until 2 a.m., ready to jump up at the slightest noise. But nothing happened.

The door of my room, the only access to our dwelling, was of solid oak at least 2 inches thick, as in the old houses of the seventeenth century. It was 4 feet wide and 6½ feet high. Its frame was of cut stone, with sockets on which the enormous hinges of the door pivoted. It was opened from the outside by a large, solid, internal lock,

---

[7] This is most significant, and we know of similar cases. See below, Chapter X., the haunting of the Morton family.

the key of which weighed at least half a pound, and turned a square bolt an inch and a quarter thick, with a catch in proportion. On the lock itself, over the keyhole, there was a sort of spring-hook pressing on the stem of the bolt. In the evening, after turning the key in the lock, I used to raise the hook, push the bolt, and release the hook, whereupon it rested on the key and made a lock which it was impossible to open. With such a door and lock one could sleep in peace. It was not pretty, but it was solid and secure, and in the circumstances I paid particular attention to the lock. I insist on this point.

One evening about 10.30, I had gone to bed after taking my habitual precautions in case of an alarm, and I remember reading in an old magazine Eugène Sue's *Les Mystères de Paris.* I had begun a page commencing with the words "The farm whither Rodolphe took Fleur de Marie," when suddenly a terrific shock burst open the door, making it rebound against the wall with such force that I can still see it trembling on its hinges. My mother started up in bed and called out: "What is the matter?" Without answering her, I jumped from my bed, hatchet in one hand and candle in the other, and rushed to the stairs, where I found all my threads in their places.

I rushed up, examined every corner, fetched the key out of the garret, opened the door, and went upstairs. Nothing! I came down again, went into my room and tried to shut the door. Then I found that the lock had remained in the "closed" position, as well as the bolt, and that the door had been opened all the same, and with what force!

Only at that moment did I feel a sensation of horror. My hair seemed to stand on end. The top of my head seemed made of ice.

I closed the door and went to bed once more, trembling in every limb, and unable to take my eyes off the door.

My mother got up, and I told her what had happened. She sighed and said we should soon hear of a misfortune in the family. But nothing of the kind happened, either to us or the jeweller, and the fact I have carefully reported *was not marked by any coincidence.*

I was so powerfully impressed that in writing these lines,

forty-four hours later, I still feel the horror which seized me when I came back to my room and could not shut the door. I do not believe in the supernatural, but I could never undestand the miracle of the spontaneous and violent opening of a solid oaken door, closed as it was with a lock more like that of a prison than of a dwelling-house.

(Sg.) ERNEST FRANTZ.

BESANÇON, *(Letter* 10 *of my general enquiry.)*
March 26, 1899.

This story, an old one, as I said before, was sent to me with all the care which might have been taken by an architect or engineer, with plans of the dwelling, the stairs, etc., which, though I consider it superfluous to reproduce them here, I have preserved. Yet the story is really fantastic and incredible, and twenty years, or even ten years, ago I should not have published it, because my readers, even those instructed in metapsychic matters, were not prepared for it. Such a manifestation appears absurd, ridiculous, a senseless farce. Yet we find happenings as incredible in the phenomena of lightning, the extravagances of which are countless, and the effects of which are formidable. It is opportune to recall some of them here which have a great resemblance to what we have just heard:

On June 1, 1903, a flash of lightning struck the church of Cussy-la-Colonne (Côte d'Or), knocked down the clock-tower, *broke a clock,* and opened a cupboard in the sacristy, totally destroying the objects within. In April, 1888, lightning demolished the clock-tower of the church of Montrédon (Tarn) to the height of 10 feet. Several bells, together with the great bar of iron which supported them, were carried a considerable distance.

At Liège, in August, 1868, lightning pierced a wall, entered a locksmith's workshop, upset all the tools, pulled out a drawer, broke it into a thousand pieces, threw all its contents on the floor, broke all the window-panes on the staircase, traversed the wall again, entered a hole containing a rabbit, killed the rabbit, and lost itself in the garden, boring a double furrow several feet long in the ground.

In July, 1896, in the hamlet of Boulens, it entered by the chimney, damaging it, threw down the rack after tearing out the socket which held it, and pierced a hole in its place. It flung a saucepan with its lid into the middle of the floor and tore up several flags in its passage. It *sprung the latch of the front door,* and flung the key into a wooden shoe under the sideboard.

In the middle of August, 1887, the lightning fell upon a house in Les Francines near Limoges. It entered the room where the master of the house was asleep. He experienced a terrible shock and found his down quilt pierced in several places by perfidious fluid. A chest of drawers was broken into a thousand pieces, with all its contents. Continuing on its way, the lightning passed into an adjoining room, *demolishing the door.*

At Niederdorf, canton of Unterwalden (Switzerland), the house of Councillor Jaller, showed, among other phenomena, doors violently opened, torn from their hinges, and bolts jumping from their catches (*Annales,* 1895, p. 94).

On April 20, 1807, a lightning discharge struck the windmill of Great Morton in Lancashire. A heavy iron chain used for hoisting the grain was, if not fused, at least considerably softened. In fact, the links, being pulled vertically by the weight at the bottom, had closed up and welded themselves, so that after the lightning the chain had become an iron bar. We might ask how such formidable fusion could come about in so short a time, during the passage of the current which passes "with lightning speed." What magic force gives to the jet of fire from the clouds the power of transforming the air into a veritable forge, where pounds of metal are volatilised in a thousandth of a second?

On July 26, 1911, at Héricy-sur-Seine, not far from Fontainebleau, lightning fell upon a tank containing water 10 feet deep, and completely dried it up! On the same day, at Bagneux, near Moulins, it transported three carts filled with sand for several yards, from the road into a ditch, without spilling the contents. But the horses were killed and the chains serving as harness had disappeared.

On October 30, 1922, at Maussane (Bouches-du-Rhône) lightning struck the farm of Mont Blanc. Entering by the chimney, the lightning passed to the kitchen table, where it fused the reservoir of the oil lamp and broke the globe, and then tore up the wax tablecloth. After those exploits it traversed the ceiling, entered the room of the widow Piquet, who was in bed, crumbled up a portion of the wood of the bed, and scorched the sheets, without touching the woman in the bed, whereas the victims are usually killed instantly.

Another example from my collection. After recounting some curious psychic phenomena, a Nice correspondent, Sgr. Torelli, wrote to me (Letter 736):

"Last November (1898) on a day I could name if required, about 2 p.m., after a great thunderstorm lasting over half an hour, I went to the upper storey of a villa of mine in Monaco and found the room flooded with rain. I went to the roof to see what had happened and found a row of six flat tiles methodically removed and transported 16 inches lower down—*i.e.*, two rows below their place, but hooked together in line as if placed there by a good workman. The tiles surrounding the hole made by the displacement of the six had not been disarranged at all."

How many more amazing singularities of lightning could be quoted here in addition to those I have already given (*Autour de la Mort,* pp. 308-311)! Some of them suggest the hypothesis of a *fourth dimension.* To deny the facts reported by M. Frantz above would, of course, simplify everything. But it is difficult, because he saw, observed, and recorded well. And then his observation is not unique; there are hundreds of similar cases.

I shall repeat once more that, while admitting the phenomena, it would be absurd to suppose that science in its present state can furnish an explanation. Yet a dynamical consideration claims our attention. Every physicist and mechanician knows the expression mV^2, and knows that the quantity of motion possessed by a moving body is obtained by multiplying its mass by the square of its speed. A double velocity is four times as powerful; a treble velocity, nine times; a fourfold velocity, sixteen times; and a fivefold velocity twenty-five times as powerful. According to this formula, we might obtain any mechanical effect we desire by simply raising the speed. It is not the bullet that kills, but its speed. Throw a bullet at the chest of a person and the shock will be hardly felt through his clothing. I remember having (1866) won a bet after lunch in a shooting-party by firing through an oak plank with a cylindrical bullet of Gruyère cheese, with which I had loaded my gun. It was the epilogue to a discussion of Force and Matter (I told this story in my *Mémoires*, p. 353).

A certain number of the noises and uproars, like several freaks of lightning, could no doubt be explained by an application of this formula. All modern scientific discoveries encourage us to think that matter is of an electrical nature, and that the cohesive forces between the particles which give solid bodies their rigidity are electric forces.

But let us not seek an explanation too ardently, since nobody knows what matter really consists of. A radio-active atom contains a formidable quantity of intra-atomic energy, enough to blow up an entire town.

Even when we cannot explain the phenomena, our scientific duty is to admit them when they are not exactly observed. These more or less strange stories, scarcely credible, or rather incredible, are not all inventions, impostures, illusions, and errors.

Here, as everywhere, it is well to look at things with eyes free from prejudice.

The conclusion from all this is that there are in us and around us unknown natural forces, and that, in spite of its wonderful discoveries, science is only the beginning. The invisible world is as real as the visible world.

The phenomena of haunting are extremely varied. They are not all open to the same explanation. They are attributable to different causes. Some are produced by the souls of deceased persons; others by invisible beings whose nature remains unknown to us; others, again, by human organisms acting unconsciously. This last cause is frequent, and many have been led to regard it as the sole cause, for the (insufficient) reason that there is always a youth or a girl associated with the production of the phenomena, the Invisible requiring an organic human form for this production.

All the men who have examined for themselves how much of these phenomena is true have emerged from their study convinced, and have been obliged to admit that the hypotheses of hallucination and illusion did not suffice to explain the observations. This fact has been well known for some time, but one affects to ignore it. Who remembers, for instance, that as early as the seventeenth century one of the most active Fellows of the Royal Society of London, Joseph Glanvill (1636-1680), discussed in his book *Saducismus Triumphatus* a collection of psychic facts similar to those we study here, but observed in 1661?[8] The Royal Society therefore preceded by two hundred years the Paris Academy of Sciences in the attention rightly bestowed upon

[8] See *Joseph Glanvill and Psychical Research in the Seventeenth Century*, by S. Redgrove. London, 1921.

this subject, and we see its Fellows in the nineteenth century—like Moor in 1841, Crookes in 1871, and Wallace in 1875—display the same courage and traveling the same independent road. Sir William Barrett succeeded them with distinction, and so did Sir Oliver Lodge. The Académie des Sciences has only recently arrived on the scene with Dr. Richet, Count A. de Gramont, and d'Arsonval. England has preceded France.[9]

Sir William Barrett has expressed his conversion in no uncertain terms, which find their proper place here:[10]

I thought [writes he] that there, where the observers were competent men of unquestioned integrity, such as Sir William Crookes and Professor de Morgan, there would be no question of fraud, but that there might be illusion like that produced in the first stages of hypnotism. My investigations proved to me that the facts completely destroyed my theory.

It was in 1876. An English solicitor, very well known and respected, Mr. C., had rented for the summer the house of one of my friends, quite near to my own house at Kingstown in the county of Dublin. Having made his acquaintance I was surprised to learn that phenomena appeared to happen at his house. Mr. C. and his people were not spiritualists. They were perplexed and rather annoyed when the sound of blows and other inexplicable noises were frequently heard in the presence of their daughter Florrie, a child of ten, intelligent and straightforward. At first they thought, quite naturally, that she was playing some trick of her own on them, but they were

[9] The English Society for Psychical Research generously puts on record the work of sincere and independent researchers, whatever their nationality, and I cannot forget that it offered me its presidency in 1923, and published my presidential address of June 26, in its *Proceedings*. I am proud to have succeeded as president such savants as Crookes, William James, Bergson, Oliver Lodge, Myers, Barrett, Richet, and Sidgwick.

[10] William Barrett, *On the Threshold of the Unseen*, p. 49.

soon convinced that this was impossible. The governess complained of hearing knocks in the schoolroom every time that Florrie was unoccupied, and the music mistress states that loud blows resounded in the piano whenever the child played her scales softly.

Mr. and Mrs. C. willingly allowed me to make a personal investigation, and I went to their house the next day after breakfast. It was ten o'clock in the morning and the sun was shining. Mr. C., Mrs. C., Florrie, and myself sat round a large dining-table without a cloth. The French windows which gave on to the lawn let in floods of light, so that the hands and feet of those present were seen perfectly. We soon heard a sort of rubbing, then blows on the table and on the backs of our chairs. The hands and feet of Florrie were closely watched; they were perfectly still at the time when the noises were heard. It was as if someone were hammering small nails into the floor, and my first thought was that there were carpenters on the floor above or in the room underneath, but we made sure that there was no one there. The blows became louder when we began a cheerful song, or when there was music; they then beat time in a most amusing way and changed into a rhythmical scratching, as if a violin bow were being rubbed on a piece of wood. I placed my ear many times on the exact place from which these sounds seemed to come, and I perceived distinctly the rhythmical vibration of the table without discovering any tangible or visible cause above or below.

The blows changed their direction sometimes, and were heard in the far ends of the room. One day I asked them to knock on a small table near me which Florrie was not touching. I was obeyed. I then placed my hands one above the other underneath the table, and felt quite well the light vibration produced by the knocks on the part which I was pressing. Whether Florrie and I were alone or not made no difference. I sometimes got other people to come in while the knocks were going on in order to see if my hallucination theory had any foundation, but everyone heard the noises.

We repeated the alphabet slowly, and the invisible intelligence knocked at each letter required to make an answer to the questions asked. We learnt in this way that the communicator was a little boy named Walter Hussey. Mrs. C. told me later that when she went to say goodnight to her daughter she often heard knocks and found Florrie chatting animatedly with her invisible comrade by means of this system. I made a note of some of the answers obtained, and they were such that Florrie herself could have made—merry and unimportant, the invisible intelligence corresponding to that of the child, also the spelling.

The sceptic will not fail to say that all this had been concocted by a mischievous child to make fun of a professor. Let him do so! I will content myself in pointing out that, after weeks of thorough investigation, all my theories and those of the friends who had joined in the enquiry forced us to reject with one accord all hypotheses of fraud, illusion, or malobservation. The phenomena were inexplicable, except on the supposition of an invisible intelligence or that of the child herself. But the force used was much beyond Florrie's. Afterwards furniture was moved. One day, in broad daylight, her parents and myself were sitting at the big mahogany table in the dining-room. Twelve persons could easily have been seated at it. Our hands were on the table, well in sight, when suddenly three feet of the table were lifted sufficiently high for me to pass mine under the castors. Anyone who tried to do it with all his force could find that even by grasping the table, which none of us did, it could not be accomplished without much difficulty, even by a clever and vigorous man.

On another occasion we heard raps after we had withdrawn our hands and had moved away from the table. While the hands and feet of all were perfectly visible, and *nobody touched the table,* it started moving sideways unequally. It was a heavy, four-legged table about 4 feet square. At my request, the two feet nearest to me rose up, then the other two, 8 or 10 inches above the ground, and the table remained there for several seconds, while nobody touched it. I moved back my chair and it advanced towards me (nobody touching it), and finally got right in front of my chair, so that I could not leave it. When it was under my nose it rose up several times, and I could convince myself by touch and sight that it did not rest on the ground, and that no human being could be directing its movements. Sceptics are at liberty to suppose that the table was moved by invisible threads worked by an imaginary accomplice, who would have had to float in the air without being seen. That was my first experience of physical phenomena. Taken with later ones and other testimony they left no doubt in my mind. There is a hidden intelligence behind these manifestations. This is an extraordinary affirmation, which destroys all the foundations of materialism.

I am not so simple as to believe that what I say will impress public opinion in any way, or that my testimony has more weight than that of any other observers. But I hope it will encourage other witnesses to give us the proofs they possess, until we have forced our opponents to admit either that the phenomena exist or to assert that the experimenters lie, trick, or are in a state of blindness and thoughtlessness incompatible with any mental state other than perfect idiocy.

Thus speaks Sir William Barrett, F.R.S. These psychic forces are also those which act in haunted houses. My long experience in the same study has led me to an opinion identical with his. All those who have wanted to see have seen like ourselves.[11]

The forces in action in these phenomena are quite unknown as yet, whatever be their affinity to electric forces, for there is evidence of mentality in them: mentality of the living and mentality of the dead.

Lombroso wrote in 1910 (*Hypnotisme et Spiri-*

---

[11] These experiences of the learned Mr. Barrett, made in 1876, are exactly the same as mine in 1862 (see *Unknown Forces*, pp. 55-66). In the same work one may read of those of Gasparin and Thury in 1853 and 1854, of the Dialectical Society in 1869, of Crookes in 1870, of Wallace, Rochas, etc. Only the ignorant can doubt the reality of these phenomena.

tisme, p. 228): "The phenomena of haunted houses bring an important contribution to a problem of the posthumous activity of the dead. They would be quite analogous to ordinary mediumistic phenomena if they were not more spontaneous than the latter, often without apparent cause, and almost always localised in a house, a room, or in a group of persons. The most frequent phenomena are loud raps, frictions, steps, transport of objects, even in locked rooms, and, more rarely, apparitions."

Another characteristic is their apparent absurdity and absence of known object in motor phenomena, like bell-ringing, extinction of lights, transportation of utensils, of footgear and headgear, etc., into the most unexpected places, clothing torn, or sewn together, etc. We must also note the great violence of the noises, the brutal projection of objects without consideration for persons or things, their vulgar triviality and sometimes evil intention, fire-raising, destruction, etc.

All this may seem trivial and mischievous. But if it results in a proof of existence beyond the tomb, we must confess that it is neither commonplace nor mischievous. Who would not, when he loses a beloved being, on asking for any sign of survival, wish to see even the raising of a little finger?

The facts are real and incontestable. The belief in haunted houses is so ancient that in every language there are words to describe it: *spuken* in German, *haunting* in English, *spiritate* or *infestate* in Italian, *hanter* in French, without counting numerous local terms. We have also seen that their reality is confirmed by numerous legal decisions.

"Haunted Houses!" The words alone, thrown at random into a conversation, are capable of calling forth the stupidest ironies and the most unreasonable anecdotes. On the one hand, a whole category of people see in them only the grossest trickery, mystification, or ventriloquism. On the other hand, superstitious stories hold sway, and memories increase and lose shape under the influence of imagination and the desire to produce astonishment. When a little shudder of mystery thrills through the organism of the women, the vainglory of the men lets itself loose. At one time everything is denied. But now the most absurd phantasmagoria are admitted. Between two such extreme and equally inaccurate positions the impartial and attentive observer must choose a middle course. Let us continue our general excursion.

When I started my enquiry concerning these phenomena, one of my readers, a well-balanced lady, already known to readers of this book, Mlle. Adèle Vaillant, a member of the Astronomical Society of France, wrote to me from Fonquevillers (Pas-de-Calais) on July 10, 1900:

On February 16 and 17, 1881, some singular noises were produced in one of the doors of the house which we still inhabit. My sister and I were then *en pension* at Arras, and I have under my eyes the letter which my mother, now present, wrote on February 28, 1881, to inform us of these strange doings. First there were sharp raps struck regularly in threes, then shakings, scratchings, grindings of the lock, and movements of the key, which was even thrown on the ground. I omit all the details for fear of wasting your time. I shall only say that there was no wind, and that care was taken to ascertain that no animal or practical joker was concerned in it. "What can it be, do you think?" was the question asked by my mother of my young brothers. "It is the soul of our uncle Edward asking for a mass at Fonquevillers," they replied, without hesitation. This uncle, an advocate at the Paris Court of Appeal, died almost suddenly on February 1, 1881, at Arras, on his passage through. He took some interest in Spiritualism, and had expressed a desire to manifest himself after his death if he could.

The morning after the second day a locksmith mechanic, M. Caron, came to us on a job of his craft. He was shown the door and the lock, but found everything in order. He was told what had happened, and he asked at once: "Have you recently lost a member of your family? For in my village, at Fampoux, something of the same kind occurred, but much louder." And he reported the following occurrence he had witnessed:

An inhabitant of Fampoux had prematurely lost his wife, and had promised her to have a number of masses said. He had commenced fulfilling his engagement, but, distracted by the project of a second marriage, he had neglected to continue it. The crockery began to dance noisily on his dresser and in his cupboard every night, and things did not quiet down until he had entirely fulfilled his promise to the deceased woman.

At a somewhat earlier epoch, in 1880, in another house at Fonquevillers, some awful noises were also produced without a known cause. Several inhabitants of the village went there expressly to investigate and try to find an explanation. I was told that every evening blows of unprecedented violence seemed to shake the blinds. My grandfather, who went into the house with another person, heard similar ones inside on the door of the bread-oven, and satisfied himself that there was nothing in the oven.

From time to time such an uproar was produced that several of the witnesses compared it with a cart of gravel emptied suddenly beside them.

All searches proved fruitless, nothing was discovered. These queer phenomena ceased after masses had been ordered for the dead of that family, but, as in the other cases, that may have been a mere coincidence.

In a third house of the village, longer ago still, noises were heard in the evening resembling those produced by throwing large stones at the shutters. When that happened in the night, all the people in the house woke up with a start, much frightened, and thinking that an enemy was in their garden. After rainy nights they looked for footprints on the ground, but always in vain. Nothing could be discovered. I ask you, dear Master, whether the souls of the dead have indeed some connection with these inexplicable noises, or whether they are due to an unknown natural cause. There is a tradition in the country that extraordinary noises, and spontaneous movements of furniture and crockery which sometimes occur in the houses, are caused by the souls of the dead anxious to obtain prayers, masses, or the execution of promises or wishes. What am I to think?

(Sg.) ADELE VAILLANT.
(*Letter* 923.)

Here we have at once a religious idea associated with these strange noises, that of a soul in distress.

These requests for masses or prayers might surprise us, but we cannot but admit that they are frequent. There are a dozen examples in *Death and Its Mystery,* vol. iii, among them the case of the picture by Van Eyck in the Bruges Museum. Must we look for the cause in the mentality of those present? We must study everything without prejudice.

And what about the exorcisms of haunted houses, which succeed, but not always (see p. 128)?

Among the numerous manifestations of haunting which I have heard of, I shall pick out the following, which is remarkable and well deserved. It was sent to me from Buenos Ayres in the following letter:

MUSEO NACIONAL DE HISTORIA NATURAL,
June 20, 1921.

DEAR MASTER,

The first two volumes of your work *Death and Its Mystery* have drawn the attention of our public to psychic questions, and forced them to ponder the serious problem of the other side.

Permit me to communicate to you a spontaneous and prolonged problem of haunting, which, if it is in time, may perhaps find room in your third volume.[12] I have only lately heard about it from one of the witnesses, a serious and intelligent man whose good faith I can guarantee. Up to the present he had not dared to talk about it for fear of ridicule.

The case is that of M. José Amadei, an Italian aged thirty-seven, who has worked as a carpenter in our Museum workshops for ten years.

On his arrival in Italy, in 1903, he went to live with his married brother, Amadeo Amadei, who lived with his wife, three small children aged five, three, and one year respectively, his mother, and a young servant of seventeen, in a small three-roomed house at Villa Devoto, a suburb of Buenos Ayres.

He was told of strange phenomena—nocturnal and other noises—of which the house had been the scene in the preceding year, with intervention of the police, who discovered nothing. He did not want to believe it at first, being an energetic man not given to superstitious beliefs. But he soon had occasion to get first-hand evidence of the reality of the mysterious facts, which recommenced with greater intensity almost immediately after his arrival.

It was usually in the night, when everybody was in bed and the lights were out. Noises and blows were heard, sometimes very violent, on the doors and windows, inside the walls, on the tables and chairs. Doors were shaken almost to breaking point, as if to open them by force. At first José Amadei, armed with a revolver, used to investigate whether this was not the work of a practical joker, and watched outside, but without the slightest result. Sometimes his bedclothes were pulled off, and the candle he tried to light was blown out several times. The same things occurred in all the rooms. The linen from the cupboards was strewn about the floors, and the crockery was taken from the dresser, but without breaking it! Once, during the day, in one of the rooms which had been locked, the three flower vases and the lamp were found carefully reversed and arranged in the form of a cross.

12 I had to reserve it for this volume.

It was impossible to sleep, life became insufferable in the house, and they were thinking of looking for another domicile, when somebody remarked that the cradle of the year-old baby had always been spared by the unknown force which upset all the other furniture. It then occurred to them that it might be the grandfather (father of M. Amadei), who was dead twenty-nine years and had been very pious, who perhaps wished the child to be baptised. This was done at once, and since then there had not been the slightest abnormal manifestation in the house, to the great joy of all the family! It had lasted fourteen consecutive days.

I must add that this family had never practised Spiritualism and never heard of it.

That, M. Flammarion, is the fact I thought it best to communicate to you. It would be easy for me to furnish further details if required, for M. Amadei is still at the Museum and in touch with his people.

(Sg.) PEDRO SERIÉ
(Zoologist at the Museum of Buenos Ayres.)
(*Letter* 4,549.)

My enquiries entirely confirmed the reality of the facts reported. A letter of August 24, 1921, contains, among other things, the attestation by M. José Amadei. The observation given above is unimpeachable. Of course there will be readers (1 per cent. perhaps) who will imagine that my correspondent is a gay *farceur* or a simple, credulous person, and will remain convinced that it is only a case of inventions, romances, illusions, and errors. Let them have their way. Without ceasing to respect these impenitent sceptics, I shall only recall the Arab proverb: "The dogs bark, the caravan passes." We are of the caravan, on its way to the promised land.

Nevertheless, we must admit that it is all very strange and impossible to explain in the present state of science. But we may affirm, at the same time, that the phenomena found at Buenos Ayres are the same as those described before at the castle in Calvados, in Corrèze, in Auvergne, in England, in Haute-Garonne, in Portugal, etc. And let us admit that to escape being convinced of the reality of the facts enumerated in this book we must deny the evidence.

Religious ideas are still associated with those manifestations in which we find a reasoning power and a purpose. But they are very diverse and varied, as we shall see.

The next story came to me from Havre, on June 12, 1902:

I am but a poor workman, without education, and perhaps I ought not to meddle with these things. But when I was about ten I witnessed an occurrence which attracted much attention at Manneville-la-Goupil, canton of Goderville, district of Havre.

It happened at the farm of Puy-Varin, in the commune of Manneville-la-Goupil. Unusual noises appear to have been heard there, because, according to what the good people of the locality said, the owner of the farm had not kept his promises to one of his relatives who died at the farm. One evening, therefore, accompanied by my grandfather, a medallist of Sainte-Hélène, and Père Votte, as I then called him, a brigadier of gendarmery at Goderville, I went to the farm at Puy-Varin to verify the marvellous things which were said to happen there.

For two hours nothing happened at the farm. As we were about to leave, Père Votte said to my grandfather: "Well, old Torquet, here is a bad bit of humbug to worry us about." Hardly had he said these words when all the furniture and crockery in the kitchen began to dance. It was like a witches' Sabbath. My grandfather's forage cap was thrown into the fire and burnt, and I, the little boy, was thrown by an unknown force against the front door.

I then heard the angry voice of my good grandfather

saying: "You who make all this pother, if you come from God, speak; if from the Devil, decamp!"

These things took place as I have told them, at Manneville-la-Goupil, and are still remembered by the old people. There was no apparatus, no medium, no conjurer, but only poor peasants, like myself, who always talked about it. These are the facts, which I consider it my duty to report to you. I hold myself at your disposal for further details if necessary.

My grandfather was then field-watchman at Manneville-la-Goupil.

(Sg.) SATURNIN TINEL.
(*Letter* 1,014.)

7, RUE LEFEVRÈVILLE,
HAVRE.

On enquiries being made, I found that the narrative conformed with reality.

Here is another and more recent observation.

In December, 1922, I learnt from an important communication on divers phenomena made to me by Mlle. Lasserre, a canal owner at La Cape, Port-Sainte-Marie (Lot-et-Garonne), that the secular girls' school of——[13] had been the scene of very remarkable haunting phenomena. In pursuance of the enquiry which I always make for my personal instruction, Mlle. Lasserre invited me to communicate directly with Mlle. X., a retired teacher living at A——, who had witnessed the occurrences, as well as other teachers. "The uproar was so great," said the narrator, "that the parish priest of —— was asked to intervene to shed some light on the matter." I wrote to Mlle. X., and here is an extract from the reply she kindly sent me under date of January 14, 1923:

---

[13] I think it right to suppress names, especially as officials are involved.

The schoolhouse of ——, which I inhabited for sixteen years, was (it may be even now) haunted. Every evening extraordinary noises used to trouble the sleep of my assistants, and I heard a good deal of them myself.

Mlle. X., now at A——, as Directrice of the École Carnot, yesterday told me of her exciting experiences. One night she saw the curtain of her bed shake, and then she seemed to see a hand, a groping hand, passing over the curtains. Fear seized her. She sat up on her bed, the lamp being alight all the time, and she still saw the hand, which finally disappeared, though the curtain continued to shake violently.

At other times it seemed to her that her wardrobe was being opened. She got up, and saw her bunch of keys swinging.

The room of the assistant teachers was over the classrooms. These ladies heard blows as of a ruler on the desks. It seemed to them that the writing-tables were shifted, and that someone was walking about. But in the morning it was found that nothing had stirred.

One night I heard a formidable noise down in the kitchen. It sounded as if a plate-rack had fallen, breaking all the crockery, and as if the kettles in the rack were rolling on the tiles. When the maid entered my room in the morning I recommended her to go down to the kitchen at once, because the plate-rack had fallen. She came back after a few minutes to tell me that nothing had moved. After some time, worn out with the uproar, I sent for the priest, who blessed the house on a Thursday morning. But the row began again soon. It was no use looking round; we never found the cause of the mysterious noise.

It would take much too long to enumerate here all we observed, but I must add that the neighbours heard a noise in the night as if a cart full of gravel were being discharged in the yard.

That is the story of one of the observers of these curious phenomena, for which we are grateful. What strikes us is the triviality of the actions.

Noises without an explanation—like the wood-splitting at Fougères—shocks making the walls tremble, plaster falling from the walls, blows responding by number to interrogations, curtains waving, the noise of furniture falling, all these correspond to no reality. They are subjective and objective phenomena, whose theoretical placing is difficult. That occult forces are acting is undoubted, but what are they?

In haunted houses and in some fantastic manifestations formidable noises are often heard: sledgehammer blows calculated to bring down the partitions; the rattling of doors and windows, the fall of crockery or glass thrown on the floor and broken in pieces; and on examining the result of all the commotion we find in general nothing broken, nothing demolished, and nothing displaced. And yet an hypothesis of illusion or hallucination is excluded by the multiplicity of observers.

In 1907 we had in Paris a "Universal Society of Psychic Studies," which was invited to conduct some enquiries on the subject of our study. Let us give the story of a haunted house on the outskirts of Beuvry, a large village of 7,000 inhabitants, five miles from Béthune, in the middle of the Black Country:[14]

> Our trip [wrote M. Chaplain, engineer] was too late to enable us to witness the phenomena, which had ceased for several days. Yet, in spite of the mistrust of the proprietor, we were able to enter the house, question the inhabitants, and examine on the furniture the incontestable traces of the violence to which it had been subjected.
>
> The first occurrences go back to January 3. M. Sénéchal, who has a small grocer's shop, lives in the house, with

[14] See *Annales des Sciences Psychiques*, February, 1907.

a wife, old and completely helpless, on account of a paralysis which has confined her to her chair for several years, and a young girl of about fifteen, who acts as a servant.

From January 3 on the furniture of the house started on a senseless dance. The chairs flew from one room to the other and broke against the tables and walls; vases and crockery broke to pieces on the floor. The till of the shop was upset, and cases of soap flew over it. Shoes walked up the stairs. A dish of meat came out of the oven and fell in the bedroom; a water-bottle fell on the floor without breaking. It was picked up, but did it again and broke.

All this took place in the daytime and ceased at nightfall. It always occurred in the room where the young servant was, and never in her absence. When the girl took a few days' holiday the house resumed its tranquillity, but the phenomena reappeared the moment she returned to the house.

Another peculiarity is that nobody ever saw anything moving. One heard the noise behind, and on turning one found what had happened. The girl herself never saw anything move.

The Sénéchal people never observed any special state about the girl. She plied her avocations quite normally.

A few days before our arrival M. Sénéchal had dismissed the servant. Since then nothing has occurred. We tried to find the girl, but did not succeed. The Sénéchal people, annoyed at what occurred in their house, absolutely refused to give their servant's address.

(Sg.) Paul Chaplain
(Engineer).

Quite naturally the servant was suspected. But the reader knows from the examples he has read already that she was not responsible.

Here is the result of an enquiry into another "haunted house," made on the initiative of the same society:

The regional papers of the Nord having published an article concerning a haunted house at Douai,[15] we went to the town on Sunday, January 13, to conduct an enquiry. The house in question is 19, Rue des Écoles. It was uninhabited for some time, but for some months it had been occupied by the D. family, consisting of the father, a postman, the mother, five children, and a young servant of sixteen or seventeen.

Here are the occurrences which attracted attention to that house. For about a fortnight Mme. D. heard the bell ring at the front door several times per day, but found nobody waiting to enter. She first thought of a practical joke, but soon the bell-ringing increased in frequency and intensity, and made a commotion in the house. In front of the frightened family, the bell rang violently, while the cord and the bell-pull moved in unison. The whole quarter assembled, and over three hundred people witnessed the phenomenon.

The police were called in, but could not find the cause. Indeed, at the end of three days, in front of a policeman, the bell fell off the wall in a last peal and broke on the ground.

Thus the papers. At Douai we first visited the central police station. The facts were corroborated, but public opinion felt unable to assign a cause.

We went to 19, Rue des Écoles, but on our arrival we were met by a formal injunction by M. D. to say nothing and not to see anybody. Although we insisted, we could obtain no information. During our short interview with Mme. D. we caught a glimpse of the famous bell. It is a simple bell, with a cord hanging down in front of the door. (The broken bell had been replaced.)

It only remained, therefore, to question the neighbours. We spoke to several people who were witnesses by eye or ear. All agreed as to the reality and loudness of the phenomenon. The bell not only tinkled, but made prolonged ringings. The cord was shaken as if by a hand.

---

15 This haunted house of Douai, 1907, must not be confounded with that of Fives-Lille in 1865.

An immediate neighbour of the haunted house gave us precise details. Several times this woman heard Mme. D. utter cries of terror; each time she rushed to help her and found *the bell ringing by itself.* One day she was amazed to see it ring on five different occasions, while the cord danced about madly. On another day, standing on her own doorstep, she made an allusion to the bell and it tinkled at once. This happened several times. "One might have thought that it was defying me," said the woman. Her opinion was that of the whole quarter—viz., that the servant was bewitched. The priest, who was sent for, came to bless the house, and recommended them to change the bell. The architect of the house paid a professional visit, carefully examined the bell, and made sure that it could not be made to ring artificially from that or the neighbouring houses. In short, he found out nothing. The police organised a watch, but it was all in vain.

One evening another alarm decided Mme. D. to send for a locksmith for the morrow. But on that morning the final carillon took place which ended in the breaking of the bell. The broken bell was replaced, and since then there has been no agitation.

But the unfortunate tenants were no better off. In the first place, heavy steps were heard upstairs. Lighted lamps went out several times. The servant espied a man in the rooms or on the stairs, and these hallucinations were frequently renewed. Furniture was shifted. A child's cot was upset, the mattress thrown on the floor, and the sheets carefully rolled up and placed in a corner of the room.

That was the situation in the house when we made our enquiry. Afterwards we learnt that all had stopped since the servant left.

We owe it to truth to add a curious detail: the girl left Mme. D.'s house in the company of her father. It appears that this man possesses the reputation of a wizard, and that before his departure he made an incantation "to drive the evil spirits from the house." The coincidence is worth recording, though the hypothesis of an understanding between father and daughter for the purpose of mystification seems to us rather improbable.

(Sg.) DHUIQUE
(Chemist).

LILLE,
February 3, 1907.

We see that there are always the same trivialities: noises, shifting of furniture, and bell-ringing.[16] In spite of the father's reputation for wizardry, we need not suppose a connivance with his daughter, since the bell was seen to move alone.

As we have said, the observations of haunted houses under the best conditions as to authenticity are as numerous as they are varied, and the difficulty is where to stop in the instructive collection we are anxious to make.

The number of documents available for this work is considerable. I owe them partly to the numerous correspondents who, like myself, are anxious to arrive at the truth, and who have taken the trouble to send me their personal observations on the results of their researches. I wish particularly to recognise the laborious and friendly help of M. Marius Guillot, of Nice, the learned secretary and librarian of the Psychical Research Society of the town, who alone has sent me 140 accounts, many of them transcribed by himself. Unfortunately, I can only quote a small number of these, the documents by themselves representing a veritable library. The number of these accounts is all the more worthy

---

[16] These automatic movements of bells without perceptible cause are relatively frequent. My readers may have noticed two in *L'Inconnu* and four in *Death and Its Mystery.* I have collected sixty-eight examples. One of the most interesting concerns the death-bed of Alfred de Musset, and was told me by his governess, Adèle Colin. The subject is worthy of a special chapter, but space is lacking. We are too rich!

of attention—eliminating illusions, errors, and practical jokes—because we must take into account the average mentality of human beings, their mental slavery and cowardice.

Let us say again that we have a plethora of choice for the proof of the phenomena of haunting. Here is another example.

Paris-Journal published on April 16, 1910, a letter sent from Saint-Nicolas-du-Port, near Nancy, of which the following is an extract:

The servant of the present proprietor of the Parisian Bazaar, an affable village girl of eighteen summers, named Germaine Maire, was washing in a yard behind the house; a chunk of bread fell at her feet.

On the following Tuesday an even more expressive manifestation occurred as she was doing the weekly washing. A long nail came whistling down, transfixed the left sleeve of her gown and planted itself in the middle of her apron.

Rebellious against superstition, Germaine suspected a practical joke of neighbours. The hour of dinner had sounded. She went down to the cellar and brought up the usual bottle of wine. An enormous pebble broke it in her hand.

This time the joke went beyond bounds. Germaine called out. A rattle of hardware responded and a windowpane fell in small pieces at her feet. The most diverse missiles fell on the wall: stones, nails, bits of wood, clamps, etc.

Two days passed, during which the young servant went as little as possible into the accursed yard. She tried to do her work in the neighbouring court, but a new hailstorm saluted her first appearance. Nails, screw-rings, and stones this time fell on the windows, breaking them into fragments.

From this day, Friday, March 25, the bombardment increased every evening with amazing punctuality, until it fell even into the shop.

A carpenter, M. Fournie, was trying on a cap, when a long nail transfixed it in his hand. The only thing was to call in the police.

M. Michelet, the local Commissary, came to investigate. He thought he discovered the point whence the mysterious nail came. His report quite simply accused the young lady herself, and he even induced her to confess.

Here we have one of the picturesque examples of the errors so often committed in the study of these subjects. It is not a rare thing for a medium to make a surreptitious and more or less intelligent addition to her real faculties. This addition does not destroy the reality of those faculties. I have personally verified this in the case of Eusapia, of Mlle. Huet, etc., as expounded in *Les Forces Naturelles Inconnues*.

The Nancy Psychical Research Society published on this point an excellent appreciation by Dr. Boucher, which brings this story of Saint-Nicolas-du-Port to a focus:

What struck me at once [he writes] was the form presented by the passage of missiles through certain window-panes and through screens placed in position by the Commissary. The hole was clean, nearly round, and hardly starred at the edges, almost without cracks, thus indicating a force acting with extreme power.

Thus, two large nails were still fixed in a pierced pane, and bits of glass were deeply embedded in a wall.

To explain the facts on ordinary lines it was necessary to assume the intervention of special instruments such as slings, airguns, cross-bows, etc., used as means of projection, and these various hypotheses had, needless to say, been envisaged by the competent authority.

But they had to be discarded at once, because they would not hold. In fact, screw-rings and stones the size of a fist are not projected with airguns or crossbows, and slings could not have projected nails with their point in front all along their trajectory. Besides, none of these instruments were found in the house, in spite of a careful search.

After examining the damage and appreciating the force with which the objects were thrown, a force infinitely superior to that possessed by human beings, I examined the different inhabitants of the house.

It did not take me long to discover the unwilling intermediary of these phenomena. It was the servant, a girl about twenty, who showed all the symptoms of lack of nervous balance required to make an excellent medium. Extraordinarily impressionable, it often had happened since her childhood that she suddenly stopped and remained as if hypnotised, hearing and seeing nothing, so that it was necessary to sprinkle her with water to make her normal again.

Thus I could, without hesitation, indicate to the Commissary and to her employers the servant as the irresponsible and unconscious author of the damage done, against the denials of them all, because the former had fixed his suspicions on a well-conducted neighbour, and the latter, pleased with the services of their little servant girl, would not have it that she was responsible for such things.

Still the magistrate was probably impressed by the clearness of my opinions, for after my departure he put the girl under a state of arrest.

She immediately confessed that she had thrown some stones at the windows. But she indignantly denied having broken more than two panes, and said that, as regarded the rest, things had happened as she had always maintained, that she had seen various objects violently thrown without ever finding whence that peculiar rain came.

Naturally this last part of her declaration was not admitted, and for the sake of everybody's peace, the servant was considered the sole conscious and responsible author of the damage.

Dr. Boucher is absolutely in the right. These erroneous reports condemning irresponsible agents are due to the psychic ignorance of the judges.

A haunted farm in Brittany, at Pleiber-Christ (Finistère), canton of Saint-Thégonnec, arrondissement of Morlaix, attracted much attention in 1909. We may read with curiosity an article about it in *Le Matin* on March 1, 1909, which is reproduced in the *Annales des Sciences Psychiques*. This Breton haunted house is a type of its kind, the mad woman of the house having grafted imaginary visions on the psychic background which we are studying.

This episode took place in 1909. Four years later, in 1913, simliar happenings in the same département, arrondissement, and canton, but on another farm, situated in the commune of Plouniour-Menez, produced a stir among the people. *La Vie Mystérieuse* of April 10, 1913, published under the signature of M. Jean Mettois, who passed a day and a night at the farm, a long report, from which I extract the following:

In the farmyard, as we entered it, the fowls were pecking away quickly, indifferent to the tragedy of the surroundings, and horses greeted us with neighings. Everything breathed calm and peace. The motor-horn sounded several times and the car snorted, but nothing stirred. It seemed as if we were not in the Devil's Farm, but in that of the Sleeping Beauty. Our noise did not trouble man or beast.

We knocked at the door of the living-house, but got no answer. We entered the classic room of every Breton farm, with its great chimney and pot-rack, its closed beds, its immense table, filling up nearly all the space. At this table was seated a woman of about fifty, her head in her hands. Our entry seemed to rouse her from a dream, and she said in Breton, "Good-day." We were in the presence of the farmer woman.

My friend, who luckily speaks Breton like a veritable Celt, explained the cause of our visit to the good woman.

We wished to have some particulars of the phenomena in her house.

"God be praised if you can stop them," she replied. "Have you the power? Are you good sorcerers?"

The farmer woman credited us with a power we do not possess. But in order to obtain precise information we told her, with the aplomb known only to reporters, that we might possibly be strong enough to destroy the miscreant.

"Tell us what happens."

"Ah, Monsieur, our horses and beasts die, our oats melt away, our corn is eaten. If you slept in the farm for a single night, you might die of fright. Every night there is an uproar which does not give us a minute's sleep. Look, there (the woman points to the chimney) stones fall one by one with a terrible clatter. It sounds as if thunder broke in the chimney. About midnight we seem to see white forms trailing burdens on the ground, the locked doors open of themselves, the horses get loose and run wildly about the yard, the cows low with fright. It is enough to drive one mad." And at the remembrance of what she had to undergo every evening, the unfortunate farmer's wife went pale, her eyes contracted and a light of terror gleamed in them.

The visitor conversed with the farmer's wife, the farmer, and his son, and eventually comprehended through their Breton idiom, with its "kers" and "brosks," that the trouble concerns a field hired from the priest, and for which they pay a tax to the State after the separation, that the soul of the late owner is not happy, that promised masses have not been said, that phantoms wander through all the rooms, etc.

Everywhere [says the narrator] I find superstition, a belief in the ancient practices of witchcraft. Not a plausible explanation conforming to our psychical theories finds any place in the explanations advanced by the people I converse with. Two or three peasants speak enough

French to make themselves understood, and in their mouths the word "devil" recurs several times. They have no doubt about it. All these manifestations, whether due to deceased relatives or to genii of the locality, are "works of the Devil."

I am invited to supper: cabbage, a chunk of pork, rabbit with garlic, red plums, and green cider. At 8 p.m. the mother says the prayer, in Latin this time—Latin in which, comformably with Papal instructions, the *us* (oos) replaces the French *üs*—and I am given a mattress and a pillow, which had been prepared for me, and a corner in the room. Then everyone disappears in the closed beds to prepare—if possible—for sleep.

In the room an oil night-light burns. Nobody sleeps, and the farmer says to me a word in Breton which I naturally do not understand.

I stretch myself on my mattress, and upon my word I go to sleep very soon, in spite of the hardness of my couch, the mattress being laid on beaten earth.

Suddenly I wake up, and my hosts start moaning. Then I hear furious blows, as if somebody armed with a battering-ram were trying to force the door. I get up. It is on the side of the fireplace that the noise is heard. And it really seems as if somebody were trying to break the chimney. I go out, and finding a ladder in the yard, I place it against the wall so as to discover any play of a practical joker. Nothing! I grip the chimney on the roof and look round upon the scene. There is absolute quiet but for the blows shaking the wall.

It is 2 a.m. I go back to the living-room. The farmer and his mother are sitting on their beds, still moaning.

Until 2.22 a.m. exactly, the blows succeed each other at regular intervals. Then they stop suddenly, and are not heard again during the night.

That is what I saw, or heard, rather, for I saw one of the phantoms which are said to pass through the room every night to commit sundry misdeeds. But what I have heard is disturbing enough to enable one to credit M. Croguennec's assertions, and to believe that other and more terrible manifestations may have occurred.

I do not wish to draw any conclusion. It is the business of those who are better instructed concerning these manifestations to say what they think of my story, which has nothing to recommend it but its absolute sincerity.

(Sg.) JEAN METTOIS.

The hypothesis of collective hallucination which first occurs to our minds is quite inapplicable here.

The manifestations, let me repeat, present the most varied aspects in their strange triviality. Let us consider the following story, communicated to me in September, 1920, from the Département of Indre-et-Loire. It recalls from the very first lines the phantasmagoria of the jeweller's house at Strasbourg, reported above, but differs in appearing to have a definite object. (In the next chapter we shall have to make a classification of characteristics.) Here is the text of this special case of haunting:

The occurrences I am about to report took place in 1865.

My father was a republican, an atheist, and a freethinker. I was still a child, and we lived in a neat and quasi-elegant little house in the commune of Mosnes, near Amboise (Indre-et-Loire). My mother kept a haberdasher's shop and my father was a farrier. Of robust health, a critic, and a great talker, he chaffed the religious people of every sort, as well as those—still numerous in the country—who believe in sorcery, the miracles of the saints, and fortune-tellers.

One day, or, rather, one night, in which my father slept the profound sleep of those who hammer iron from dawn to dusk, he was awakened by an unusual noise on the stairs. It seemed to him that a ball descended step by step, with great regularity, the stairs of the two storeys of the house.[17] At that time we had a working farrier of the name of Angevin. At that time, when guilds were

[17] This inexplicable but incontestable noise is not rare.

flourishing, every workman provided himself with the name of his province or native town. At the first sound of this noise my father ran up the stairs and inspected the garret. Having found nothing, he came down and went to bed again. As the noise returned in great force, he dressed and went to knock at the door of his workman, who slept on the first floor. "Angevin, are you asleep?" "No, master. The infernal noise in the house annoys me. I have barricaded my door and am waiting for it to finish." "Put on your clothes, you coward, and come up to the garret with me." "I have been, master, and saw nothing." "Let us go again, together." Having found nothing, the two men looked at each other, alarmed and out of countenance.

"What can be making that noise, Angevin?" "I don't know, master" (his teeth were chattering). "Neither do I. Let us return to bed."

The noise only stopped at 3 a.m. That day the smithy was hard at work earlier than usual. Long before dawn the workshop resounded with the noise of hammers falling on ringing iron, and the astonished neighbours said: "The farrier is early to-day." Next night the noise started afresh, and it was impossible to discover the cause. The free-thinker was no longer so assured. As regards Angevin, he was terrified. On the fourth day, in the morning, he accosted my father, his bag in his hand and his bundle on his shoulder. "Master," he said, "I am going. If I remained here another day I should go mad. If there was somebody to fight, even—but there is nothing, nobody. I am going at once, master."

After having drained a bottle of white wine as a leave-taking, they shook hands and parted. Angevin was sad and disconcerted, and my father sombre and quiet. "It is the first time I have shirked, master."

Those were Angevin's last words. My father followed him with his eyes on the road leading from Mosnes to Amboise until he disappeared from view in the long avenue of poplars which skirt the road.

But the commotion went from bad to worse in the house. The invisible authors of the strange noises grew daily more audacious and enterprising. They took possession of the room where my parents slept, the furniture cracked, the crockery danced, and they were rocked in their bed. "My shirt was often wet," said my father, in telling this truthful story, and he accompanied his narrative with the oaths usual among men of his occupation.

What was he to do with his secret? Should he continue to chaff those who believe in soothsayers and burn candles in the chapels of the Virgin and the Saints?

"Above all, don't tell this to anyone," he said to my mother, "or they will laugh at me."

Every month there was a fair at Amboise. He went there to distract himself. He found friends from the neighbouring country, with whom he breakfasted. What he concealed from his neighbours with the greatest care for fear of being chaffed he freely confided to strangers. At the meal everybody recounted a story, which might be more or less questionable. He would then tell his own rather eerie tale and would feel relieved. Everybody laughed and was ready to chaff and inundate the narrator with ridicule. Roars of laughter, difficult to restrain, were breaking out, when one of the blacksmiths began to speak with peculiar solemnity:

"There is no occasion to laugh, friends, about what our comrade Bourdain has just said. It is more serious than you think. Nobody here knows what this is. I do, and am going to tell you. My old friend, there are ghosts in your house, and it is they who make the noise you hear. Yes; they are ghosts, or spirits of the dead. They exist, and what will surprise you more is that means have been found of communicating with them."

He then gave a lecture on spiritism which caught my father's attention. He had the curiosity to be present at experiments made in a neighbouring house. Gradually he became convinced and spoke to his wife.

"But you told me that that was all nonsense, and that there were no ghosts. The priests say the same."

"The priests know nothing about it. Ghosts exist. I believe in them now, but there is neither heaven nor hell, only it appears that there is a God. I am not quite sure of that yet, but, as it has been explained to me, it no longer seems unreasonable, and I understand something about it."

In the spiritualist séances he was told concerning the noises in our house that the invisible world was at present making great efforts to attract the attention of human beings to other-world questions, and that spirits exercised some ingenuity in producing effects proving survival, that our case was not an isolated one, and that the choice made of our house was made with the object of leading my father—and especially myself, who was then twelve years old—to the knowledge of spiritualistic truth.

We were assured that the object had been gained and that the noisy manifestations would soon cease completely. As a matter of fact, the noises diminished in force and soon ceased altogether. I remember that we were told at a séance: "The considerable forces required for the production of the remarkable effects intended for you are now dissipated, and you will now be left in peace."

Well, it seemed to me that when my father had to be content with raps and movements observed in groups, and phenomena among which it is sometimes difficult to say what comes from Beyond, and what must be attributed to suggestion or auto-suggestion, he sometimes regretted the cessation of the infernal noise which raged at the beginning of the adventure, and which had given him and my mother so many frights. He had become interested in it.

(Sg.) EDMOND BOURDAIN.

This curious and true narrative is here reproduced without alteration of any kind.

It is difficult not to see in these queer manifestations the action of an invisible intelligence. Was there really an intention connected with spiritualism? That is another question.

We have before us so great a number of manifestations that it is impossible to recount them all. But we cannot pass over the haunted house of Valance-en-Brie, which roused so many echoes in 1896.

My much-lamented friend, Dr. Encausse ("Papus"), who for over twenty years made a special study of magic, the cabbala, and witchcraft, sent me a remarkable report on this case, which was no less surprising and certain than the preceding cases. Here is his letter, abridged:

MY DEAR MASTER,

The phenomena of Valence-en-Brie are very interesting to occultists. In this village of 700 inhabitants, a house, up to that time peaceful, in which live two maid-servants, an invalid lady and two children, is the scene of disturbing occurrences. It belongs to M. Lebègue. Mme. Lebègue senior is in bed worn out with excitement.

1. First of all, a gruff voice, very loud and uttering coarse abuse, was heard by a young maid-servant in the cellar. This voice made such an uproar that a dozen neighbours came in and confirmed the fact.

2. The following days, "the voice" continued to be heard, but spread itself over the house to such an extent that a week after the commencement of the phenomenon the voice could be heard not only in the cellar, but even in the vestibule, at the front door, in the kitchen, and in all the rooms of the first floor.

The voice seems to come from the ground, but the tone is so high and it breaks out in so many different places that any trickery seems impossible.

3. Some enormous planks, as well as a cask, were on three occasions moved from one end of the cellar to the other, furniture was turned upside down in the unoccupied room and things upset more or less everywhere.

4. And to crown all, from the fourteenth day of the persecution, the window-panes flew into pieces, in broad daylight at four o'clock in the afternoon, and under the very eyes of the bewildered tenants.

Things reached such a pitch that a formal complaint was made to the authorities by M. Lebègue.

These occurrences happened for the most part when the master of the house was in Paris. The latter could therefore not have had anything to do with them.

In the evening the two maids left the house, and the things happened exactly as if they were present. It is sufficient to say that they are not to be reckoned with either in this affair.

Finally, the children were sent away, *successively* and *separately,* and the phenomena continued.

Then the sick lady herself was taken away to another house, and the phenomena followed her there. The bed was pushed about and almost turned upside down. More than fifty creditable witnesses are certain of the facts and have testified in the courts of justice.

What sort of phenomena have we to do with?

Is it some ill-natured practical joke, as it so often is? Is it a domestic trying to make fun of a whole village by imitating ghost stories?

I do not think so, and here are my reasons:

Phenomena due to fraud are generally produced at night, and always in the same place. Furthermore, they cease when the trickster is removed. In this case they happened in the daytime as well as at night, and continued in the absence of all the members of the family.

It is therefore necessary to suppose the complicity of several persons. That, again, only accounts for some of the clumsy physical phenomena, but not for *the voice* and its instantaneous changes of direction.

Further, a mirror was broken in such a way that it was impossible to reproduce it artificially. In fact, this mirror showed a very clean circular hole with a convexity *between the wood and the hole,* which indicated that the hole was made from within outwards, as in the case of an electric discharge.

Artless people who profess to explain everything have not failed to say: "There was a ventriloquist hidden somewhere." Now, one only needs to have studied ventriloquism to eliminate this idea. It is impossible to produce effects of this kind from the bottom of the cellar to the first floor, and if any one in the house was master of this art the phenomena would have ceased with the departure of this person, and such was not the case.

In short, the householder made considerable borings and excavations in his cellar to make sure that there were no electric wires, or acoustic apparatus of any kind connecting the cellar with the house.

All those whom one interrogates in the near neighbourhood, whether they are credulous or not, affirm the reality of the voices heard: persons, the most respectable, the least capable of trickery, the most exempt by their age or temperament from any hallucination or influence of any kind, have distinctly heard the voice: M. Hainot, Mayor of Valence, the teacher, and the priest, who, by the way, does not see any diabolic activity in these strange phenomena.

The young servant was not afraid of the inconvenient guest, although she was the origin of his pleasantries. She was in the cellar getting coal when he snuffed her candle. That was the prelude to the mystifications which, alas! finished the poor helpless invalid.

The authorities have been sent for. There is an enquiry on foot. It will have the usual result.

Dr. Encausse
(*"Papus"*).

This haunted house of Valence-en-Brie (Seine-et-Marne) must not astonish us more than the others. The mysterious voice we have already met. We also know those displacements of objects and broken windows. These are unknown forces in action.

My readers are well informed. Do they not remember in vol. iii of *Death and Its Mystery* a curious haunting which revealed a theft committed by a former chambermaid?

We said just now that all countries and all times furnish material for us. The city of Turin alone furnishes a large number. Here is, among others, a curious case discovered by M. Vesme in 1901, and published in his *Revue des Études Psychiques*:

La Stampa, of Turin, one of the most important papers of Italy, published in its number of May 10 the following article:

A strange occurrence was observed yesterday in a small dwelling consisting of two attics at No. 6 Corso Valdocco, inhabited for some time by a certain Juvenal Menardi with his wife and their children.

About 5 p.m. this man was surprised to see several small pieces of furniture move. After that a number of objects and kitchen utensils which were on the mantelpiece or hung on the wall detached themselves and fell with a clatter.

Everybody can imagine the consternation of these good people.

Mr. Menardi, after giving the alarm to his neighbours, remembered that on the first floor of the same building the police commissariat of the Montcenis quarter had its headquarters. So he descended the stairs four steps at a time and went to the police to inform them of the adventure and ask for their help.

A constable at once went up to the attics, where he was able not only to verify the disorder among the objects there, but he and the family Menardi, as well as some neighbours, saw a smoothing-iron leave the mantelpiece and fall on the floor.

It is even added that some moments afterwards a jug full of milk, without being touched by anybody, was upset and emptied. People asked whether the foundations of the house were solid.

Meanwhile the rumour of what had happened spread like wildfire, and people came from all quarters to be present at the show. But Mr. Menardi and his family had no wish to remain in the dwelling. They locked it up and all went elsewhere.

On the following day *La Stampa* went back to the subject:

Yesterday afternoon we visited the house in the Corso Valdocco, in order, if possible, to witness some of the phenomena we wrote about.

The Menardi lodging is on the third floor. When we arrived no member of the family was in the place.

In leaving Mrs. Menardi had left the key with the concierge, Mr. Adolphe Schiappa, so that he might be able to admit to the lodging any visitors who might come. The floor of the two rooms is almost covered with fragments of pottery and bottles.

While we were examining the débris we saw a good old woman come up, Mrs. Teresa Francesetti, who held in her arms the youngest son of Mr. Menardi, a pretty baby of barely six months. She had been present at the appearance of the first phenomena, and here is her story nearly literally:

I was in the rooms, sitting down there by the window. I was sewing. All the Menardi children were about me. The mother had gone out to buy milk.

Suddenly, about half-past four, I saw the little table upset. I first thought it was the wind. I picked up the table and set to work again. A moment afterwards the table fell again. I picked it up again. The same thing happened several times more. Losing patience, but still thinking it was the draught, I carried the table to another corner of the room. Then it did not fall. But a few moments afterwards I was amazed to see a china dish fall from the chimney-piece and smash on the floor. I got up to see what was happening, but a bottle jumped and broke on the floor. Several neighbours ran up, among them Mrs. Menardi, the concierge Schiappa, and Constable Andries. Mrs. Menardi sent for her husband and a priest.

Abbé Valimberto, curate of the Parish of Cormina, soon arrived. The scene is depicted for us by a neighbour, Miss Kreifemberg. When the Abbé arrived, I was in the Menardi lodgings with some other people. The priest blessed the two rooms. We were kneeling and responding to prayers. Some women had in their hands those olive branches which are distributed on Palm Sunday. When the prayers were finished, the priest had some holy water put into a glass. The glass was put on the table where, among other objects, there was a small statue of the Virgin. Suddenly this statue fell on the floor and was broken, and the glass of holy water went to join it.

The vandalistic phenomena then continued without interruption. In the whole dwelling not a single glass or china object is intact, except a mirror and a decanter. Everything is in smithereens, including the oil lamp. Needless to say, nothing else is talked about in the house or in the rest of the town.

The poor Menardi family is in a piteous state. The mother, a healthy and robust woman, is prostrated and weeps all the time. The children, especially the eldest girl are much frightened.

Finally, on May 14, the same paper wrote:

The Duke of the Abruzzi has visited the house and remained for ten minutes among the visitors, asking among them and especially among them the eyewitnesses for detailed information concerning the phenomena. He once more showed his devotion to science, that science which took him to the summit of Mount Saint Elias and among the icebergs of the Arctic Pole.

To sum up, the affair caused much commotion, everybody talked about it, and there was no explanation.

Another haunted house of Turin was the object of a special enquiry by Professor Lombroso. He writes: [18]

In November, 1900, I heard that strange and inexplicable movements had been observed at No. 6, Via Bava, at Turin, in a cellar owned by the innkeeper named Fumero, which was exclusively used for depositing bottles. If anyone entered the cellar, the bottles, full or empty, started breaking, always by the action of the same unknown agents. In vain did a priest bless the place. The police were equally powerless. But they gave a hint to poor Mr. Fumero that it would have to stop.

When, on November 21, I called at the cabaret without mentioning my name and asked for details of the alleged phenomena, I was much surprised to hear from the pro-

[18] *Annales des sciences psychiques*, 1906, p. 266. See also Lombroso, *Ricerche sui fenomeni spiritici*, Torino, 1909, p. 247; and Richet, *Traité de métapsychique*, p. 737.

prietors that the occurrences had really taken place, but that, fortunately, "Professor Lombroso had come, and since then everything had ceased"! Much interested by this reply, as I had never set foot in the place, I revealed my identity and demanded an explanation, wishing to make sure whether somebody had not misused my name for a purpose concerning which I reserved my action. Mr. and Mrs. Fumero then admitted that, having heard that I would probably come, they conceived the idea of saying that my coming had put the "spirits" to flight! They thus succeeded in ridding themselves of the police and sightseers, and for that purpose they saw no harm in attributing to me the powers of Grand Exorcist! But these good people then told me that, unfortunately, the phenomena were continuing, and that probably I could verify them with my own eyes if I would go down into the cellar.

I eagerly accepted the offer. I entered into the cellar, at first in total darkness, and I heard the noise of breaking glass and of bottles rolling at my feet. The bottles were ranged on five shelves, one over the other. In the centre there was a rough table, on which I made them place six lighted candles, thinking that the bright light would stop the phenomena. But, on the contrary, I saw three empty bottles, standing upright on the ground, roll as if pushed by a foot and break against the table. To guard against trickery I touched and minutely examined with a candle all the full bottles on the shelves and made sure there was no thread or wire which would explain the movements.

After a few minutes two bottles, then four, and then two more bottles of the second and third shelf, fell to the floor without a shock, as if they had been carried. After their descent—one could not call it a fall—six of them broke on the moist ground, already impregnated with wine, while two remained intact. A quarter of an hour later three more bottles of the last row fell and broke on the ground. And as I was just leaving the cellar, I heard another bottle break.

Among the testimony of eyewitnesses I shall only report that of the accountant, Pierre Merini, whose deposition completes my own. It is dated January 9, 1901, and is as follows:

"Down there (in the cellar), in the company of several other persons, I saw the bottles breaking without apparent or plausible cause. I wanted to be alone in order the better to verify the phenomenon. The others having agreed, I shut myself up in the cellar while everybody else retired to the end of the passage at the foot of the stairs leading to the floor above. I first made sure by means of a candle that I was really alone. This was easy, on account of the smallness of the cellar and the difficulty of hiding behind the few utensils in it. Along the long side of the cellar was a set of strong planks resting at each end on upright beams. These planks were entirely covered by bottles, full and empty. I should mention that the window onto the yard, which formerly lighted the cellar, was then obstructed by a plank.

"I then saw several empty and full bottles break of their own accord under my eyes. I brought a step-ladder up to the place where the breakages occurred. I took down a bottle which had just broken, and of which only the lower half remained. I separated it from the others, placing it some distance away. After a few moments the bottle finished cracking and burst into fragments! This is one of the things I can most distinctly certify.

"Carefully examining the manner in which the bottles broke, I found that the breakage was preceded by a cracking such as usually occurs in glass which splits up. I have already mentioned that the empty bottles broke also, so that the explosion cannot have been due to the evolution of gas by fermentation (which in any case is improbable).

"To give an idea of the noise made by the breaking and crumbling of the bottles, I can compare it with that of the drops of glass which reduce themselves to powder on scraping them, and are known as 'Rupert's drops.'"

On November 22, Mrs. Fumero, wife of the innkeeper, left for her native place. She remained there for three days, and during that time nothing unusual occurred. On her return to Turin the phenomena reappeared. On November 26, Mrs. Fumero again went away, but on this occasion the phenomena continued. Then it was decided to send away the potboy, and the phenomena finally ceased. Must we conclude that the phenomena were produced by his mediumship? This seems very probable, as there is no question of trickery on his part. We have seen that the phenomena took place in the cellar when the boy was not there. In the shop, displacements of objects had been observed when he was there, but under the eyes of all.

Everything goes to show that the boy was the unconscious agent. He showed no abnormal peculiarity. The intensity of the phenomena shows some relation to his physical state. For some days, when he was ill, the noises were less loud. This fact, which is rather disconcerting, has been observed in the case of other mediums.

In connection with haunted houses, it is interesting to note that such things can now be talked about, as they are numerous and well attested, whereas formerly there was a tendency to ignore them.

At present they are being noted and studied. Yet they are easily forgotten, and men of science sufficiently courageous and unprejudiced to concern themselves with them are still few in number. As we have seen, if I had not turned up, the public, misled by the very inhabitants of the house, would have thought that the arrival of the police or myself had sufficed to stop the phenomena; in other words, though the author of the deception was not found, they would have thought that the phenomena were due to trickery, and therefore unworthy of being studied.

For my part, if I made the mistake of denying the facts before I observed them, I have not thought it right to go on denying them for the simple reason that I could not explain them.

(Sg.) DR. LOMBROSO.

That illustrious savant is straightforward and independent. In Turin alone he examined ten haunted houses. His conviction is definite and unshakable. He remarks that if in 28 cases out of 100 one finds the action of mediums, that action is the more remarkable as the great energy of the phenomena observed is contrasted with the weakness of children and women associated with them.

Let us examine all objections for the sake of our general instruction, but let us not be misled by mirages. The reality of the facts is undoubted; and as regards the causes, they are yet to seek.

I could, perhaps, add at the end of this chapter a special case, which made a great commotion at Grenoble in 1907. An *esprit frappeur (Poltergeist)* manifested its presence every night in the dwelling of a lady of the name of Massot. But it was not the spirit of a dead person. It was the spirit of a young girl very much alive, who wished to get married!

Here is a summary of the case according to a private account sent to me:

M. de Beylié, ex-president of the tribunal of commerce, and owner of the haunted house, conducted a singular enquiry in the presence of M. Pelatant, central commissioner, and Police-Inspector Berger. Constables had been stationed on the roof, others in the neighbouring rooms and in the street, in order to eliminate all trickery.

The persons present surrounded the wall upon which the rapping spirit was in the habit of operating. The raps seemed to be struck from both sides at once.

The phenomena are only produced when Mlle. Alice Cocat, Mme. Massot's niece, is present. But there is no question of fraud on the part of the girl, who remains among those present and is watched by them while the raps are sounding. For five years she has been engaged to a nephew of Mme. Massot, aged twenty-five, who is a working electrician, and has served in the second regiment of artillery at Grenoble. His description tallies with that furnished by the mysterious rapper. As the raps are not considered as emanating from the spirit of a deceased but a living person, they are probably only a function of the faculties of Mlle. Alice.

One naturally thinks of a well-acted comedy. But the wall against which the spirit raps is only 4 inches thick, and it separates two rooms which have been inspected and examined by professors of the University, the chief of police, and numerous detectives, in the presence of the Massot family. And as it was impossible for a person to hide in the wall, all trickery seems excluded.

This particular haunting, revealing the ideas of living persons, has been much discussed. The Grenoble papers added my portrait to their special editions, and invented comments which I did not make, having remained an entire stranger to this story. My friend, Colonel de Rochas, who came from Grenoble to see me at the time, declared that he could not understand it at all. It seems to me that it was the girl's subconscious self which was at work.

It is time to terminate this general excursion. I still have several hundred stories before me, including a very strange one from Neuville (Aix), dating from 1900, and a similar one from 1909 at Florence. But these would but repeat what we have learnt. We shall now classify the phenomena, and pay special attention to those associated with the dead.

CHAPTER X

CLASSIFICATION OF PHENOMENA. HAUNTINGS ASSOCIATED WITH THE DEAD

THE general excursion which we have just made among haunted houses has unrolled before our eyes a series of pictures of great variety which it would be interesting and instructive to classify. We shall attempt to do so. We may succeed in discovering the causes and approach the long-sought explanation.

In this classification we shall have to consider the production of physical forces not associated in any way with the problem of survival, while others are so associated beyond a doubt, as we have seen in the last chapter, particularly in the first case described there. This association has been obvious in several cases, and we are the better prepared to accept it as we have had experimental proofs of survival solidly established. We shall commence this classification with hauntings associated with deceased persons, leaving the others for the next chapter.

Let us not blind ourselves in either direction. Some phenomena are clearly associated with the intentions of deceased persons, while others are quite independent of them.

The exclusively anthropological theory has been refuted in the present work by direct observations (see particularly pp. 66, 150 to 177, 183, 202, 210, 217, 231, 247 to 261). These observations clearly show the insufficiency of that theory. We must therefore decide between manifestations of the dying and those of the dead, both exterior to ourselves.

Let us, above all, remember that at all times and in all countries these unexpected phenomena have been attributed to the dead. Was it an illusion of ignorance or fear? Everything goes to prove the contrary.

It were superfluous to go back to what has been said in the preceding chapter. Each of the examples mentioned could be paralleled by several similar ones. With a coincidence so frequent that it cannot be fortuitous, unknown deaths are instantly marked by physical phenomena. Broken mirrors are not rare, and have, indeed, created quite a legendary tradition. There can be no question of auto-suggestion or illusion. On this I have a recent letter (April 30, 1922):

I am a printing compositor. I was working at 20, Rue Turgot. Opposite me a girl of seventeen was working, Ida Schaub. One day, at midday, this girl, about to leave the works, she was powdering her face with the aid of a small mirror she was holding in her hands at the level of her eyes. Being free-spoken with her, as with all those in the shop, I chaffed her about her powder and her coquetry, and was looking at her, when the mirror broke into a thousand pieces in her hand, without her making any movement. "Oh, my mother!" she exclaimed.

On going home to the Rue Trézel, half an hour's walk, she found her mother lying across the door dead. She had succumbed to apoplexy and was still warm.

(Sg.) AUGUSTE PAUTRÉ.

31, RUE MAZARINE.

Now here is a material, objective fact, and no illusion is possible. If it was produced by the girl's organism, the coincidence with the mother's sudden death is undeniable. Chance again? The little god must indeed have a broad back!

Here is another fact among a thousand, communicated to me by M. G. Brochenin, of 2, Rue de Conflans, Place des Écoles, Charenton, on February 25, 1922:

Since you are, in the interests of humanity, continuing your vast and laborious enquiry concerning the mysteries of the Beyond, I consider it my duty to place you in possession of a fact which enters within the purview of your studies.

In my household, Mme. Colassot, now about sixty years old, told me of an occurrence which she remembers precisely, though it happened thirty-three years ago, and of which a material trace remains. At that time she was nursing a very sick baby of twenty-two months with the passionate devotion of a mother. The baby died in spite of the care lavished upon it by the family. It is then that the remarkable occurrence took place. At the moment of death a very loud noise was heard, and Mme. Colassot found that the top of her dining-room sideboard, more than a yard long and an inch in thickness, had split along its whole length. The occurrence struck her all the more as it corresponded to the death of her baby son, and she saw in it a supernatural phenomenon impossible to explain.

Mme. Colassot was a loving woman, with an exaggerated devotion to her own, and excessively serviceable to everybody. Prostrated with the intensity of her suffering, may she not have unconsciously projected some fluid comparable to some extent to lightning, and sufficiently powerful to split the wood?

Forgive me, dear Master, if in my ignorance I put forward such a risky hypothesis.

This electrical hypothesis is what occurs naturally to every enquiring spirit.

We have there, as in the case of the small mirror broken in the girl's hands mentioned above, a material occurrence coinciding with a death.

And now for another kind of material movement.

In *L'Inconnu* I announced the following occurrence, reported to me by an esteemed artist:

About a year and a half ago my father, my sister, and a cousin staying with us, were conversing in the dining-room. The three of us were alone in the dwelling when they suddenly heard the piano playing in the salon. Much surprised, my sister took the lamp, went into the salon, and clearly saw several keys descending together, sounding the notes, and coming up again.

She came back and told what she had seen. At first we laughed at her assertion and suspected a mouse in the *affaire,* but as the lady has excellent sight and is not in the least superstitious, we thought it strange.

But a week afterwards a letter arrived from New York announcing the death of an old uncle who lived in that city. But, what was even more extraordinary, three days after the letter arrived the piano started playing again.

As in the first case, the news of a death came a week afterwards: the death of my aunt.

My uncle and aunt were a perfectly united couple. They were also greatly attached to their relatives and the Jura country, where they were born.

The piano has not played since then.

The witnesses of this occurrence will testify any time you wish. We live in the country round Neuchâtel, and I assure you that we are not high-strung people.

(Sg.) ÉDOUARD PARIS
(Artist-Painter).

Victorien Sardou told me of an identical observation made on his own piano when he lived on the fifth floor of the house situated at the corner of the Quai des Grands-Augustins and the Place Saint-Michel. He saw with his own eyes the keys going down, concurrently with the emission of the sound, and attributed the incident to his recently deceased sister.

In the work referred to, a good many similar examples of movements observed at the moment of death are given, particularly the one on p. 112 (xl.) —two persons awakened by a friend dying at Granville; and that on p. 188, of the uncle of Jules Claretie, knocking on the window of his people at Nantes at the moment when he was killed at Wagram.

Of course, we cannot understand at all how an individual dying at Wagram can knock on a window at Nantes. But we must either admit these facts or deny them. To attribute them all to illusions, errors, misinterpretations, etc., seems to me an unscientific expedient, however convenient it may be, and quite inadmissible.

We have heard the sound of untouched piano keys. Here is the cover of a piano rising of its own accord at the moment of a death. On July 6, 1922, a Paris student, whose name it would be discreet not to mention, wrote to me to say that when he was living in a Government building together with a student of the Sorbonne, they were one evening playing the piano and dancing within a hundred yards of a youth who was on his death-bed. Their noise could not, however, be heard at that distance.

We were five in the salon, two of us dancing, a lady playing, myself standing behind her, and her sister beside her. The cover of this heavy grand piano rose before my eyes some four or five inches, without the objects on it sliding down.[1] The cover only rose and fell. We afterwards heard of the young man's death, and thought he had wished to show his displeasure in that way. I confess I am only sixteen, but I am not inventing anything. I only tell you what I saw. Please excuse a schoolboy's anxiety to let you know what he saw to help you in your search for truth.

These are direct and unexpected observations. I can understand lies and illusions, but my enquiries have always proved the veracity of the narrators.[2]

---

[1] This observation, which contradicts gravitation, is not rare. I have several times found this absence of gliding myself.

[2] The only case which remains, not, indeed, doubtful, but in-

We seek an explanation in electrical transmission.

What is electricity? We do not know.

What is the magnetic element which, coming from the sun 93 million miles away, comes and moves the magnetic needle of the compass? We are equally ignorant.

What is the transmission of telegraphy or telephony through air, over mountains, and over seas, which can be caught in its passage in a closed house? Mystery also.

Let us therefore be modest in our blind and deaf denials.

Subjective phenomena can become objective. In *L'Inconnu* we can read in the chapter on "Phantasms of the Dying" a letter from an inhabitant of Valabre (Vaucluse), who wrote (Letter 714):

I may have been twelve years of age. My poor father, one of the heroes of Sidi-Ibrahim, had passed the night and part of the day at the bedside of his mother, who was seriously ill. He had left, and about 4 p.m., one of my uncles went to find him and tell him that his mother was worse and had expressed a wish to see the two little sons. My father wanted to bring us along. My younger brother obeyed, but I resisted so wildly that nothing could shake my resolution, all because I was very much afraid of the dead.

I therefore remained alone in the house with my mother, who, after supper, wanted to put me to bed. But I refused

---

sufficiently reported, is that of the premonition associated with Lord Dufferin. Its verification is still pending. I know three different versions of the story: (1) The version published by myself (vol. ii, p. 231). (2) That contained in *Liliana,* by Sienkiewicz (Madrid, 1921, p. 154); Sienkiewicz died in 1917. (3) That published by Stainton Moses in *Light,* 1892, p. 181, and 1907, p. 64, reproduced in Bozzano's *Phénomènes prémonitoires* (Paris, 1914, p. 397). It sometimes happens that the same story is given in several different forms, and that is why I much prefer first-hand stories written by the witnesses themselves. But we must not trust ourselves to mendacious negations of interested parties.

to go, being still afraid. She then put me into her own bed, promising to join me soon.

About half-past seven I was slapped in the face with extraordinary violence. I started to cry. My mother came on hearing me cry, and asked what was the matter. I replied I had been beaten and my cheek hurt. My mother found, indeed, that my cheek was red and swollen. Alarmed by what had taken place, she longed for the return of my father and my uncle. My father did not come in till about nine. My mother told him what had happened to me, and when she told him the hour he said: "That was just when his grandmother breathed her last."

For over six months I had on my right cheek the impress of a right hand, which was very apparent, especially after playing, when my face was redder. This was observed by hundreds of people. The trace of the hand was white.

(Sg.) A. MICHEL

(Dyer at the Valabre Dye Works).

This memorable slap, received by the boy who obstinately refused to go and see his dying grandmother, is, of course, rather burlesque; but we may admit that it is logical enough and apparently justified. To explain it is more difficult. Is it, perhaps, an effect of auto-suggestion, due to remorse or fear? A subjective phenomenon which became objective? We shall later on have to discuss similar peculiarities, such as stigmata.

That the dead manifest themselves at the time of death by unexpected and inexplicable incidents such as visions, sounds, movements, noises, and diverse sensations, has been shown by hundreds of accounts I have published, and in the preceding chapter we have the positive observation, made by three friends who, expecting a comrade for the opening of the hunt, received from him a singular manifestation which was perceived at the same time by the dogs of the house. We have also seen the remarkable fall of the portrait observed in the bishopry of Monaco, coinciding with a death, and subsequent observations. We also remember (*L'Inconnu*, "Phantasms of the Dead," p. 123) the letter of a professor of St. Petersburg, announcing that, at the hour of his sister's death, the sister's portrait, though solidly fixed, fell without the nail being torn out, and that the clock stopped. These observations are significant, for great though chance may be, it has its limits.

Here is another account worthy of attention:

From an absolutely reliable source I have an extraordinary and authentic fact. My people had been called to the bedside of a neighbour who was dying. They went there and joined some assembled friends who waited silently for the sad end. Suddenly they heard in a clock hanging on the wall, which had not gone for years, a great uproar, a deafening noise, like a hammer striking on an anvil. Those present rose up in alarm, wondering what the noise signified. "You can see it," said someone, pointing to the dying person. Shortly afterwards the latter breathed his last.

(Sg.) H. Faber
(Agricultural Engineer at Bissen, Luxemburg)

I add the following to the above observations (p. 178). Another communication of the same period (1899) gave me a description of an occurrence not less curious, although subjective. M. Ferdinand Estève, of Marseilles, wrote to me:

I was sixteen years old. I was on a visit to the village of Les Gavots. My cousin, newly married, put me up in a neighbouring house, the home of an aged relative, who thought to do me a great honour in giving me the room *in which her husband had died.*

It was a vast room without a door. From the bed one could see the enormous well of the staircase. I went to bed without even shutting the window, for it was a warm night in August, and I slept very soundly.

Suddenly I was awakened by an infernal uproar, by a frightful noise of saucepans being thrown about, broken dishes, of plates flying into pieces, which I heard clattering on the concrete floor of the kitchen. One would have said a regiment of cats was upsetting everything in the house. This last idea reassured me. However, the uproar lasted for more than an hour, with some interruptions. When silence was re-established I heard, rushing towards me from the foot of the staircase, and saw some kind of animal, which I took for a cat, jump with one bound on to my bed and with another out of the window, whence it disappeared.

I went immediately to shut the window. What was my astonishment to find that it was already closed on the outside by wire-netting of one-third of an inch mesh. My surprise was greatly increased when, day being come, I saw everything in order in the kitchen—not a scrap of broken crockery!

Three days after my mother slept in the same room and witnessed the same phenomena.

Hallucination? We can discover no reason for that in this young man of sixteen who observed with such composure. All this is very complex. Yes, the first impulse is to see nothing but hallucination in it. But the slap received by M. Michel was no hallucination; and if M. Estève's cat was but an illusion, and the noise of unbroken crockery in the kitchen the same, how is it that the mother received the same impression, and what is the cause of the sensation?

In these last cases we may see subjective impressions which are yet produced by external causes, the former by the dying and angry grandmother, and the latter by the shades of the dead relative.

These incomprehensible noises recall numerous observations of the same order which we have already studied. The verifications are innumerable. Here is a rather striking one:[3]

M. Baechly, of Saverne, aged twenty, was alone with his father in the house, when a terrible uproar was heard about midnight. The father and son both started up, not knowing what it could be. The uproar came again. The father and son, having gone to bed, got up again and met at the open door. The door opened violently a third time. They then bound it with thick twine. Some time afterwards, a letter announced that M. Baeschly's brother had died in America, precisely on the day of the uproar, at 1 p.m. It appears that the dying man, waking up out of a prolonged coma, said: "I have been on a great voyage; I have been to see my brother at Brumath.

There can be no doubt that material movements are associated, both far and near, with the physical and psychical phenomenon of death.

These noises at the moment of death are of the same order as those of haunted houses, and must be due to the same cause. There are many other examples.

The following letter was sent to me on February 11, 1899, by Mme. de la Garde:

For your interesting researches I consider it my duty to tell you that a remarkable manifestation occurred at the death of Monseigneur du Lau. All the windows of his castle of la Cotte, commune of Biras, Dordogne, opened at once, which led the good people of the country, who witnessed it, to say that the saintly Bishop had just died.

Actually they found afterwards that their master, whom they had not seen for many years, had breathed his last on that day. I believe Mgr. du Lau was a martyr. His life has been written by a priest of Périgord, M. Pecout (now senior priest at Hautefort). He mentions this strange

---

[3] Chevreuil, *On ne meurt pas*, p. 334; Richet, *Traité de Métapsychique*, p. 358.

fact, which was reported to him by inhabitants of Biras who had witnessed it.

Here is another communication of the same epoch (received June 3, 1899):

To the innumerable letters sent to you for your very useful work you may add the following:

In the last days of February, 1868, I had to go to Tauligran, a large commune of Drôme, not far from Montélimar, at the request of my mother, who was dying. I arrived in time to see her expire.

On the very day of her burial, March 1, I was in her death-room, alone with the servant and the latter's child. There was not enough breeze to stir a leaf. Suddenly the door of the room, wide open to the landing, banged with a loud noise. We opened it at once to see whether anybody was on the stairs, but we could see nobody. My mother was the sole occupant of the house. The servant, mad with fear, fell on her knees and cried: "That must be your mother, who wants our prayers! And she began to tell her beads. The child cried and called for "Mama Alançon." I was more affected than I can tell you. The scene is engraved on my memory, and in reading your writings it vividly returned to me, and I asked whether the Beyond really existed.

Your assiduous and respectful reader,

Alançon
(Agent of the Union Co. at Moulins).
(Letter 726.)

In this, as in the preceding case, the phenomenon is very objective.

It is by a comparison of all the facts observed that we must form our opinion. (Note, in passing, these frequent religious associations.)

Another letter sent to me from Poitiers on June 7, 1922:

DEAR MASTER,

After seeing your psychic trilogy I must make my modest contribution to your researches on the Unseen.

The following event was witnessed by my wife and her aunt, who attest it below.

Some days after the decease of my wife's maternal grandfather, François Coudreau, on September 30, 1899, noises were heard in the house where he died. My wife, then quite a young girl, had gone to bed with her grandmother. Her aunt, now the widowed Mme. Roy, had gone to bed in the same room.

It was 10 p.m. They all heard something like pebbles thrown at the window-panes. As there was no storm or wind they thought of some practical joke. The grandmother called out, "Who's there?" but there was no reply.

The noise continued for some ten minutes, intermittently. They also heard something like the noise of a shovel stirring the heap of coal in the yard, which sounded as if it were being thrown against the wall.

I must tell you that the deceased had been in the habit, during his lifetime, of shovelling this heap.

Also, the latch of the door seemed to move noisily, as if somebody wanted to enter.

Much frightened, the three women started praying, as they believed the soul of the deceased was there. Finally my wife's aunt called in a loud voice: "If that is you, father, speak to us!" The noise stopped immediately.

Next morning they found everything in its place outside the house. There was no trace on the windows nor on the walls. The shovel was lying on the heap of coal as usual.

Masses were said, and the noises did not come again.

A detail which may be important is this: On the day when the event occurred, the grandmother had found in a trunk which the deceased had always forbidden her to open a beautiful plait of hair of his first wife, whom he had loved much. She had burnt the plait.

The witnesses maintain that it cannot have been a practical joke, since the windows would have been broken with the violence of the blows (the windows have no shutters).

Nobody could enter the yard to throw the coal against the wall, and indeed no trace was found next morning.

Yours, etc.
(Sg.) POUILLART.

ATTESTATIONS.

We confirm the above narrative of M. Pouillart and declare that he has faithfully described what happened.

E. POUILLART AND WIDOW ROY.

To suppose that all this has been invented has no sense. But we cannot refrain from remarking on the triviality of these manifestations. In any case, the duty of the researcher is to study everything. These noises were purely subjective and correspond to no material movement.

The same applies to the observation made by a student of Buckingham, M. René Gautiers, which we summarise here:

My father lived in a lonely castle in the middle of the wood. We were in the dining-hall, talking at length after supper, and waiting for my grandfather, who was expected back. The night went by without fatigue when, at 2 a.m., everybody in the dining-hall, including two soldier uncles, who were very sceptical, distinctly heard the door of the salon shut with a violence which made them all jump from their seats. There was no mistake. The door which banged, or was heard to bang, was an adjoining door. It was the bang of a door, and of an inside door. My mother often said to me: "We heard the door close as if a prodigious gust had got into the house and had violently struck the door." This gust of wind, quite unreal, had this amount of reality, that my people felt it on their faces, and that it left them in a sort of cold perspiration as one gets it in a nightmare. Conversation stopped. The violent banging of the door seemed strange to them and gave them an undefinable feeling of uneasiness. Soon my uncle burst into laughter at the piteous faces of his mother and his sisters. He organised a spirited hunt. My uncle, a man of courage, went ahead to see the door of the salon. Everybody thought it had been shut. But it was found locked and bolted. All doors and windows were shut, and no draught could enter the house on any floor.

My grandfather returned next morning and announced the death of his brother-in-law. "At what hour?" "At 2 a.m." "Two o'clock?" "At two precisely." The banging of the door had been heard by seven persons at 2 a.m. precisely.

Subjective impressions, caused by an unknown death (same case as that of General Parmentier, *L'Inconnu,* Case 1).

It is very strange and incomprehensible that the death of a person should produce at a distance the sensation of a gust of wind which opens a window. Yet it has been frequently observed. Here is another case which, though old, is as yet unpublished. It dates from Buda-Pesth, April 16, 1901:

Dear Brother,

If I allow myself to write to you under this title, it is because we are brothers in our ideas of the hidden faculties of the human soul and the importance of studying them.

I consider it my duty to acquaint you with a phenomenon, similar to those you study, which happened to me long ago.

My father had been ill for several weeks with acute neuralgia, which made him so feeble that at his age of sixty-five years his death was feared. My wife and I were in a state of continual unrest until on the night of 4th to 5th April we awoke with a start on hearing a terrific gust opening the window of the neighbouring room with a great noise, though we had heard the servant close it the previous evening.

We felt the gust coming under the door which separates the two rooms.

At the moment of waking up, I had at once the feeling

as if my father might have died at that moment. I lighted up and found it was a few minutes past three.

I said nothing to my wife, in order not to disturb her sleep. But when next morning we received a telegram with the fatal news of my father's death, my wife confessed that she had also had a similar feeling at the moment of awakening, but more positive than mine, because whereas I felt the possibility of the death, she was sure of it.

I must add that the gust was one of exceptional force, that it only lasted one or two minutes, and terminated in a light draught which lasted until morning.

When we arrived at my father's dwelling-place (Trencien, in Hungary, 112 miles from here in a straight line), one of my first questions was an enquiry as to the hour of his death. The reply given by my sister, a girl of twenty-one, who had watched by him, was that he died a few minutes after 3 a.m.

Permit me to add that I am of a thoughtful disposition, a mechanical engineer and electrician, used to minute observation, to clear ideas, and to caution in arriving at conclusions.

I give you my word of honour that I have added nothing to, and omitted nothing from, the facts which seem essential to arrive at a conclusion, and at the same time I authorise you to publish this with my name and occupation. You can make enquiries about me from M. Désiré Borda, Director of the Electric Service of the Fives-Lille Company at Paris, Rue Caumartin, and from M. Maurice Loewy, Director of the Paris Observatory

Yours, etc.

(Sg.) LEOPOLD STARK.

BUDA-PESTH,
COVOHAZ, 34.

(Letter 988.)

On enquiry, I found that this letter must be accepted as worthy of confidence. The author is a man of scientific standing. In reality, this phenomenon was subjective. The window did not open. There was only a sensation—an impression. But whatever our view of it, the sensation is incontestably proved.

Now comes a strange case of haunting, corresponding to the anniversary of an execution, reported to me in 1899 (Letter 614*c*):

> A lady of my acquaintance had rented a flat in a country house for change of air.
>
> There were several tenants. One morning at four everybody was awakened by extraordinary noises. The furniture in a large room seemed to roll about with a noise of chains. It was quite an uproar. All the tenants were women, and one became hysterical. My friend's servant slept in a room adjoining hers. She came in trembling and said that a man in heavy boots had been walking round her before the noise commenced.
>
> My friend, much concerned, went to the town and told people of the occurrence in the evening. Several people told her: "But this is the date of the death of Sainlouis, executed at 4 a.m. a year ago." My friend's servant had been Sainlouis's mistress. She had left him to be converted, and he, in his fury, had decided to kill her. He shot at her—but killed another person. Sainlouis, condemned to death, had been executed on the date and at the hour when the strange noises were produced in the house where his concubine lived. I forgot to tell you that the room in question was found locked, with all the furniture in proper place.
>
> (Sg.) H. COTEL.

Among the phenomena of haunted houses, some are objective, material, and external to the percipients; while others are subjective, perceived by the spirit, but as real as the former, produced by a more or less distant telepathic cause, generally an unknown death. It is necessary to pay special attention to these singular noises, of which there is no explanation, and which one is inclined to discredit.

Probably none of my readers will contest the reality of telepathic transmissions to any distance, for such incredulity were inexcusable. But what a variety in transmission! The following observation, made under perfect conditions of security, is very remarkable.

M. A. Riondel, advocate, of Montélimar, wrote on May 23, 1894, to Dr. Dariex:[4]

I had a brother much younger than myself (he died in his fortieth year, on April 2, last), who was employed on the telegraph lines at Marseilles, and was an agent of the *Messageries Maritimes.* Affected with anæmia owing to a long stay in the Colonies, my poor brother was attacked by marsh-fever, to which he succumbed, though nobody could have foreseen the terrible rapidity of the disease. On Sunday, April 1, last, I received a letter from him to say that his health was excellent. Well, on the night of that day—*i.e.,* from Sunday to Monday, I was suddenly awakened by an unusual and violent noise, resembling that of a paving-stone rolling on the floor of my room, which I alone occupy and which was locked. I noticed that my alarm clock pointed to 2 a.m. Getting out of bed, I looked for the object which had disturbed me, but did not find it. It gave me a singular feeling of terror.

Well, on that night my brother had died, without suffering or agony, and without saying a word. I asked the friend in whose arms he had died for the exact hour of his death. It was a quarter to two.

To complete the particulars I send you I must add that our old mother, totally blind for the last fifteen years, also heard loud nocturnal noises on the door of her bedroom. I must tell you that I left her ignorant of this death, and she is still unaware of it.

Under the impression that she had heard noises, my mother came to me just as I returned from my brother's funeral. In my wife's presence she told me sharply:

[4] *Annales des Sciences Psychiques*, 1895, p. 200.

"Two or three nights ago I had a premonition concerning the health of your brother. You must go at once to Marseilles, for he must be worse and they are concealing it from you. Go and help him."

I soothed the apprehensions and presentiments of my poor mother, treating them as chimeras, as dreams and nightmares.

That is my narrative. If it comes within your purview, you may print my name outright, or put my initials and address. These facts cannot be put down to imagination. They are tangible.

I need not repeat that at present my mother still believes that Benjamin is of this world. My duty is to leave her in that ignorance as long as I can. Such a fatal piece of news would kill her on the spot, so extremely feeble is her state of health.

(Sg.) A. Riondel
(*Advocate*).

Here are precise facts of observation, which, however, remain incomprehensible. How can these noises be produced? A paving-stone rolling on the floor! To imagine (1) an auditory hallucination of such a noise; and (2) a chance coincidence with this unexpected death is an hypothesis difficult to sustain. And the mother's telepathic sensation? These phenomena are so frequent that they must enter into the purview of modern science. Perhaps it is time to seek an explanation.

We already met the impression of the rolling stone in the haunted castle of Calvados (see p. 124).

The case is so remarkable and represents so many similar ones that I must not simply publish it without comment, but must seek an explanation. Well, this dying person was particularly fond of his brother. At the supreme moment a psychic current was established between him and his brother, and translated itself in the latter's brain into the sensation of a noise, perfectly heard, as if a paving-stone had rolled on the floor of his room, and the noise was accompanied by a feeling of anxiety. There is *the fact*. We know many similar ones, notably those which have been published in vol. ii of *Death and Its Mystery,* in the chapter on "Deaths Announced by These Noises." These telepathic transmissions are incontestable. Noises are heard which differ according to the state of receptivity of the percipient. They are subjective and non-material noises. There is a projection between the cause and the effect, between the dying person and the percipient, and we are led to believe that in these cases we have not to deal with spherical waves spreading out and enlarging, like those of sound or light. It was probably not a wave of this kind which started from Marseilles in every direction, to be picked up in Paris by the brother of the dying man. Rather do we suspect a psychic current, like the magnetic current produced between a bar of iron and a magnetic needle.

Such a psychic current would recall the link established between Captain Escourrou, killed in Mexico on March 29, 1863, and his mother, who was living at Sèvres, near Paris. The latter on that day saw on his portrait one of his eyes destroyed and the blood flowing over his face. In publishing this remarkable telepathic occurrence in vol. ii, p. 375, I did not add the numerous attestations and official documents which prove its authenticity, on account of lack of space, but those interested may look up the *Annales des Sciences Psychiques* for 1891 (pp. 148 to 156), and they will find that no doubt is possible. Here, as in M. Riondel's observation, we have obviously subjective phenomena. The portrait had not one eye destroyed, nor did blood flow over it. But at the moment of death the officer projected his last thought towards his mother, and that psychic current translated itself visibly in the aspect of the portrait. Such transmissions are so numerous and clearly established that they must be received within the purview of positive science.

Let us now listen to another story.

A man appears to two persons, in two different rooms, at the moment of his death. Miss Tverdianski wrote to Dr. Richet in November, 1891, from Dormelles (Seine-et-Marne):[5]

I had just established myself in a small village of Seine-et-Marne to pass the summer. My hostess, an excellent old woman, had given me her own room, and as her bed was a good one I passed the first night in great comfort, sleeping soundly, and awakened late by the good woman, who brought me a hot cup of milk.

It was different the second night. Hardly had I gone to sleep when I was awakened by a formidable concussion. The window, in spite of closed shutters, opened with a bang. As the window looked out upon a lonely road I thought that malefactors who knew the house was only inhabited by women had burst the springs of the shutters to get into the room. With a bound I was at the window to shut it and closed the shutters as firmly as I could.

But I could not get to sleep again. It seemed to me that someone had come in by the window, and I fancied I heard this somebody or something the whole night long.

The sun had just risen when I heard the steps of my landlady in the kitchen. I called out to her to get me my cup of milk as soon as possible.

"Oh," I said to her, when she came, "I believe some great nightbird opened my window last night by flying at the shutters, and perhaps some bats came in at the time, for I assure you that I heard movements about me all night. I did not sleep a wink."

"Like me," she said smilingly—she was gay and fond

---

[5] *Annales des Sciences Psychiques*, 1892, p. 129.

of a joke—"I was awakened by the visit of my wicked neighbour, the farmer Dufour. I shall tell you some time how he set about stealing all my fortune without the law being able to punish him. Well, this precious man, whom I have not seen for years, paid me a visit last night. Did I dream it? I bet that I was awakened by his voice, that he stood in front of my bed and said, 'Forgive me, Victoire.' Think of his impudence, calling me by my Christian name! Well, I have wept enough real tears on his account not to be angry with him in my dreams."

Just at the moment somebody knocked at the door and told us that that neighbour had died that very night.

(Sg.) JULIA TVERDIANSKI.

This narrative is accompanied by other letters from Mlle. Tverdianski, of Mme. Veuve Petit, and an attestation by the Mayor of Dormelles of the death of Edmé Firmin Dufour, on April 10, 1891, at 4 a.m. These I cannot reproduce from lack of space.

To attribute to chance this double, or rather treble, coincidence of two impressions perceived independently of each other by the women, and of the death of this man, seems to me as impossible as to deny the very striking case quoted in vol. iii of *La Mort,* p. 373—J. Lewis, killed by a train and himself announcing his death. That occurrence led us, without a break of continuity, from "Telepathy between the Living" to "Telepathy between the Living and the Dead."

The dead Lewis wanted to have his corpse identified, and tried to communicate with those in charge of his funeral, but without success. So he tried elsewhere, and found in a certain family the sensitives susceptible to telepathic influence, which enabled him to attain his object.

It is impossible to think that all these narratives are false. We cannot explain them, but we are bound to affirm their reality. That is a beginning, because, until now, they have been doubted. We are collecting the stones which will go to the building of a future science.

Astronomy, that universal science, offers us examples which can often be applied to other studies. Here is one which I pointed out long ago. Certain spiral nebulæ, photographed with the help of powerful instruments, show stars symmetrically distributed along their gaseous twists, and thus indicate the secret of the formation of these bodies. The coincidences are so numerous and so concordant that they cannot be attributed to chance, and we are led to recognise a causal connection. It is the same with these coincidences of deaths with manifestations and apparitions. Chance plays no part here.

But let us confess that explanation is difficult. The human soul has not yet been dissected.

Plato wrote in *Phædrus*: ψύχης οὔν φύσιν ἄξιως λόγου κατανόησαι οἴει δύνατον εἶναιἄνευ τῆς τοὺ ὅλου φύσεως; "Do you think that the nature of the soul can be sufficiently known if we do not know the nature of the universe?"[6] This maxim could be applied to all reasoning about life. The judgments passed on human beings by their equals are almost always false, because we do not know the direct or indirect springs of action. The studies we are making here have a far-reaching significance.

The psychical and physical faculties of the human soul during life and after death are almost all yet to be discovered, and the observation of the phenomena of haunting sheds an unexpected light on this subject.

Thus, well-observed movements of objects not

---

[6] Schopenhauer, *The Foundations of Morality.*

touched by anybody turn out to be due to souls of the dead. Here is an example which is hardly credible and is of Romanesque appearance, but which had been scrupulously studied by F. W. H. Myers and Mrs. Sidgwick, and published in the *Proceedings of the English S. P. R.* (vol. vii, p. 183). The story is long, and I shall only give the essential passages according to Bozzano.[7]

The scene is laid at the village of Swanland, near Hull, in England, in a carpenter's shop, where Mr. Bristow served as an apprentice. He relates the following:

On the morning when the phenomena took place I was working at the bench next the wall, where I could see the movements of my two companions and watch the door. Suddenly one of them turned round and called out: "You had better keep those blocks of wood and stick to work, mates." We asked him to explain, and he said: "You know quite well what I mean; one of you hit me with this piece of wood," and he showed us a piece of wood about an inch square. We both protested that we had not thrown it; and I for one was quite certain that my other companion had never stopped working. The incident was being forgotten when, some minutes afterwards, the other companion turned round like the first, and shouted to me: "It is you, this time, who threw this piece of wood at me!" and he showed me a piece the size of a match-box. There were two of them accusing me now, and my denials counted for nothing, so I laughed and added: "Since I did not do it I suppose that if someone was aiming at you it is now my turn." I had hardly said this when a piece hit me on the hip. I called out: "I am touched. There is a mystery somewhere; let us see what happens!"

We searched inside and out, but could discover nothing. This strange and embarrassing occurrence gave us much to talk about, but in the end we set to work again.

---

[7] *Les Phénomènes de hantise,* p. 254.

I had hardly started when some Venetian blinds, held above by beams let into the wall, started shaking with such a clatter that it seemed as if they must be broken to bits. We thought at once, "Somebody is up there." I seized a ladder, rushed up and craned my neck, but found that the blinds were immovable and covered with a layer of dust and cobwebs. As I descended and found myself with my head on a level with the beams, I saw a small piece of wood two fingers thick hop forward on a plank, and with a final bound of two feet, pass close to my ear. Dumbfounded, I jumped to earth, and then I said: "This is nothing to laugh at. There is something supernatural. What do you say?" One of my companions agreed with me, the other still maintained that somebody was making fun of us. During this little dispute, a bit of wood from the entrance end of the workshop flew and hit him on his hat. I shall never forget the sheepish look on his face.

From time to time a piece of wood just cut and fallen upon the floor jumped up on the benches and started a dance amidst the tools. And it is remarkable that in spite of innumerable attempts we could never catch a piece in movement, for it cleverly eluded all our stratagems. They seemed animated and intelligent.

I remember a piece which jumped from the bench on to an easel standing three yards away, whence it bounded on to another piece of furniture, then into a corner of the shop, where it stopped. Another traversed the shop like an arrow at the level of three feet above the ground.

Immediately afterwards a piece took a flight with a wavy motion. Another went in a slanting line and then alighted quickly at my feet. While the chief of the works, Mr. Clark, was explaining the details of a drawing, and we were both holding our fingers on it in such a way that between our fingers there was a distance of rather less than an inch, a pointed piece of wood passed between our two fingers and hit the table.

This state of things continued with more or less intensity during six weeks, and always in broad daylight.

Sometimes there was comparative quiet for a day or two, during which one or two manifestations occurred, but then followed days of extraordinary activity, as if they wanted to make up for the time lost. In one of these periods, while a workman was repairing a Venetian shutter on the bench next to mine, I saw a piece of wood about 6 inches square and 1 inch thick rise up and describe three-quarters of a large circle in the air and then hit the shutter with some force just at the spot at which the man was working. It was the largest piece of wood which I have seen in the air. Most of them were no larger than an ordinary box of matches, though they were of various shapes. The last flying piece that I saw was of oak and about 2½ inches square and 1 inch thick. It fell on me from the far corner of the ceiling, and described in its course a screw line like a spiral staircase of about 20 inches diameter. It is necessary to add that all these objects, without exception, came from the interior of the shop, and that not one came in by the door.

One of the strangest peculiarities of the manifestations consisted in this, that the pieces of wood cut by us and fallen on the ground worked their way into the corners of the shop, from where they raised themselves to the ceiling in some *mysterious and invisible manner*. None of the workmen, none of the visitors, who flocked there in great numbers during the six weeks of these manifestations, ever saw a single piece in the act of rising. And yet the pieces of wood, in spite of our vigilance, quickly found their way up in order to fall on us from a place where nothing existed a moment before. By degrees we got used to the thing, and the movements of the pieces of wood, which seemed to be alive and in some cases even intelligent, no longer surprised us and hardly attracted our attention.

In reply to a question of Myers, Mr. Bristow wrote on July 19, 1891:

There was no connection between the manifestations and the people concerned. The workmen of the shop often worked in private houses, and the three of us, who were present the first day of the manifestations, worked repeatedly and alternately outside during the period that they took place, and more than once we were all absent. It was the same in the case of the other workmen, who were all absent successively during the six weeks' haunting. In spite of that the phenomena never ceased.

Except in some special cases, the projectiles fell and hit without any noise, although they came at such a speed that in normal conditions they would have produced a fairly loud clatter.

Nobody ever saw a missile at the time it started. One would have said that they could not be perceived until they had travelled at least six inches from their starting-point. Which brings one to the consideration of another aspect of the mystery—namely, that the missiles only moved when nobody was looking and when they were least expected.[8] Now and again one of us would watch a piece of wood closely for a good number of minutes and the piece would not budge; but if the observer stopped looking at it, this same piece would jump on us. . . . We were never able to make sure whether the pieces began their flight invisibly, or whether, on the contrary, they profited by a moment's distraction on our part. Sometimes the direction taken by the projectiles was a straight line, but more often it was undulating, rotatory, spiral, serpentine, or jerky.

. . . Numerous visitors were profoundly impressed by the manifestations, but the one who was most struck was Mr. John Gray, for a particular reason.

He had lost a brother, who died in financial difficulties. This brother had left a son, named John Gray like his uncle, who was taken into the shop as an apprentice, but who died shortly after of consumption. In the district it was said that his father's creditors had not received all the money due to them (about £100), and that the uncle

---

[8] This is not a unique case. There are other examples to be seen in *La Magie*, of Charles Du Prel (i, p. 232)—projectiles becoming visible only at the moment when they arrive. That is a fact often noticed in these phenomena, as inexplicable as the rest, and which the sceptics make the most of without scruple.

was responsible for this. Further, it came to be known that the last wish of the nephew had been that his uncle would pay his father's debts. The uncle did not, however, grant the desire of the dead boy.

I can testify personally, adds Mr. Bristow, to the excessive fear with which he was seized when the manifestations broke out. One day he made me go with him to do certain work, and on the way he began to speak to me about the phenomena, apparently wanting to hear me say that they could be explained on natural grounds. His behaviour was that of a man petrified with terror, and I felt sure that he had made personal observations on his own account of which he did not speak.

One day we heard that he had paid his brother's creditors: the manifestations *stopped immediately*. No tombstone had been put on the grave of the nephew, but when the phenomena began, the uncle hastened to accomplish this duty also; the stone is still in the Swanland cemetery, and one can read there the name of John Gray, died at the age of twenty-two years, January 5, 1849.

I have published this very curious observation in details in spite of its length, because they are really instructive from all points of view. I may add, with Myers:

We do not find in this case any intellectual manifestation, but only the projection of pieces of wood in all directions by intentional acts, with the object of attracting attention without causing harm to anyone. The eyewitnesses agree in regarding them as provoked by a deceased person with the wish of attracting the attention of a living person and inducing him to pay a debt of conscience. The end was gained. If we consider this point of view plausible, and if we take concomitant proofs of another kind into account, we must admit that the apparent indefiniteness and horrid absurdity of the manifestations do not constitute an objection, because nobody knows what powers are possessed by a discarnate entity. In any case, it is certain that the movements of objects as effected had a connection with the trade practised in life by the supposed agent, and the testimony goes to show that the acts were efficacious for attaining the desired end. It is also very remarkable that the manifestations seem to have been independent of the presence of particular persons. Such observations, judiciously pursued, have shown how well-founded is the hypothesis of the intervention of discarnate intelligences in certain material manifestations, however commonplace they appear to be.

This interpretation is quite admissible. It agrees with what we concluded above: (1) That invisible beings exist; (2) that they may be human beings formerly alive; (3) that they may not be very different from what they were in life.

The forces in action are not unconscious, like gravitation, weight, or heat; they are *thinking forces,* acting intentionally. The proofs here collected are numerous and demonstrative.

We saw that in the haunted castle of Calvados the lady of the house, hearing movements in the haunted room, where all the furniture moved and loud noises shook the walls, wanted to go into the room, and put forth her right hand to open the door, when she saw the key detach itself, turn in the lock, and hit her left hand a blow so hard that its trace could be seen for two days. She had a witness with her, the clerical instructor of her son. It was Wednesday, December 29, 1875.

That is a clear observation. No illusion, any more than in the case of the various missiles thrown through narrow apertures (pp. 83, 86, and elsewhere; see *La Mystique,* by Gorres, vol. iii, p. 361). Bishop Guillaume d'Auvergne said, in the thirteenth century, that stones thrown in haunting rarely hurt anyone (see also *Mystique,* iii, p. 351, for 1746; and Carré de Montgeron, *La Vérite des Miracles du Diacre, Pâris*). These proofs of the intelligent acts of the Invisibles are so well known that it is childish to insist upon them.

We have seen passing before our eyes a number of cool-headed observations for which there is no normal explanation. Another example, certified by authentic attestations, and dating from 1882 to 1889, is one recorded with confirmations by the London S. P. R., and published in Myers's great work, *Human Personality,* published in 1904. Here is a summary of it:

Captain Morton's family came to inhabit in 1882 a house built in 1860, which was first occupied for sixteen years by an Anglo-Indian, then by an old man, and was then unoccupied. One evening the Captain's daughter, Miss Morton, heard a noise near her door, and believing it was her mother, she opened it. She did not see her, but on looking in the passage she saw near the staircase a tall woman dressed in black. The unknown woman was afterwards seen by the whole family, Miss Morton's three sisters, the father, a little boy, and the servant, and perceived by the dogs, who whined. On enquiry it was found that the phantom was that of the Anglo-Indian's second wife, who drank and often quarrelled with him, then separated and went to live elsewhere, and died in 1878. Between 1882 and 1884 Miss Morton saw the phantom six times. One of her sisters saw it during the summer of 1882 and thought it was a nun. In the autumn of 1883 the servant met it. In December of the same year Miss Morton's father and a little boy noticed it in the dining-room. On January 29, 1884, Miss Morton spoke to the phantom for the first time; but it did not reply, and seemed to be deaf. She often tried to touch it, but it always moved away. In the night its steps were heard, very lightly. In fact, it appeared to inhabit the house without wishing for anything, and finally they got accustomed to it. Some twenty people saw it. Efforts were made to photograph it, but were unsuccessful. Loud noises were heard from time to time. But let us tell the story.

Mr. S., a land-owner, lost his wife, whom he loved passionately. In order to drown his grief to took to drink. Two years later he married again. His second wife hoped at first to get him to give up his habit of intemperance, but she herself succumbed to it and took to drink also, which resulted in a very stormy married life, constantly troubled by quarrels which degenerated into violent scenes. Some months before the death of Mr. S., on July 14, 1876, his wife separated from him and went to live at Clifton. She was absent at the time of his death, and it seems that she never returned to the house. She herself died on September 23, 1878.

After the death of Mr. S., his house was bought by a man of a certain age, who died less than six months after. The dwelling then remained empty for several years.

My father acquired the house in 1882. Our family is numerous, I have four sisters and two brothers. I was nineteen at that time. Not one among us had ever heard anything about the house being abnormal. The removal took place towards the end of April, and it was not until the following June that I saw the first apparition.

Having gone into my room, I heard someone at the door before going into bed. I went to see who it was, thinking it might be my mother. Nobody. Taking a few steps down the corridor, I saw the figure of a tall woman, dressed in a black woollen gown, who made hardly a sound in walking; her face was hidden by a handkerchief held in her right hand. The left hand was partly hidden in a wide sleeve on which was a black armlet characteristic of a widow's mourning. She wore no hat, but on her head there was something black which seemed like a bonnet covered with a veil. I was not able to observe anything else, but on several occasions I succeeded in seeing a part of her forehead and hair.

In the two following years—between 1882 and 1884—I saw the figure five or six times.

Several times I followed her. Generally, she went downstairs, entered the small sitting-room, and remained standing in the right corner of the veranda where she stayed for some time. Then she retraced her steps and proceeded along the passage up to the garden door where she suddenly disappeared.

The first time that I spoke to her was on January 29, 1884. As I mentioned it two days later in a letter to a friend, I quote this passage of my letter: "I softly opened the door of the sitting-room and entered at the same time as the figure. The latter, however, got before me and went near the sofa where she stayed motionless. I advanced immediately and asked her in what way I could be useful to her. At these words she trembled slightly and seemed about to speak, but she only uttered a light sigh. She then went towards the door. When she arrived at the threshold I renewed my request, without result. She went into the drawing-room and proceeded as far as the garden door, where she disappeared. . . ."

On other occasions I tried to touch her, in vain, for she avoided me in a curious manner: not that she was impalpable, but she seemed always to be *out of my reach*. If I pursued her into a corner she suddenly disappeared.

The apparitions attained the greatest frequency during the months of July and August, 1884, after which they began to decrease. I kept a record of these two months in a collection of letters—a diary which I addressed to a friend. I take from it this passage, bearing the date, July 21:

"It was nine o'clock in the evening and I was sitting with my father and sisters in the small sitting-room, near the veranda. While I was reading, I saw the form enter by the open door, cross the room and come and stand behind my chair. I was astonished that nobody present saw it when I could see so clearly. My brother, who had seen it before, was not in the room. The figure stayed behind my chair for about half an hour, afterwards moving towards the door. I followed it under the pretext of going to look for a book, and I saw it cross the room, go towards the garden door and disappear on arriving there. When she got to the foot of the staircase, I spoke to her without receiving any answer, although, like the first time, she seemed to tremble and wish to speak."

During the night of August 2 the sound of footsteps

was heard by my three sisters and the cook, who slept on the upper floor, and by our married sister, Mrs. K., who was on the second floor. In the morning they all related how they had heard footsteps of someone who came and went past their doors. They were characteristic steps, quite different from those of any member of the family; they sounded slow and light but firm. My sisters and the maids were afraid to go out when they heard them.

On August 12, towards eight o'clock in the evening (so it was still daylight), my sister E. was practising her singing, when she stopped abruptly and ran into the drawing-room to tell me that, while she was at the piano, she had suddenly perceived the figure at her side. We went into the room. She was there, motionless, standing in the usual corner of the veranda. I spoke to her, for the third time, but still without result. She stayed there for about ten minutes, after which she crossed the room, passed into the passage, went as far as the garden door and disappeared.

A moment after, my sister M. came in from the garden calling out that she had seen the form go up the steps outside the kitchen. We all went out into the garden, and my sister K., who was at the window, called out that she had seen her cross the lawn and go towards the kitchen-garden. That evening there were four of us to see her.

I will observe that, if we made arrangements to watch for the apparition at the times when we expected it to manifest itself, our expectations were invariably disappointed.

During the rest of the year 1884, and that which followed, the apparition continued to show itself often, especially in the months of July, August, and September, in which occurred the date of the three deaths: that of Mr. S. (July 14), that of his first wife (August), and that of the second (September 23). Everybody saw the same sort of apparition, passing several times in the same places.

Up to the year 1886 it appeared to be so solid and real that it could have been taken for a living person, but after that it began to be less and less distinct, although right till the end it intercepted light. There was no opportunity of observing whether it cast a shadow.

Several times, before going to bed, and after the other members of the family had retired for the night, I fixed some very fine threads across the staircase, placing them at various heights.[10]

I fastened them on each side with small lumps of paste, in such a way that a very slight push was sufficient to make them fall without the passer-by being aware of them, and so that they could not be noticed by the light from a candle. *Twice I saw the form pass through the threads, which remained intact.*

We came to the conclusion that the apparition was connected with Mr. S.'s second wife, for these reasons:

1. The history of the house was quite well known, and if the mysterious form had to be identified with any of its former inhabitants, Mrs. S. was the only person who resembled the phantom.

2. The phantom appeared dressed in mourning, which could not apply to Mr. S.'s first wife.

3. Several people who knew the second Mrs. S. also identified her with the phantom we saw. I also saw a photograph album from which I picked out a photograph as showing the greatest resemblance to the form I had seen. It was a photograph of her sister, who, according to people who knew both, was very much like her.

4. Her daughter-in-law, as well as other people who had known her, told us she spent her days in the small sitting-room where she appeared so often, and usually just in the corner of the veranda where she stopped.

The accounts of the other witnesses all agree with Miss Morton's account, and it appears that the phantom always took the attitude of a woman prostrated by grief and weeping, with her face partly covered by a handkerchief held in her right hand.

The *Proceedings of the London S. P. R.*, from which this account is taken, and the strict enquiries

---

10 Same observation made at Strassburg in 1855.

of Myers published there and in his great work on *Human Personality* render its authority incontestable. The hypothesis of a collective hallucination of eight persons *independently of each other*—and of two dogs—is quite simply absurd. Eyes and ears perceived the apparition. Its reality is as certain as that of the Obelisk on the Place de la Concorde.

Here is a case of a haunted house not less worthy of attention than the preceding ones. It was made by a group of children who had no idea of the importance of our problem, by the servants of the house, and by a man of solid sense who only accepted the fact with the greatest reluctance. Gurney devoted a close study to this curious manifestation, and published it in the *Proceedings of the S. P. R.* (vol. iii, p. 126), as did Bozzano in his *Phénomènes de hantise,* p. 86. The occurrence took place in 1854, and a report was made on it at the time, with all the details of this remarkable apparition. This is the account written by Miss Mary E. Vatas-Simpson:

I have a very clear recollection of an old lady who appeared to us when we were children (I was the eldest and had a little sister and several little brothers), and it was the greatest trial of our childhood, first because the lady was a mystery to us, and then because she brought down upon us some severe paternal scoldings.

We lived in a very ancient house, with the dining-room on the top floor, with three windows, and two doors facing the windows. The staircase was narrow and the steps were very high, with frequent landings, from which we loved to lean down to see what was going on below, especially if the servants brought any visitor into the drawing-room.

One day when I was leaning over at one of our posts of observation, I saw a very frail old lady come slowly up the stairs and enter the drawing-room alone. It surprised me greatly, because the free passage of the stairs was interrupted by a supplementary door separating my father's study from the offices in the ground floor, so that persons wishing to enter had to ring, as at the front door. Now I had seen the old lady come up the stairs on this side of the door, though nobody opened it. There was a whispered conversation between me and my brother Walter, who was sitting astride on the upper banisters, and we resolved to go and see who the intruder was. We went quietly down to the drawing-room, feeling sure of finding the lady there, and were greatly disillusioned when we found nobody there. I came back on tiptoe, knowing that we were forbidden to go into the drawing-room; but as I went up the stairs again I gave a cry of astonishment because I saw the old lady pass out, by a door which was always closed, on the landing where I had been a short time before. I went back to the drawing-room to tell Walter and then went to watch on the landing, and saw the lady going slowly, having passed the door at the foot of the stairs. Just as she turned and disappeared from our view our father rushed out of his study and chastised us for the talking and the noise we had made.

Some days afterwards we were busy with our favourite game, which consisted in reversing two chairs, which represented a post-chaise in which we sat, and putting a rug over our heads to represent the roof. At one moment my brother Garry hurt me, and I revenged myself by throwing the rug into the air. The first thing I saw was the old lady, dressed the same as before, a very worn black garment, a velvet cape on her shoulders, and a big bonnet on her head. I thought that she wanted to go into my father's study and had gone too far by mistake; but she continued on her way up. I ran up to catch her in the passage, but saw her no more. Then I ran on to the landing and down the stairs, where I met Walter, who ran after the old lady who was just quickly going down the stairs and keeping close to the wall. But in the middle of our pursuit my father came out of his study and threatened to beat Walter if the noise did not stop.

We then asked the servants for some information about the old lady, and saw them making mysterious signs to each other, and explained to us afterwards that it was an old lady come to see Mama.

Though we saw her often, and were not in the least afraid of her, it seemed that nobody wanted to believe us, and we spoke of her often between ourselves, but never with grown-ups. But we took our precautions, and when we played "post" a postilion was placed outside to give us warning as soon as she came. She had seemed to look at us too insistently, and we thought that if she surprised us with our heads under the rug she would do us some terrible harm. And under the rug we also concealed a defensive weapon in the shape of a heavy ruler to throw at her if she dared to touch us.

It is clear from all this that we took the phantom for a real person, and in spite of the long years which have passed, I still have a very vivid recollection of her and seem still to see her.

(Sg.) MARY E. VATAS-SIMPSON.

Here the text gives long quotations from Mrs. Vatas-Simpson's diary, and we learn that, besides the phantom of the old lady, another phantom, that of an old man, was also seen, and that noises of all sorts were heard. The house was very old and was reputed to be haunted. A family who had previously lived there had left on account of the noises in the night, which awakened and frightened the children.

Here is a significant passage of the diary in question:

My husband was very incredulous about all this. But last night his unreasoning incredulity received a great shock, for he saw the phantom himself and felt a terror quite unknown to him before. This is what happened to him:

In consequence of his recent illness, heaps of letters and documents had accumulated on his desk. He resolved to devote the evening hours to the task of going through his correspondence and classifying the documents, giving the servants strict orders not to admit anybody and not to disturb him in any way. For my part, I took all the measures necessary to assure him absolute quiet.

Last night, then, when the house was perfectly quiet, my husband had gone to his study after dinner, and had not come out when eleven struck. I was sitting in the drawing-room with the door open, as I usually did when I was alone. Suddenly I heard a noise in the direction of the study, I heard the door open and heard my husband furiously denouncing the servants for allowing a stranger to enter his study. Who had contravened his orders? He was told that nobody had, and he said: "Don't deny it. Where is the woman? When did she come? What does she want? I receive nobody at night. Let her come to-morrow if it pleases her. Now show her the door."

All this was said as if the intruder were still in the house, and with the intention of making her hear. Meanwhile the servants were protesting that they had not shown in anybody, and had seen nobody go up or down stairs. Suddenly my husband's face changed. He said no more and stood motionless. He seemed remote from all external expressions, as if he had been struck with a stupor or confusion. Then he pulled himself together. He seemed to shudder, and, stepping forward a few paces, he ordered the servants to go to bed, saying that in the morning he would find out who had taken the liberty of showing a woman into his study. And if the woman came again he would ask her.

He said these words to hide his thoughts, for he spoke very differently when we were alone. He told me that when he was looking among his papers for a very important document, and was much preoccupied, he had happened to raise his eyes, and had seen a frail little old lady on the threshold. Though she came at an inconvenient time he did not fail in courtesy, but got up and asked her to come in. Seeing that she did not move or speak, and only kept looking at him, he advanced to repeat the invitation. But the lady remained silent and immobile, and seemed to regard him with a sad expression. Thinking that she was out of breath from mounting the stairs, my husband waited some time, but since no reply came he came forward, the lady imitating him with a gliding movement. The room being large, there was always some distance between them, and my husband took several steps towards her. At last he walked resolutely forward, decided to probe the mystery of the silence. But then he saw her no more. She had disappeared!

Having proceeded to that point, my husband paused and fell into a profound meditation. He seemed extremely agitated, and his lips trembled. He was evidently making a supreme effort to master his emotion. After some time he seemed to awaken from a dream and concluded his narrative.

He said his study was brightly lighted with the gas lights, and that he did not remember the door opening when the phantom appeared, nor when it disappeared, while he was certain he had shut it on entering the room. He had never thought he was face to face with a phantom. He had taken the lady for a person in grave difficulty, who had come to consult him, and the urgency of her motives, and her advanced age had seemed to him sufficient excuse for the unreasonable hour at which she presented herself. These considerations had led him to receive her with deference. But her inexplicable dumbness had finally irritated him, and he had made her understand that by his voice and gesture. He described the phantom in these terms: "It was an old lady, small and frail, very pale, dressed in dark garments, with a large bonnet on her head, tied under the chin, and the hands always crossed." She had come forward with a soft gliding motion, had always looked him in the face, and had never moved her hands.

Then he summed up his impressions: "I have told you what happened exactly. I cannot doubt what I have seen. I admit I cannot explain it, so let us not talk about it." I am sure he will no longer laugh at our "absurd visions of ghosts." Indeed, he is so much struck that he does not know what to think. Much time will pass before he forgets the visit of the "pale little old lady" who often visits us.

That is Gurney's story. This multiple observation, first made by children, discourages, if it does not entirely suppress, the hypothesis of hallucination, an hypothesis which I know in all its forms, for I always have the classical work of Brière de Boismont on my table. Who was this singular person? Everything leads us to believe that it was a deceased lady who had lived in the house. Let us seek another hypothesis to accord with the facts!

We can apply to this apparition what we said above about the Morton family: "It is as certain as is the existence of the Obelisk on the Place de la Concorde."

Let us admit without reserve that we are here in the realm of complete mystery, as we were in the case of the haunted castle of Calvados and all our other examples. Let us admit that we know nothing, and that it is permitted to be curious and to want to know. This is worth all the fantastic romances published every day, generally on the same fascinating subject.

Nothing must be affirmed but what is surely observed. But it is neither reasonable nor honest to refuse to recognise a verified reality on any pretext whatever.

Sir Arthur Conan Doyle published in 1919 a remarkable book called *The New Revelation,* in which he tells that, as a member of the Psychical Research Society, he was sent with two other delegates to pass a night in a haunted house. There we have another personal observation. Incomprehensible noises and blows were heard, recalling the story of the family of John Wesley at Epworth in 1726, and of the Fox family at Hydesville in 1848, which was the foundation of modern Spiritualism.

The result of this enquiry was the observation of phenomena corresponding to those described in this work and their probable connection with a burial preceding them.

How many problems there are besides those presented by the ghosts of the departed!

All the entities, all the forces, all the invisible causes, all the spirits which reveal themselves in any way in the numerous phenomena which we are studying, are not necessarily the souls of the dead. Apart from the fact that the souls of the living can externalise themselves, and that we can ourselves sometimes act unconsciously, we are surrounded by psychic elements, both known and unknown. Does the very curious observation which follows denote an action of the living, the realisation of a wish or a determination, or does it denote the action of the dead person concerned? Appearances are in favour of this last interpretation. Let us weigh everything in absolute liberty and without prejudice.

What is the part played by our human organism in metapsychic phenomena?

I have already announced (*Death and Its Mystery,* vol. iii, p. 351) an observation by M. Oscar Belgeonne, Secretary to the Bench of Antwerp in the Court of Summary Jurisdiction, an observation which the abundance of material prevented my inserting in that volume and which I had to reserve for this. This case is interesting from the point of view of the question just raised. Here it is (Letter 4,421, of April 5, 1921):

I had had over twelve years in the service of the Administration which I am still serving. One day some friends came and offered me an important and highly paid post in a private organisation. They strongly insisted on my immediate acceptance, as the matter was urgent. In order to speed my decision, they sent one of my intimate friends with a mission to convince me. I asked for twenty-four hours.

That night there was a bitter frost. I had had a long walk through almost deserted parts of Antwerp, and all the way I had weighed the pros and cons of the position offered. I went home about 11.15 p.m., and found sitting in the kitchen two of my sisters, who were reading while waiting for me. They told me that as the fires had gone out in the dining-room and on the veranda they had shut all the doors and had settled in the kitchen by the blazing fire. They knew that the offer I had received concerned my whole future, and they wished to know my decision.

All three of us were seated by a table moved against the wall. Our faces were towards the fire. A shelf was fixed to the wall beside the fireplace. Kitchen utensils were upon the board, and two inches below was a lath holding some hooks, from one of which hung a towel by a loop of cord.

Nobody was walking about the room. There was not, and there could not be, the trace of a draught.

We discussed the question which occupied me so intensely. My sisters did not wish to influence me. I was perplexed. What was I to do? The future depended on my decision.

"If only," said one of my sisters, "we could consult somebody."

"Or if father was still alive," I added, "he would give me good advice."

At the name of our father, who was all goodness and honesty, everyone became pensive and silent.

After some time I said again: "Should I accept?"

Suddenly the towel began to swing on its screw as on a pivot, to the right and left, all in one piece, not as if moved by a draught, but without a fold stirring, as if it were rigid and someone had, by light friction on the loop with his fingers, given it a pendulous motion to the right and left.

The towel said "No." Nothing more.

We had all seen it. It was so sudden, so uexpected, so very much to the point, so manifestly due to an invisible force, that my sisters' eyes were full of tears and I felt a sort of shudder.

I accepted the advice. And now, after nine years, I can only congratulate myself that I took the hint. The war has changed matters a good deal. It was in 1912. The organisation which had offered me the important employment no longer exists. Had I accepted, I should now be without a job.

I should be glad if the facts I report to you, and which I declare on my honour to be absolutely authentic, could be of some use towards the scientific monument you are building with such competence and impartiality.

(Sg.) O. BELGEONNE.

PARQUET D'ANVERS.

In a further letter of the following May 14, M. Belgeonne adds:

What I note with the greatest interest is that the "force" which by means of the towel (perhaps the only means at its disposal) gave me an adequate answer to my question *saw into the future.*

What was that force? How did it foresee? Is it not similar to the force which one day at Folkestone during the war rapped on a piece of furniture and made me arrive in time to prevent a fire? I have already reported this to you.

I admit that my first impression on reading this narrative was that of a rather forced interpretation of a rather trivial and almost ridiculous incident. But a man accustomed to juridical discussions is not a nobody. The simplest thing to suppose would be an illusion. This I shall not presume to adopt, in the presence of the concordant testimony of three witnesses. And, after all, is this swinging of a towel more ridiculous than the agitation of Galvani's frogs' legs? We can still ask if it is not M. Belgeonne's subconscious self which was in action. But how? To move an object without knowing or expecting it? Let us admit that the problem is not solved.

In the course of the enquiry which the narrator kindly allowed me to make, I obtained from Antwerp a certain number of official documents concerning the death of the elder M. Belgeonne (February 3, 1900, at the age of sixty-seven), and the separate attestations of the sisters, as well as several writings to elucidate the problem. The theory of an action by the deceased, whose paternal affection was known to his children, remains a possible one. Let us go on studying and *comparing*. Let us not forget that it was by means of *comparative anatomy* that Cuvier made his palæontological discoveries.

I have constantly expressed my surprise and regret to see the communications of the dead so insignificant and their manifestations so trivial, and our adversaries have relentlessly turned this triviality and insignificance against me. But is not sincerity the first requisite? We are studying and verifying and searching. We should (and I should certainly) prefer having more revelations concerning the spiritual life and other worlds. If the result of our studies is that certain souls do not communicate and that there are only fragmentary acts in these manifestations, imperfect echoes of spirits bound to earth, or even unconscious personal productions, we could but register the fact frankly. There is everything to learn. Truth above all.

CHAPTER XI

HAUNTING PHENOMENA NOT ATTRIBUTABLE TO THE DEAD. RAPPING SPIRITS. POLTERGEISTS

IN the previous chapter we collected a certain number of cases showing an association of the phenomenon with the dead, cases which a more or less definite object indicates intentions or promises awaiting fulfilment, and posthumous actions. We had noted some of these already in our general excursion. At the same time we also found the existence of singular phenomena devoid of any indication of origin or purpose. We gained the impression that these mysterious facts are extremely varied, that they are far from having the same explanation, and that they place us on the frontier of a whole new world to explore. In the present chapter we shall only deal with phenomena not indicating a connection with the dead. I do not say, in contrast to the last chapter, "without association with the dead," for we know nothing about that, and the whole extra-terrestrial world remains to be studied, so that we must be extremely careful, but say "without any indication of a connection."

In our preliminary survey of the subject, in the stones thrown in the Rue des Noyers at Paris and a certain number of cases, we already saw the absence of any indication of a psychic order. Nor did we see any in the phantasmagoria of phenomena of Calvados, nor in the vicarage of the strange noises. Though unexpected posthumous intentions have been suggested in some cases, it looks as if there were something else.

For a long time already a whole class of haunting phenomena has been collected under the name "rapping spirits," particularly studied in Germany under the name of *Poltergeist* (*polter,* to make a commotion; *Geist,* a spirit), and comprising noises, raps, uproars, various auditions, blows, steps, movements, murmurs, sighs, etc., produced by indeterminable causes.[1]

In the preliminary survey which we gave above (Chapter II), we witnessed the strange phenomena of stone-throwing, upsetting of furniture, and were stupefied by their vulgar triviality. We asked what might be the cause and purpose of such actions. The typical examples which followed showed us that these phenomena are as varied as they are fantastic.

If there are some which, like those in the last chapter, reveal the occult action of the dead, there are others, like the following, which seem entirely different. They deserve a distinct chapter to themselves. What can be their cause? Unknown faculties of the human being, animism, vitalism, non-human psychic agents, fragments of the world-soul, unknowable entities?

We must in these first lines not lose sight of the irrefutable verifications published above, such as the phenomena of the Rue des Noyers, 1860, in the Rues des Grès, 1849, the Ardèche, 1922, in Fives-Lille, 1865, the castle of Calvados, 1875, the house in Auvergne, the haunted vicarage (p. 161), the teacher's house (p. 173), the broken door of Strassburg (p. 233), and all similar cases, in which no source is indicated but anonymous rappers and *Poltergeists.* Let us specially collect here and com-

[1] A remarkable technical study of these has been compiled by Professor Barrett in the *Annales des Sciences Psychiques* for May, 1911, and a more detailed one in Miss Grove's *Night Side of Nature,* 1849.

pare some of these cases. The following case, surely a very singular one, was sent to me from Cherchell (Algeria) on July 17, 1922:

In 1913, when we lived in Tonkin, my wife and I went to take a rest for a few weeks in the town of Mong-Zen (Yunan). We lived in an isolated bungalow in a sort of camp constituting the French concession, the nearest house being twenty yards away. We were accompanied by our "boy," a young Annamite of about sixteen.

A day or two after our arrival we were startled by a formidable noise, which seemed to be outside and vibrating through the roof. I thought of a thunderclap. Looking at the sky I found it clear, without a breeze or a cloud. But we had found during our stay in Cambodia that thunderclaps without wind and without perceptible clouds often disturbed the atmosphere, and this observation duly led me to enquire of my neighbours next morning, but they had heard neither noise nor thunder.

Some days after that there was another noise in the night. It was impossible to sleep. We passed the night waiting for the day, and I had ample opportunity of studying the character of the sound. I attributed it to a rock detached from the neighbouring mountain, which had rolled down, or to a slight earth tremor (so frequent in that region). Yet this explanation did not entirely satisfy me, for the noise, though very loud, was, so to speak, muffled and unique. To carry out my suggestion, it would have to be a rock falling flat on level ground, which is absurd. Again, nobody in the concession had heard anything, and no seismic shock had been registered.

These two manifestations might have been forgotten if a third one of the same kind had not occurred. Again, at the same hour of the night, under the same meteorological conditions of perfect calm, a noise, appalling this time, resounded on the roof. In a second we were up, and our boy (God knows the Annamities are sound sleepers!), who slept in the next room with the door open, stood up also, stupefied.

I thought there would not be a tile left on the roof.

I thought of an unexpected cyclone. I went out, but found that the house was undisturbed and there was quiet everywhere. Seeing a light in the neighbouring house I called them and asked: "Did you hear that?" They seemed astonished, but said they had been quietly reading and had not been disturbed by any noise.

In view of these circumstances, and after reading the various reports on these things, I no longer doubt that entities must have haunted that bungalow.

It was let every year for a month or two to birds of passage, and it is therefore difficult to ascertain whether previous tenants noticed similar manifestations. The sources of these unexplained noises is still to seek.

(Sg.) Max Roussel
(Estate Receiver at Cherchell).

This must have been a subjective phenomenon, but how, and why? We see no connection with the spirits of the dead.

There can have been no illusion. Audition is certain.

As we saw in our general excursion, these cases are numerous and varied, and occur in all countries. Here is another, even more grotesque than the last.

A mysterious fall of stones, reminding us of that described above (p. 78) and observed by the Protestant pastor Laval in the Ardèche, was reported to the English S.P.R., and reproduced by Bozzano in his *Phenomena of Haunting*. I give it from a report by Mr. Grottendieck, of Dordrecht, Holland:

In September, 1903, I happened to witness an abnormal phenomenon which I was able to observe carefully in all its details.

I had succeeded in traversing the jungle from Palembang to Djambi (Sumatra), with an escort of fifty native Javanese, for purposes of exploration. On returning to my point of departure I found my usual residence occupied. I therefore had to take my sleeping-sack to an unfinished hut made of beams stuck together and covered with large dried leaves plastered over with "Kadjang."

I spread out the sleeping-sack on the wooden floor, arranged the mosquito-net, and soon went to sleep. About 1 a.m. I woke up, hearing an object falling near my pillow outside the mosquito-net. I looked around and saw black pebbles about an inch long. I got up, took the lamp from the foot of the bed, and watched. I found that stones fell from the ceiling in a parabolic curve and fell near my pillow.

I went into the next room to waken the Malay boy who was with me, ordering him to inspect the jungle round the hut, and while he did this I helped him by lighting up the foliage with an electric lamp. All this time the pebbles were falling inside. When the boy came back I put him on guard in the kitchen, and in order to watch the falling of the pebbles better I knelt by the pillow and tried to catch them as they came. But it was impossible, for they seemed to jump into the air as I grabbed at them. Then I climbed up the palisade and examined the roof at the point where they came from. I found that they emerged from the layer of Kadjang leaves, which, however, had no holes in it. Again I failed to seize them up there.

When I got down, the boy entered and told me that nobody was in the kitchen. I was sure some practical joker was hiding somewhere, and, taking up my rifle, I fired five times from my window into the jungle, with the result that in the hut the stones came hailing down with greater force than ever.

But in any case I wakened up the boy completely. Before the firing he had seemed somnolent. When he saw the stones falling he said the Devil was throwing them, and was so terrified that he fled into the jungle in the night. As he disappeared the stones ceased to fall. But the boy disappeared and I lost him for good. The stones showed nothing peculiar, except that they seemed rather warmer to the touch than usual.

When day broke I found the stones on the floor, and

I found under the window the five cartridges I had fired. I again examined the roof but found nothing, not even a chink in the leaves where the stones had emerged. During the short time the phenomenon had lasted some twenty stones had fallen. I put several in my pocket and kept them. I first thought they might be meteoric stones, as they were warm to the touch, but how explain that they went through the roof without making a hole?

To conclude: The worst of the adventure for me was that the flight of the boy forced me to make my own breakfast and give up my usual toast and coffee.

In reply to questions put to him by the Council of the S. P. R., Mr. Grottendieck added some particulars, among which we note the following:

I was alone with the boy in the hut, which was entirely surrounded by the jungle. From the point of view of fraud, the boy is beyond suspicion, for while I was bending over him to awaken him (he was sleeping on the floor near my door) two stones fell one after the other, and I saw and heard them fall, the door being open.

The stones fell with astonishing slowness, so that even if fraud must be assumed, there would still be a mystery to explain. It seemed as if they went slowly through the air, describing a parabolic curve and hitting the ground with force. Even the noise they produced was abnormal, for it was too loud relatively to the fall.

I said the boy had been somnolent up to the moment when the shots woke him up, and his state showed itself in his abnormally slow movements. He had got up, had gone into the jungle and come back in an extraordinary slow manner. The slowness of his movements made on me the same strange impression as did the slowness of fall of the stones.

Those are the essential points of Mr. Grottendieck's account.

In another case, which occurred in Sicily in June, 1910, in full daylight, Mr. Paolo Palmisano saw stones falling slowly without causing any damage, and says that one of them, near a place where the young deaf and dumb daughter of a peasant was sitting, detached itself from the wall, and, after describing a slow semicircle in the air, deposited itself in the hand of a friend. We looked at each other dumbfounded, but the rain of stones continued (*Giornale de Sicilia,* June 7, 1910).

In connection with missiles issuing from a point where there is no aperture, and their abnormal heat, we must note that although these facts are incomprehensible they are usual in *Poltergeist* phenomena.

We cannot resist these facts. We must note, in the three cases of Cherchell, Sumatra, and Sicily, the presence of a young and unconscious human being.

In seeking the causes of these mysterious actions we find no indication of activities of the departed, and yet there are certain marks of intention, of purpose and intelligence. Have we to deal with invisible beings, different from human beings? It seems to me that this hypothesis is not necessary. If we admit survival there must be millions of mediocre or inferior human spirits capable of amusing themselves in this way.

Amuse themselves! The word may sound strange, but it is particularly appropriate to the observations in their infinite variety complicated by unexplained movements.

In February, 1913, I received several Belgian periodicals, including *Le Sincériste* of Antwerp, *L'Étoile Belge* of Brussels, *La Fraternité, Le XXme Siècle,* etc., containing various accounts of a haunted house at Marcinelle. The best account of this was published in the *Annales des Sciences Psychiques* of 1913 (p. 152). I give it here:

All the papers of this country have reported the singular case of stone-throwing without known cause produced at

Marcinelle, near Charleroi, in the house occupied by M. Van Zanten, Rue César-de-Paepe. These manifestations, which began on Thursday, January 20, ended on Sunday, February 2, lasting only four days. They set the local police in motion, as well as the gendarmerie. They led to a visit by the bench of magistrates, but all these investigations remained without result. We visited the place on February 5. The house is the last of a row of similar ones. Beside it, facing the street, is a large, well-wooded garden extending to the corner of the first crossroad, and surrounding the ends of the yards and closes of the small dwellings in the line terminated by the Van Zanten house.

A little after our arrival we were able to talk with a representative of the authority which took a leading part in the organisation for watching the house. What had struck him most in the circumstances, he said, was the singular accuracy of aim, the missiles appearing to hit exactly the place chosen by the delinquent.

"I have seen," he added, "a stone arriving in the middle of a large window-pane, and then came others in a spiral round the first point of impact, so that the whole of the glass was broken up methodically. I even saw, in another window, a projectile caught in the fragments of glass of the first hole it made, and subsequently ejected by another passing through the same point.

"The stones, according to our observations, can only come from a house situated on the opposite side of the quadrilateral, about 150 yards from the target. To obtain such accuracy of aim the guilty person must dispose of a very powerful and perfectly adjusted catapult."

I told him that that did not solve the problem. The objects were said to differ in weight, shape, size, and density, so that every missile would have to describe a trajectory different from that of the others, on account of differences in the resistance of the air. Besides, the wind would noticeably deflect the stones to one side or the other. It can be said with some assurance that such correct aiming with missiles so varied is beyond human ability.

A few minutes after I had an opportunity of seeing Mr. Van Zanten, who very kindly consented to show me the property, the damage done, and the missiles which had been preserved. Furthermore, he gave detailed replies to the questions I thought necessary to ask. I spoke to him first of all about what had been told me by the public official.

"The first fact is perfectly correct," he replied. "The first stone did, indeed, hit this window-pane exactly in the middle, and the following ones struck it systematically in a spiral round the first hole."

But what surprised us most was that not one of the 300 stones thrown hit anybody. The first day my little boy was in the garden and my little girl was sleeping in her cradle near an open window on the first floor. They were not disturbed in any way. The nurse, it is true, was struck on the head by a piece of brick, but she was not much hurt. My father-in-law was hit on the arm and cried: "Well, I did not feel anything."

That is one of the signs, I believe, by which, according to the theory, one can distinguish missiles thrown supernormally from those by human agency.

As the servant came back just at that moment, I questioned her also. It is well known how often one meets in haunted houses a person of the feminine sex arrived at the age of puberty. This one seemed to me barely fifteen years old. The phenomena appeared to have some connection with her for they hardly ever began until she was up. She showed me the place on her head where the stone had hit her; neither chignon nor cap protected this spot. "Were you much hurt?" I asked. "Oh! yes, I have been crying with the pain during the day." "However, it did not bleed; you have had no swelling or lump?" "No, nothing like that." The projectile was about the size of a quarter of a brick. It seems to me very unnatural that it should have produced so little effect, coming so far and consequently falling from a height.

Armed with a search warrant the police of Marcinelle, after having gauged the approximate direction of the missiles, visited from top to bottom four houses which they vaguely suspected of serving as a base of operations for the enemy.

Nothing was found, and the tenants of the houses in question seemed as mystified as Mr. Jacob Van Zenten himself.

Such is the narrative of the Antwerp editor.

We agree with Bozzano, who also reported this case of Marcinelle, that we must take into account the quantity of missiles sent, which indicates a supernormal origin of the phenomena. A human operator who threw 300 stones without changing his place would have been caught red-handed by the police.

It must also be noted that when projectiles hit anybody they did not hurt them or did so much less than they would have done normally, while in hitting objects they did damage corresponding to their weight and volume.

The peculiarity is usual in *Poltergeist* phenomena and invites us to admit the existence of a will and intention governing the manifestations. These intentional acts suggest another observation on a commentary following the Sumatra narrative, in which projectiles were said to have described their parabola in air with relative slowness. The phenomenon is of theoretical interest, but very rare. The missiles are inoffensive to persons, but produce their maximum effect in hitting the windows, doors, and furniture.

Cases of this kind occur to some extent everywhere. Professor Perty, of Berne University, published in 1863 a little work [2] on the haunted houses of Councillor Joller of Niederdorf, near Stans, canton Unterwalden. Here is a summary of it:[3]

---

[2] *Die Mystischen Erscheinungen der Menschlichen Natur.*

[3] *Annales des Sciences Psychiques,* 1895, p. 94. See also C. Richet, *Traité de Métapsychique,* p. 744, and Bozzano, *Les Phénomènes de hantise,* p. 261.

In the middle of August, 1862, from the 15th to the 27th, tables and chairs were upset by invisible hands. Raps came on the doors and floor, doors opened and shut of their own accord. Finally the noise became appalling, bolts gave way, and the demolition of the house was feared. To persons in the room the noise seemed to come from the cellar under the floor. To those in the cellar they seemed to come from above. At the same time blows were struck as with a hammer on tables and chairs. In spite of the most careful searching, no visible cause could be found for all this. Yet a few days later a Lucerne paper, *Der Eidgenoss,* alleged that the most palpable explanation had been discovered: rapping instruments had been found which made the noise for the purpose of depreciating the house and inducing its owner to sell it for a song.

Councillor Joller replied to this unfounded allegation in *Der Bund* of September 4, declaring categorically that this strange phenomenon, in spite of the official inquiry and the measures taken, could not be reduced to any rational cause. The uproar continued, concentrating on a smaller circle, until August 27, and then ceased for a time.

For a numerous family those were days of terror which had cruel consequences.

The sceptics pretended to give a mechanical explanation, and the religious suspected the work of the Devil. The occurrence made a great deal of noise in the Press, and, as always, there was talk of illusion and trickery. In the *Allgemeine Zeitung* of September 28, a Berne correspondent said the last word had been spoken; the cause of the uproar was Mr. Joller's son, aged eighteen. He had, among his Bohemian friends, learnt all sorts of tricks, and had practised this one to frighten his people and amuse himself. In reply to my enquiry, Mr. Joller wrote to me as follows on October 2:

"In reply to your esteemed letter of September 30, I beg to inform you first of all that the mysterious phenomena, without the tumultuous violence they displayed in the beginning, still continue in the house, and that the papers you mention contain not a word of truth on the subject."

After regretting that the committee of enquiry had not heard or recorded the testimony of the many honourable people who had been eye and ear witnesses of these strange phenomena, Mr. Joller added:

"Exposed on the one hand to a coarse and fanatical populace, and on the other to an incredulous, slandering, and jeering Press, I was abandoned in my misfortune with a numerous family, and now my wife's and my children's shaken health force me to find another home. At first I wanted to keep the secret. But the noise was so great that I could no longer keep silence. The phenomena, of whose existence I was convinced in spite of myself, and in broad daylight, for six weeks, were of various kinds.

"At first we heard raps on the walls and floor, and especially on the doors of the house. Sometimes these phenomena were so violent that the doors opened and shut, being torn out of the latches. Then the noises diminished and passed into a light jolting. Tables, chairs, and crockery were upset, sometimes with noise, sometimes without. Pictures were taken from the walls, vessels taken from tables and cupboards, and put upside down on the floor. All sorts of objects were hung on nails. Finally, pictures were turned with their faces to the wall under our eyes, and stones, fruits, clothes, etc., were thrown about and hidden in dark places, in spite of locks and bolts.

"Stones were often thrown down the chimney. Nothing was broken or damaged, and, strange to say, the stones which, coming down the chimney, hit one or other of my children did not cause a shock or appreciable pain. We have been made to feel the touch of an icy hand and the ends of fingers, and we have felt a cold wind like a beating of wings, which was felt by every inhabitant of the house. We also heard a perfect imitation of a watch being wound up, of splitting wood, of counting money, of rubbings and songs, and articulate sounds as from a human voice. Generally these sounds, often very loud, had some relation to the work and conversation of the people in the house. The night before last, about 8 p.m., a stone wet with dew was thrown up the stairs nearly in front of the door of our dwelling. Seven weeks ago these stories would have made me smile and shrug my shoulders, but now I must assert them with all the force at my command."

Professor Perty adds: "National Councillor Joller, who is known everywhere as a truthful and enlightened man, will find some consolation for the annoyance and disturbance he suffered on account of these mysterious phenomena, in the thought that they contribute to the enlarging of our spiritual horizon, and open a vista of a new order of things, while the false judgment passed on him by some is but the result of ignorance."

We might think, with Professor Perty or with Bozzano who comments upon him (and repeat what we said before), that these trivial, vulgar, material manifestations, similar to so many others in this work, are operated according to the principle of least resistance (like lightning flashes) and might be directed by invisible intelligences, with the object of impressing the witnesses by shaking their indifference and inviting them to meditate on the possibility of the existence of a soul surviving death, with all the moral and social consequences implied in that. If we admit that interpretation, we also admit that a very noble aim is attained with very moderate means, adapted to the largely vulgar nature of man; for we must admit that most people only know material life, remain deaf to philosophical and psychological arguments, and are only struck by brutal facts. A hard knock in the back impresses them more than a discourse of Plato, of Buddha, or of Jesus Christ.

We may now state that in the totality of haunting phenomena the *Poltergeists* or independent rapping spirits, having no connection with the dead, are much more numerous than the cases of association such as those described in the last chapter. Yet the accounts now on my table would represent some thirty pages. They are quite similar to those already published.

That some invisible intelligence is at work in *Poltergeist* phenomena is incontestable. Missiles hit chosen targets, slow down so as not to hurt spectators, describe capricious trajectories, fall from no one knows where, pass through narrow slits and even penetrate into hermetically closed rooms. Such acts belong to a supernormal world. To attribute them to queer faculties of the subconscious seems to me an hypothesis difficult to sustain. We have pointed out that the triviality and vulgarity of the manifestations may be explained by the simple object of attracting attention and by the facility of taking the line of least resistance. There may also be vulgar spirits, as there are in our world, and probably even a large number. Why should there not be practical jokers on the other side of the barrier as well as on this side—or even imbecile and wicked entities?

A laborious compilation made by Ernest Bozzano led him to the following conclusion:

> Among 532 cases of hauntings, 374 belong to the category of "haunting by the dead," and 158 are *Poltergeist* cases. The latter are, therefore, 28 per cent of the total. Examining the categories separately we find that among the *Poltergeist* cases there are 46 cases of stone-throwing, 39 of spontaneous bell-ringing, 7 fires, and 7 auditory cases in which unknown human voices were heard.
>
> Among the phenomena of haunting proper, 374 out of 532—*i.e.,* 72 per cent—show a connection with a death—mostly tragic—which took place in the building or the locality haunted.
>
> The 374 cases in question can be divided into several very distinct and suggestive groups. Thus, in a first group of 180 cases—mostly of great certainty—the origin of the haunting coincided with a tragic event which had occurred there. In another group of 27 cases the absence of documents was compensated by the discovery of human remains buried or walled in in those places—a manifest indication

of bloody tragedies enacted there and forgotten. In a third group of 51 cases, deaths are associated with the place, and in a fourth group of 26 cases the person deceased and manifesting did not die in the haunted place, but had lived there a long time.

In 304 cases out of a total of 374 there is, therefore, a death coinciding with a haunting. There remain 70 cases without a death precedent, or at least without a discoverable one. This enormous majority of cases succeeding a death seems sufficient to justify the hypothesis of a link between the two orders of facts.

The conclusion of all we have reviewed is that these extraordinary and inexplicable phenomena certainly take place, in spite of difficulties of observation and special illusions inevitably associated with their study. They are as certain as the existence of the sun and the moon. But it is easier to verify them than to explain them. Yet we must devote a last chapter to a search for an explanation, pausing, however, to deal with Spurious Haunted Houses.

CHAPTER XII

SPURIOUS HAUNTED HOUSES

SPURIOUS haunted houses are as numerous as true haunted houses. The matter lends itself largely to fraud, trickery, practical jokes, illusions, hallucinations, and hysterical errors, as well as lies by children of both sexes. I have gone to the trouble of collecting hundreds of narratives, including those discussed some time ago by the Psychical Societies of England, the United States, France, and Italy, and published in various French and foreign journals. These various narratives present a volume nearly as large as this, and it seems superfluous to publish them separately. I have spent much time on this, and I shall spare the reader's time. Those who wish for full information need only look up the files of the Paris *Annales des Sciences Psychiques,* the *Proceedings of the Society for Psychical Research* of London and New York, and of the Rome review *Luce e Ombra.* These are the principal periodicals on the subject, and they give much authentic information.

The facts and happenings associated closely or remotely with Spiritualism are particularly exposed to illusions, errors of interpretation, and particularly frauds of impostors. In spite of the infamy of false mediums who cynically speculate with the sorrow of bereaved human beings hungering for consolation, such vile impostors are numerous, and cannot be too carefully avoided. I myself have exposed more than one, so that they were driven from the countries they exploited so grossly and unscrupulously. Also, there are persons endowed with real psychic faculties who, when their powers give out, do not hesitate to give a *coup de pouce.* Students of the subject whose time is precious have often had to complain of this sort of thing.

As we have seen, among other cases, from a letter of the eminent astronomer Schiaparelli, which I published before, savants are often discouraged in spite of their anxiety to gather information, to the great detriment of science. Men imbued with the scientific spirit are naturally frank and sincere, and do not understand mendacity.

It is more interesting and more important to discover the causes of the true phenomena observed.

One thing we cannot refuse to admit—viz., that haunted houses belong to all times and all countries.

CHAPTER XIII

THE SEARCH FOR CAUSES

Origin and mode of production of phenomena of haunting—The fifth element.

"This is a book of good faith."—MONTAIGNE.

"FELIX *qui potuit rerum cognoscere causas!"* (Happy is he who is enabled to know the causes of hings!) said Virgil 2,000 years ago in his admirable *Georgics* (ii, 489), referring to the happiness of those whose vigorous spirit penetrates the secrets of nature and rises above commonplace ideas. Does the material collected in the present work enable us to attain that happiness?

In this force and independent documentation, devoid of all prejudice (*præ-judicium,* anticipated judgment), my readers know that my only object has been to instruct myself and to give them the result of the investigations. May they allow me, therefore, to remind them that my personal study of this occult world commenced in November, 1861, in the company of Allan Kardec, the founder of modern Spiritism and without doubt the best informed man of the epoch, and that from those far-off years till now (1923) I have been in a position to know nearly all the work done on the subject in the whole world. I am, therefore, I confess, singularly astonished to find these phenomena denied by people who seem to be intelligent, well informed, and sensible.

As I have already said, it is usually considered "good form" to profess an absolute scepticism with regard to the facts which form the subject-matter of the present volume. For three-quarters of the citizens of our planet, all the unexplained noises in haunted houses, all the displacements of more or less heavy objects, without contact, all the movements of tables, furniture, and other objects met with in so-called spiritualistic phenomena, all the communications dictated by raps or automatic writing, all apparitions, partial or entire, of phantom forms, are illusions, hallucinations, or tricks. There is no explanation to seek. The only reasonable opinion is that we have to do with errors, that all "mediums," professional or otherwise, are impostors, that these phenomena do not exist, and that the witnesses, are idiots.

The subject is indeed complicated, and the problem is an equation with several unknown quantities. But science has solved many others like it, from equations of the first degree to the transcendental functions of the integral calculus. In the first place, there are two elements present—viz., human faculties to be analysed and determined, and an invisible psychic element external to ourselves.

We may read in the *Unknown Forces of Nature* (Final Edition, 1906, p. 591):

> The field of Spiritualism is open to all explanatory hypotheses. It is found that the communications dictated by the tables are in *rapport* with the state of mind, the ideas, opinions, knowledge, attainments—even the literature of the experimenters. They reflect the assembly.
>
> The name "medium" is quite inappropriate, inasmuch as it prejudges what has to be proved. It supposes that the person endowed with these faculties is an intermediary between spirits and experimenters. Admitting that this is sometimes the case, it is certainly not usually so. The rotation of a table, its tilting, its levitation, the displacement of a piece of furniture, the swelling of a curtain, the noises

heard, are caused by a force emanating from that person or from the totality of those present.

We can surely not assume that there is always a spirit responding to our fancies. And the hypothesis is all the more superfluous since these alleged spirits teach us nothing. Our own psychic force is surely in action most of the time. The person exercising the force would more appropriately be called the *dynamogen,* because he or she engenders the force. That would, in my opinion, be the term most appropriate to that state. And it expresses what every observer witnesses.

That was an invitation to use scientific methods.

Our studies on these subjects require, perhaps, greater care than all the others. Already in 1869, in my speech at the grave of Allan Kardec, I remarked that Spiritualism must not be treated as a religion but as a science to be studied, and that the causes at play are more varied and numerous than one might suppose.

We do not know all the human faculties. The precept of the Temple of Delphi (Γνῶθι σεαυτὸν, Know thyself) is still appropriate. Our own powers certainly have something to do with the phenomena we are studying. A faithful servant of the experimental method, I hold that we must examine every natural hypothesis before we have recourse to others.

When, in *L'Inconnu* (1900) I essayed a first methodical classification of these very varied occurrences, I started with the best-established telepathic transmissions and with the manifestations of the dying and the living, which were open to verification by creditable witnesses worthy of entire confidence.

It has always seemed to me that we cannot use too much caution in the interpretation of the facts, especially when it is a question of a scientific proof of the survival of the soul. For our normal impression is that the soul is intimately bound up with the brain, with its evolution and its end. It is a matter of provng the error of this appearance. Are certain phenomena occurring at the moment of death to be placed before or after that moment? I naturally assumed at first that they were due to the psychic force of the living person, while agreeing that a careful analysis might yield the proof of an action after death. This caution has been brought against me as a reproach.

M. A. Erny wrote in the *Annales des sciences psychiques* of 1900 (p. 22):

It is a complete error of M. Flammarion to believe that it is only the *dying* who can manifest themselves and not the *dead*.

A deceased person can manifest himself in a more or less objective manner, being disengaged. His psychic body can act instantaneously and transport itself to enormous distances, like the electric fluid.

Besides, it is only to relatives or friends that a dead person manifests himself, as a rule, because the affection which united them in life attracts them once more towards those who loved them.

As for the dying, they cannot possibly manifest themselves, for the excellent reason that at the moment of death all the psychic elements struggle painfully to disengage themselves from the physical body, and in that supreme crisis they are unable to act in any manner whatever.[1] The dying person is in a sort of comatose state, in which he seems to suffer a good deal, but is in reality insensible during the crisis and on account of it. I myself remember that when my father was dying he seemed to suffer terribly during his agony, and I said to him: "One would think that you are in great pain, but if you are not suffering, press my hand." Though he could not speak, my father lightly pressed my hand which held his. It was a palpable

---

1 This is contradicted by facts (see *Autour de la Mort*).

and clear proof that he was not suffering, and that his state was not painful. My father firmly believed in the immortality of the soul, and after his death his face, contracted by his illness, took on a look of grandeur and elevation, which greatly impressed my mother and myself.

I never said or thought that the dead *could* not manifest themselves, and I have found no hypothesis of theoretical analysis. On the contrary, I believe that such manifestation is now proved by observed facts and that we must admit it, on condition of not being misled by illusions and errors.

M. Erny was then (1900) specially dealing with my work *L'Inconnu,* which had just appeared and which does indeed occupy itself principally with telepathy and manifestations of the dead. That was to be the beginning of our studies. He quoted the cases I published, including the case of General Parmentier (*L'Inconnu,* pp. 64-67), of René Kraemer (p. 70), of Mme. Fèret (p. 74), of Clovis Hugues (p. 76), of Baron Deslandes (p. 81), and of Baroness Staffe (p. 82), and concluded that I was mistaken in attributing these cases to dying persons or to hallucinations, whereas, according to him, they were certainly due to the dead.

I desire this as much as my critic, but I am more exacting with regard to proofs. We cannot be too exacting. The scientific method is inexorable. I am often caught between two reefs—that of scepticism which denies everything, and that of credulity which accepts everything.

May we not even ask ourselves whether we are not all mistaken, whether these phenomena are not produced either by the dying or the dead, but simply by ourselves, by human faculties, as yet unknown? The question arises very naturally. The permanent fact that a medium is necessary for the production of spiritoidal phenomena is not negligible. On a former occasion I called mediums *dynamogens.*

Man certainly does not know himself.

The comparative studies of Aksakoff have shown that more than one phenomenon of haunting can be put down to an action at a distance due to the psychic force of the living. In many cases this is indeed quite probable. Kerner tells us the following story of the poet Lénan:

> I must mention an event which proves how little his ethereal body was attached to his physical body. One day, when he was dining with us and we were conversing over our dessert, he suddenly went silent and pale, and sat immovable in his chair. But in the adjoining room, where nobody was, we heard glasses clinking as if somebody were moving them. We called him by name and asked him to explain. He arose as out of a magnetic sleep, and when we told him what had happened he said: "That has often happened to me. My soul is then, so to speak, outside my body."

Without occupying ourselves for the present with the theory of "ethereal bodies," let us only repeat that the human being is endowed with some as yet unknown faculties.

In his ingenious researches on the physical phenomena attributed by his wife Gisèle (an excellent medium) to a dead woman (Gisèle's mother), Dr. W. de Germyn [2] was led to the following curious remarks:

> The noises produced in the house continuing from time to time, I took occasion one night when Gisèle was asleep, and I was awakened by sounds imitating pans and furniture being upset, to convert her ordinary sleep into hypnosis. She repeated, with many hesitations and searches,

---

[2] *Contribution to the Study of Certain Misinterpretated Cerebral Faculties*, p. 441.

what she had already told me when she was impersonating her mother. I then ordered her to remember the next day on waking up all she had told me when she slept, to have a mass said for the repose of a soul in torment, and to pray that we might be delivered from her presence.

I do not know whether Gisèle had the mass said or not, but I know that since that time no more sounds have been heard.

The sounds attributed by Gisèle to the spirit of a dead person were evidently produced unconsciously by herself. There is a medium in every haunted house. Ours was decidedly haunted. Often the covering was pulled off my bed, and invisible hands touched me through the bedclothes. On one occasion, when I was awake and sitting on my bed, I felt a hand which seized one of mine and pressed it strongly. I sometimes distinctly heard somebody coming up the stairs, reach the door of our room, and try to open it. The furniture seemed to move and be upset without any visible effect. These were imitative sounds, but of wonderful perfection.

I believe the subconsciousness of Gisèle was led by the desire to convert me to Spiritualism. My incredulity made her suffer. And she had, to attain her purpose, used this absurd means derived from popular beliefs.

In spite of the title of *dynamogens,* which I formerly applied to mediums, I think that term is rather too exclusive. The unknown faculties of the human being act, but they do not suffice to explain certain posthumous manifestations. But let us not lose sight of it.

Among other examples in favour of the idea that the *dead* manifest themselves, M. Erny quotes the following (*Annales,* 1900, p. 98):

Alfred Ohagen has communicated to me an account of a case which happened to a friend of his, M. H., a materialist convinced that death is the end of everything. His belief was considerably shaken by what happened at the death of his brother-in-law, whom he loved very much and who showed his materialist opinions. M. H. was sitting by the bed on which his brother-in-law was lying some hours after his death. The door was half open and there was only one candle, burning near the door. He placed his hand on the rigid forehead of the dead man and said: "Albert, can you tell me, is there survival or is there not?" Hardly had he pronounced these words when the half-open door slammed and the candle went out. M. H. quietly arose, and, unconvinced that it was a strange phenomenon, he lighted the candle afresh, thinking that a draught might have made the door bang and extinguish the candle. But in order to find where he stood, he got a piece of chalk and made sure that the door had no tendency to shut of its own accord by some inclination and that there was no draught in the adjoining rooms, the doors and windows of which were shut. M. H. placed the candle in front of the door several times and it did not flicker. Then he put the door in the same position, and made a mark on the floor with the chalk to fix the position exactly. The door did not move. Then he repeated his appeal: "Albert, if that is really a sign from you, shut the door again." It immediately banged as at first. His sister, who lay on a couch in the adjoining room, asked him angrily why he had twice banged the door so violently. He asked her if the door ever shut of its own account. "Never," said the sister. Next day he made some more experiments with the door, but found it did not close by itself. Also, the servant removed the marks of chalk in his presence, so that he was sure he had not been dreaming; and the fact that his sister had been troubled twice in her sorrow by the noise proved that there was no hallucination.

This very characteristic case was reported in *Light* of February 27, 1894, from which I translate it. I ask M. Flammarion to consider it, for as the case comes from a materialist it is all the more striking.

Well, this remarkable case does not strike me as absolutely conclusive. What is there to prove that the personality of the experimenter was not able to produce the phenomenon unconsciously? The action of the deceased is indeed very *probable,* but is it *certain?*

I am far from being opposed to assuming the actions of deceased persons. On the contrary. If I commenced by considering those of the dying, of the living, it is because it seemed best to prove first of all the reality of these, from which we might naturally pass on to a discussion of those of the dead by a continuation of the methodical order which should be observed in affirmations of such importance. Let us not forget that for our personal conviction we must neutralise by positive psychical observations the capital objection of the parallelism between the birth and development of the intelligence of the infant and the material evolution of its brain.

And let us not lose sight of the physiological and psychological faculties of the human being, especially its possible doubling. Everybody knows the great discovery made at Bordeaux by Dr. Azam of the two alternate mental states of Félida.[3]

---

[3] It will be remembered that, born in 1843, this girl in 1858 had violent hysterical fits which seemed to presage lunacy, and for which Dr. Azam was consulted. She was observed to fall into cataleptic trances which lasted several minutes, after which she woke up in quite a different state, a different person, gay instead of sad, with a sprightly character; and this second state, which at first lasted but a few hours, ended by dividing her life into two nearly equal periods, the second state forming a life almost entirely distinct from the first. It got so far that in the second state she fell in love with a neighbour, became pregnant, and gave birth to a child (without being aware of it when in her first state), who, in 1875, when Dr. Azam published his study, was sixteen years of age. The second state was gradually lengthened at the expense of the first, and finally spread over her whole existence. Naturally this story was received with a general smile. The girl was accused of acting a comedy, and the eminent observer was considered to have been duped. The latter, in reply to the general ignorance, published his observations under the title *Hypnotisme, Double Conscience et Altérations de la Personnalité.* Félida was then forty-four years old, had been married for a long time to the mysterious father of her first-born, and was the mother of a charming family, the second state having finished by absolutely dominating the first.

When we get to know these examples we can guess how vast is the unexplored territory of the human psychical and physiological world, and we are disposed to assign it an important part in the production of the phenomena we are studying. All this agrees with what we found in vol. i of *Death and Its Mystery* as regards the existence of unknown human faculties. We are only in the forecourt of knowledge. We know nothing. Let us say with Millet, in his beautiful book *En lisant Fabre:* "I know nothing, but I hope to know."

At the International Congress of Psychical Research held in Copenhagen from August 28 to September 2, 1921, of which we have an excellent Official Report, edited by M. Carl Vett, Dr. von Schrenck-Notzing, expounded under the title *Der Spuk in Hopfgarten,* a judicial verification of the phenomenon of telekinesis of which my learned colleague, M. Louis Maillard, has given, in the review *Psychica,* a scientific summary which shows how uncertain the explanation of haunting phenomena still is.

This case of haunting presents a double outlook, inasmuch as it brings up certain hypotheses concerning its cause, and also because it was the subject of a judicial enquiry which established its authenticity in an indisputable manner.

In Hopfgarten, a village near Weimar, there lives a clockmaker of the name of Sauerbrey, married a second time and having a son by his first marriage. The latter, who lives in a neighbouring locality and occupies himself with occult sciences, visited his father about February 10, 1921, and found his stepmother in bed with a chronic malady from which she had suffered for a long time. The subsequent enquiry failed to ascertain whether he tried to

---

Other cases of the same order are to be found in the excellent work of Jules Liégeois, of Nancy, *De la Suggestion et du Somnambulisme* (1889).

treat her by hypnotism or whether he restricted himself, as witnesses report, with examining her pulse and placing his hand on her forehead. But after his departure the patient complained of pains in her head.

On February 17 her condition grew worse. She had hallucinations, and seemed to see the eyes of her stepson constantly fixed upon her. About 11 p.m. raps were heard in her bedroom, on the walls, the table, the door, the ceiling, etc. They lasted until morning, and then ceased the next day and following nights.

They recommenced some days afterwards. Various objects moved without contact, such as chairs and the table. A cup was thrown on the floor and broken. These phenomena took place by the light of an electric lamp, but grew stronger in the dark.

The inhabitants of the house, disturbed in their sleep, sent for the Weimar police, and on February 24 the *Commissar* with eight men arrived on the spot and posted them through the house in order to discover the supposed trickster. But the same phenomena took place in presence of police and the commissary could but put it into his report. One of the men placed various objects about two yards from the patient and saw them move without anyone touching them. The other men, as well as a nurse and a neighbour, also witnessed the movements. The dog of the house, ordinarily very lively, showed himself much depressed while the phenomena lasted. A clock stopped,[4] though Sauerbrey found it had not deteriorated.

Finally, on February 28, a mental physician arrived from Weimar. He treated the patient by suggestion and persuaded her that she had a stronger will than that which had influenced her. His efforts were successful, and the patient exclaimed that she was delivered. From that moment all the phenomena above described ceased.

Thereupon the younger Sauerbrey was prosecuted for carelessly causing harm by the hypnotic manifestations he was suspected of having used. He was brought before the Sheriff's Court at Vieselbach and appeared on April 19, 1921. The case against him being insufficiently established,

---

[4] Compare the stopping of clocks mentioned above (p. 154).

he was acquitted. But the official report of the trial, giving the evidence of the various witnesses and that of the police commissary, as well as a statement by the president of the court, establish conclusively the reality of the facts and the impossibility of the patient having carried them, as her extreme weakness made it impossible for her to leave her bed.

The hypnoid state of the patient seems to be a necessary condition of the phenomena observed, because it accompanies them, and they cease as soon as that state does. And the author of the pamphlet here summarised concludes that the animistic hypothesis fully accounts for the manifestations, which, by the way, did not any time acquire a religious or spiritoid character.

But he hastens to add that this explanation is far from being applicable to all manifestations of this kind. There are several which are produced in the absence of any person who can be considered an agent, and which seem to be more dependent upon a locality than upon a person, etc.

If, then, in the present example we can, so to speak, seize the mode of production of the phenomena on the wing, we must not generalise hastily. It is wiser to recognise that the etiology of the phenomena of haunting is still surrounded by deep mystery.

This reasoning of M. Maillard is exact and judicious, and agrees with numerous cases brought forward in this book. The living human being enters largely into the production of these phenomena. But they are not yet explained.

We do not know how they are produced. There are, no doubt, fantastic stone-throwings and veritable destructions of buildings, committed unconsciously by women and hysterical girls, by the externalisation of their nerve force. I shall mention another case, still more amazing, published by the *Annales de sciences psychiques* (1899, pp. 302-309), a case which is almost incredible and yet sufficiently verified.

Under the title "A Haunted Young Lady at Ooty," the *Madras Times* of May 7, 1897, tells how a certain Miss Floralina had gone with one of her friends to visit a Catholic cemetery. Three days before, a man had committed suicide and was buried there.

Of a light and thoughtless disposition, these young persons had chosen the cemetery that evening as a place of recreation. Carried off by their own merriment they jumped and danced on the grave, and even dug into the earth and demolished the cross which had been placed there. On arriving home they fell ill, and it is said they are truly possessed by the Devil.

But let us listen to the story of those mad victims of hysteria, who recall the convulsionists of Saint-Medand, the possessed ones of Loudun, and other psycho-physiological cases.

They were agitated, looked at everybody with wild eyes, and became so strange that it was thought better to keep them confined to the house. They tore their clothes, and if women came near them and endeavoured to make them quiet they simply sent them rolling on the ground. On the other hand, they would give way to men, whether because they were stronger or for another reason. The days passed, and these singular girls, perpetually tormented, let their hair hang uncombed and in disorder, and sometimes broke into fury.

One of them, Miss Grace, got married (which was the best she could do) and left the house.

On Sunday evening, the 25th April last, I had the privilege of being introduced to Miss Floralina. She seemed calm and quiet. But I was told the following:

Since April 20, between 10 p.m. and midnight, stones were thrown with force from outside, and glasses were broken, though the stones hurt nobody.

On the evening of the 27th I went home at 7 p.m. and heard a large window-pane fall heavily to the ground. Advancing a few paces, I heard sounds as if stones were being thrown on the four sides of the house. A little while after that I heard several glasses fall and break on the floor. The inhabitants of the house called for help. I hurried home to find a friend and a policeman (the station was close by). We went to Miss Floralina's house together and, to our great astonishment, saw glasses broken into a thousand pieces and almost reduced to powder by large stones which seemed thrown with great force. What astonished us most was the breaking of the glasses, which could not have been accomplished by stones thrown from outside. While stones were being thrown, Miss Floralina told us that a large stone had fallen from the ceiling, grazing her head, which she was just combing in her dressing-room at about 2 p.m. She also told us that the throwing of stones and breaking of glasses had commenced at noon.

Feeling certain that practical jokers were at work in all this, we fetched some more police and posted ourselves round the house in the thickets and ditches. We kept guard in vain till 11 p.m., for during the whole time while we were watching outside, stones continued to fall inside.

On Wednesday, April 28, a number of constables, led by two head constables and myself, came back about 7 p.m. We then saw stones thrown at glasses, and glasses falling on their own account. This excited our curiosity still more. Miss Floralina complained of being tired, and wanted to retire to her room. While she was going a piece of granite of medium thickness fell and broke a glass quite close to her with great force.

Soon afterwards her brother came to tell us that she had fainted on her bed. Entering her room, we found her not breathing, speechless, and stiff. With much trouble she was brought to. Some minutes later she fell into a worse trance. But eventually she recovered her senses.

On Thursday, 29th, about noon, we heard more glasses break. In the course of the evening we returned to the house and found a large assembly of head constables, all willing to obey orders given to them. We asked the young lady how she felt, and she said: "The shades of the evening are falling; a sensation of cold pervades my whole body, and my hair stands on end. I am very tired." From

5 p.m. till 7:30 p.m. a rain of stone fell, which reduced all the panes of the casement windows to atoms.

She sat down on a chair in a corner of the room, and after she had resumed her ordinary gaiety she fell quietly into a trance, and then became so wild and strong that five men could not keep her quiet. It is worth mentioning that while she was unconscious no glass was broken. Some minutes afterwards she rose from the chair with such force that some of us who held her were thrown over sideways. She remained standing, and nearly upset all those who held her. Using all our force, and with great efforts, we got her to sit down again. She sat down, her whole body as stiff as a piece of wood, and some seconds passed. She got up again, and gave us a lot of trouble. She wanted to go out. She was forcibly taken to her room and put to bed. She kicked everybody all round, and used her hands with such violence that several of us were afraid to go near her. A few minutes after she had been taken to her bed a large mirror on the door of the room—the central room of the house—fell to the ground and was smashed to atoms. The police then sent for a Malayali to expel the demons.

While we were waiting for this man, still holding Miss Floralina to prevent her from rising, her prayer-book, which was in a chest of drawers in the adjoining room, came flying through the window, which had been broken several minutes before, and fell near her right hand. We were quite surprised at this incident. She remained quiet for some minutes, but then wanted absolutely to go out. I asked her why. "To see two women." I asked her who were the two women. She gave the astonishing reply: "Two women without heads." She became very agitated and determined to get out. We had to use force to keep her quiet. She also said: "I must go to the cemetery." My friend asked her what was her object. She replied: "I must go to the cemetery to see Miss Grace." Miss Grace is the young married woman who was with her in the cemetery.

The Malayali, the exorciser we were waiting for, entered the room, and as he approached the bed, the girl, who had

had her eyes closed all the time, opened them and looked at him in a terrible manner. She made an effort to rush at him. The Malayali spoke to her in a violent tone, and she kept her eyes fixed on him. The Malayali (named Kunjini Gandhu) then wrote something on a long tape of paper, then mixed some "ghee," pepper, etc., and made a sort of cigarette of it. He first rolled up the tape and placed it in Miss Floralina's hair. She put out her hand to tear it away but with a quick movement the man bound it up with her hair. Then the girl spit at him, but the Malayali pointed at her with a cane of Malacca (which he alleges to have a certain power), went boldly in front of her and dared her, in Malayalee, to spit upon him. She no longer ventured to do so. He then lighted the end of the small roll in the shape of a cigarette, and got one of us to hold it so that she could breathe the smoke through her nose. After some time she felt quite well. It was 11 p.m., and she spoke to us as usual till a quarter to twelve. Then a glass broke with a great noise. She fainted. The Malayali had left the house at 11 p.m. We used the same small roll, blowing the smoke into her nose, and she seemed quite to recover, and drank a cup of tea.

On Friday, April 30, stones commenced to be thrown at noon and continued until 11 p.m. She fainted once, but not so deeply, though she looked terrible. On Saturday, the 1st inst., she told us that she went to fetch a plate from the dining-room, and that it had been pulled away from her. That evening she was in a much better frame of mind. But glasses were broken. She went for a walk the same evening, and as she re-entered the house an isolated window-pane which was still in one of the casements broke near her head and fell to the ground. Talking to one of us about her misfortune, she said every night she could see two women without heads. Some time afterwards a large cobble-stone flew into the room, and a glass broke of its own accord.

The father was telegraphed for, and he arrived at Goodalur (132 miles from Ooty) the Monday evening after. On that day the damage in broken windows was formidable, but fortunately the girl did not lose consciousness.

Yesterday (Tuesday) she and her father packed their luggage to leave Ooty and go to Goodular. As Miss Floralina passed from room to room, packing up her belongings, glasses were thrown near her, but no stones were thrown or windows broken. They left Ooty last night. M. F. and his children departed in another direction.

In my long account of this possessed girl I have not exaggerated the facts, and I have told them just as they happened. The house has a desolate appearance and is completely ruined. When night falls people are afraid to pass near it.

This article in the *Madras Times* (which I have abridged as much as possible) was accompanied by the annexed letters dealing with this case of lunacy:

I.

OOTACAMUND,
July 1, 1897.

I send you herewith the authentic testimony of two gentlemen who are my personal friends, and who sent me their letters to be transmitted to you with authority to publish them. One of them is a Captain in the Navy (retired), and the other a licentiate in medicine and surgery, who was one of the physicians consulted. I can vouch for their veracity. Hoping that this will be of use to you, I remain, yours, etc.

G. BURBY.

II.

OOTACAMUND,
MADRAS PRESIDENCY,
May 28, 1897.

I can testify to the accuracy of the report made in the *Madras Times* by its Ooty correspondent under the heading "Ghost at Ooty." The correspondent is known to me and has reported real occurrences. I was an eyewitness of the phenomena, and though I looked for the cause with much care I could find none. I may mention that several people who joined my search when I visited the "possessed" house are quite in agreement with me.

(Sg.) JAS. T. KELLY, Z.M.S.
(*Superintendent of St. Bartholomew Hospital*).

III.

HOPE VILLA,
OOTACAMUND,
May 9, 1897.

DEAR MR. BURBY,

I must tell you at once that I do not believe a word of Spiritualism, but I was at Ethel Cottage the night before the departure of your namesake for Sudabar. Windows were broken on every hand, without a human agent. I stayed there for more than an hour, but discovered nothing. Some of the persons present attributed these strange doings to a supernatural intervention, but I require proofs before accepting such an explanation.

Yours sincerely,
(Sg.) W. M. BURTHELL.

These observations, taken with those we have read on the preceding pages, show a certain association of the human organism with the production of phenomena, even with those which appear most independent of it, such as stones thrown, glasses broken, objects displaced, phenomena which cannot be denied, as they are incontestably real. This dynamogenic girl was their unconscious cause and their victim.

It is sad to think that hundreds of women "possessed" were burnt alive by the Inquisition for the crime of witchcraft. Let us also remember that one of the purest women of history, Joan of Arc, was also burnt as a witch. Humanity is a little more enlightened now. But how much of the road is still to travel!

Here follows a psycho-physiological manifestation which closely resembles the last. I shall pick it out from among the large number of those I have here. It is extracted from the *Gazette de Lausanne* of May 1, 1914, under the signature of a correspondent of the paper:

About a league from Sion, on the hills on the right bank of the Rhone overlooking the Saint Léonard road, there is a pretty little village of Molignon, which has given its name to a famous wine.

The hamlet consists of a chapel dedicated to Saint Anne, the centre of a favourite pilgrimage, and half a dozen houses and granges. Five minutes farther in the direction of Grimisuat, there is, facing a steep and rocky road, a pretty chalet of brown wood, bearing the date 1874 on its gable.

In this isolated village lives a young family consisting of father, mother, and a boy of eleven years.

On April 18 last, the young lad was suddenly seized by nervous attacks accompanied by strange phenomena.

Under an unknown influence the boy was convulsed, hit out with legs and arms, rolled his eyes, jumped, shouted and fell down flat. At the same time, sand and stones were thrown in the room. Cheese, knives, and other objects which were on the table rolled on the ground. A holy-water stoup was broken with a stone at the moment when a Capuchin friar was pouring holy water into it. A glass of wine was broken in the hands of a relative who had come to see the poor boy. When he was in bed, he felt himself violently pulled, and was hit in the face with stones, etc.

The lad was taken to Saint Anne's chapel, but this made it worse, and the attacks became so violent that two men had difficulty in holding the child, and at one moment he was thrown violently on the ground and drawn along the floor.

A blessed medal had been attached to the boy's neck, but the fastening soon undid itself and the medal was thrown into the air by invisible hands.

A Capuchin of Sion, the parish priests of Savièze and Grimisuat, and a canon of Saint Bernard came to the haunted chalet, but did not succeed in bettering the state of the patient, whom the parents declared to be smitten with a curse. The famous "mège" of Hérémence, of whom M. Victor Tissot tells us at length in his *Suisse Inconnue*, was called and soon arrived. Installed in the room of the chalet, and surrounded by the family and some relatives and friends, he read from a grimoire the prayers and invocations suitable to the occasion. While he was reading the stones did not spare him, and several fell on his head and on his book.

These events took place last Sunday. Now, since Monday evening, the attacks and the phenomena which accompanied them have completely disappeared.

In listening to these stories one seems to be dreaming. However, nothing of all that I write has been invented. During the ten days that these phenomena were produced, hundreds of people from Molignon and the surrounding villages, Sion and even Conthey, saw them, were present at the seizures and were profoundly moved.

I went yesterday to Molignon, passed the chalet and chatted with the little boy, pretty enough with his soft shy eyes and bloom of health; also with his father, an honest peasant with a sad face; and with his mother, whose eye is still sore from the handful of sand which was thrown in her face in the closed kitchen. All told me in the most natural manner the facts I have related, saying they were sure a *sort* had been cast on their child.

Until April 18 nothing unusual had occurred at the chalet, which has been in existence for forty years. On the question of *mauvais sort* the parents seem to have some preconceptions, but they say nothing positively. They live on good terms with the people of Molignon, and do not know whom to accuse of their misfortune. As regards the child, he has a good constitution, nothing in his attitude suggests any weakness, and before the attacks of April 18 he had experienced nothing like it.

Here we see once more that these strange phenomena are associated with the organism of an adolescent child.

A learned and distinguished man, Mr. Hjalmar

Wijk, of Gothenburg (Sweden), published in 1904 a remarkable work on these phenomena. It is "an experimental study of inexplicable noises and movements." It can be read in the *Annales des sciences psychiques,* of September, 1905, and it is interesting to summarise it here. The conclusion indicated by this case is that the raps were due to the unconscious action of a person whose presence was necessary to their production.

In the spring of 1904 the inhabitants of a villa situated in the south of Sweden noticed some noises which seemed to be produced by vigorous blows inside the flooring and the walls, and impossible to account for by any known cause.

The occupants were the forest inspector, N., and his wife, their servant, and a German official. Before long it was observed that the phenomena were connected with the person of Mme. N. by some indefinable link, for the blows were only produced when she was in the house; and always in her immediate neighbourhood, but were in no way influenced by the presence of the other inhabitants.

Here is, first of all, a sketch of Mme. N. who, for the sake of brevity, is called by her Christian name, Karin.

Karin is twenty-seven years of age. She is of a delicate constitution, and there is something childlike in her face and her whole being. She has lost a little of her gaiety and light-heartedness in consequence of disappointments and sorrow, without, however, suffering any alteration in her original disposition. Hers is a frank and trusting nature which quickly expresses its inmost feelings.

Her whole person seems healthy, and one has the impression that the nervous attacks to which she has been subject during the last few years are not the consequence of her original pathological condition. There seems to be no family defect. Karin has been married since 1897, and has no children.

Her first observations go back ten years. She had then, on several occasions, auditory sensations in the shape of sighs, footsteps, etc. More important than these few isolated cases appears to be her talent for clairvoyance, which was discovered three years after the appearance of the attacks of hysteria, and the manifestations of which show certain similarities with those attacks.

The information obtained from the clairvoyant is not of any great interest. At first she believed she saw people whom she knew, deceased friends and relatives of Karin and her husband, sometimes two or three at the same séance. One day in the spring of 1903 the glass which Karin held in her hand began to dance gaily on the table and a personage of the name of Piscator came on the scene. This Piscator gave only a little vague information about his life. A familiar, impertinent, coarse, and jovial individual, he overwhelms Karin with declarations of love, and is totally different from the other personalities; violent and irritable in the extreme, he ended by becoming for Karin her *bête noire.* As she believes that her clairvoyance only reveals her own subconscious, imaginative life, it seems to her as if the personality of Piscator hangs over her like a cloud, and, representing as he does in some way the lower part of herself, he has become odious to her.

Piscator gives quite the impression of being a product of the imagination, and it is perhaps in this capacity that he supplants more and more his predecessors with the clairvoyant.[5]

On April 18, Karin and her husband moved into a villa, which they rented for the first time, near a factory. It is built of wood in a clearing between the edge of the forest and the road, and comprises a ground floor and several large attics. A cellar runs under a part of the house and a garden surrounds it.

The house has a deserted look. For a long time it had a bad reputation. When it was uninhabited and shut up, lights were seen shining in the windows and disturbing

---

[5] This case is analogous to that of the American medium, Mrs. Piper, with the secondary personalities of Phinuit, Pelham, Imperator, etc. See the work of M. Sage, *Madame Piper et la Société Anglo-Américaine des Recherches Psychiques,* with a preface by Camille Flammarion, Paris, 1902.

noises were heard through the walls. Tradition established a connection between these tales and certain crimes, real or imaginary, which must have been committed there. Of all that, however, Karin and her husband heard nothing until the phenomena which occupy us had given a fresh impetus to the gossip.

On May 9 the manager of the factory received a visit from some people whom he detained until the next day. In the evening these strangers were assembled in a workroom of the villa, which was opposite Karin's room and communicated with the lobby.

Mr. N. was away on business. Karin, who had gone to bed early, was kept awake for a long time by the noisy conversation of the guests. At last, towards midnight, she heard the party break up. Two of them, who were to sleep at the manager's house, left in search of their lodgings. The third, who was put up at the villa, locked the door and retired to his room. Silence reigned, and Karin was on the point of going to sleep when she heard heavy footsteps mounting the steps of the veranda. Immediately afterwards three loud knocks resounded. When she had recovered from the first shock, she dressed and went to open the door. Before her stood one of the two men who had just left. They had not been able to find their way in the dark and wanted a lantern. Karin gave him a lantern and went back to bed. She was falling asleep when three more knocks, just like those which had recently frightened her, made her start. She got up, went to the door and found nobody there. Back in bed, she heard the same three knocks resound repeatedly for about an hour, then all was quiet until three o'clock in the morning; the three knocks then came once more, the last for that night.

Karin had no thought but that these knocks were a practical joke on the part of the guests of the evening before, or of some other person, so she did not worry about them much.

But the following night hardly had she got into bed and put out the light, when the three knocks began again and were repeated, with intervals of silence, for about two hours. They were also heard distinctly by the maid who, that night, was sleeping in the dining-room next door. The maid was extremely frightened by this inexplicable uproar.

The next day Mr. N. came back to the villa. The row having begun again at night, he resolved to throw some light on the subject and catch the disturber of the night. A watch was established inside and outside, and the house was inspected from cellar to attic, but without result. Nothing was discovered and yet the blows did not cease. Mr. N. and his wife changed their room, they even installed themselves in the attic; the noise followed them everywhere, and it was not long before they perceived that it was connected with the presence of the lady.

Except for one day when the latter absented herself in order to visit the town, the phenomena were reproduced every night until May 30. Worn out, Karin then went away for a week's rest. Silence returned to the villa, and it was not troubled at the place where she stayed, but, from the second night after her return, the knocks started again. From that date, however, they were less regular and not a daily occurrence.

The day when Karin and her husband reoccupied the villa the knocks began again, but considerably feebler than before, and often at intervals of several days. In the middle of October the phenomenon ceased completely. It happened only once more, the day before our arrival. That day Karin received a telegram which caused her a moment of keen anxiety; immediately several knocks resounded in the floor at her feet. A little later some fairly loud knocks were heard.

During her residence at the villa Karin frequently had an indefinable feeling that some evil being was present in the room. This sensation was particularly strong immediately before or during the manifestations, and when these took place in complete darkness, Karin often thought she heard a sort of muffled footsteps and sometimes a slight noise resembling that made by shoes gliding softly over the floor. These various sounds were frequently heard by Mr. N. when he was near his wife.

Besides the auditory sensations relating to the knocks, Karin had, in the course of the summer, several other strange sensations. During the first period of the knocks she often had a presentiment of the return of her husband, whom she heard come in, take off his coat in the other room, etc., a quarter of an hour before his actual return from the town. Twice, when sitting in the dark, Karin saw in her room a strange light. On one of these occasions the light, which was quite distinctly the shape of a small flame, appeared near the shoulder of Mr. N., then it slowly withdrew and disappeared. Mr. N. saw the phenomenon as distinctly as his wife. Many times Karin, and sometimes other people, thought they heard certain objects in the room being moved, a chair for example. These occurrences also happened unexpectedly nearly always in pitch darkness, and it was always impossible to make sure if anything had really been moved. One afternoon that Karin was writing, alone in the dining-room, she heard a noise in the kitchen. It seemed as if someone were moving the chairs and cleaning the floor. Knowing that the maid was outside, she went, much astonished, to the door of the kitchen, through which she heard the sounds just as distinctly as before. She dared not open the door, but went to find the maid, who was working in the wash-house. When they both together entered the kitchen the noise of cleaning had ceased, but they both experienced a strange sensation as if someone were moving the chairs and knocking very gently. The floor of the kitchen had been scrubbed that morning in the presence of Karin.

Karin's perfect good faith showed itself in her efforts to find out the cause of the mysterious knocks. Her natural good sense made her reject, from the first, the thought that they could be the work of some "spirit." She thought that she was herself, by some incomprehensible process, the cause of the phenomenon. For his part, Mr. N. was just as interested in the solution of the puzzle. Stories of the phenomenon had revived the old gossip about the haunted villa, and the landlord began to give his tenants to understand that he believed them guilty of organising a hoax with a view to strengthening the bad reputation of his house. To sum up, Karin and her husband were equally interested in throwing light on these various incidents, and, in the course of the summer, several of their friends who came to see them had entire liberty to make every possible investigation.

Naturally these investigations consisted chiefly in making sure that there was no question of a hoax. Karin, for example, had to place herself on a cushion apart; if she was lying down her legs and arms were held. The phenomenon diminished then in intensity, but continued.

It was only in the month of September, through an article in a newspaper, that we heard, Dr. Bjerre and myself, of the existence of the phenomenon. When we made known to Mr. and Mrs. N. our desire to study it on the spot, they immediately invited us to their house.

The case appeared to us singularly interesting. We had to do with a person who seemed to present in a slight degree several of the psychical peculiarities of mediums, and one of these peculiarities appeared in an exceptionally pure and well-marked form. The numerous analogies between the state of trance and the phenomena of mediumship on the one hand, profound hypnosis and hypnotic suggestion on the other hand, had already led us, in previous researches, to believe that hypnotism furnished the best means of studying phenomena of this kind, by enabling us to deal with them with the instrument *par excellence* of the exact sciences—namely, experiment. The phenomena of mediumship are most often, like the unusual knocks in the present case, manifestations of an intelligence which has its roots—one can admit this in a general way—in the subconscious life of the medium. Could we not, thanks to hypnosis, reach this subconscious life, model it to our liking by the aid of suggestion, and even by that means submit to our will the physical phenomena which are its manifestation, provoke the phenomena, stop them, modify them.

Such is the narrative of Mr. Hjalmar Wijk. The reader will have noticed more than one analogy between this report and certain cases published in the present work. The experiences we have just mentioned take up a large number of pages and can be summarised as follows:

1. There seems to be in this case a causal connection between a known nervous disease (hysteria) and the obscure phenomenon of raps. This last has been intimately mixed up with psychic phenomena emanating perhaps from the same nervous disease, such as hallucinations and the imaginative subconscious associations developed by clairvoyant "psychography." Also, a certain part has been played by ulterior psychic influences, stories of ghosts, atmosphere of haunting, etc.

2. The raps can be brought under the influence of the will by hypnotic suggestion.

If the results of our researches are exact, they imply important consequences, on account of the practical importance of raps in Spiritualism and their probable relationship with other mediumistic facts. These results would furnish a solid basis for judging the psychic value of spiritualistic "typtology" and their dependence on the medium and the circle, and would confirm the conclusions already arrived at in this respect by methods of less certainty. Besides, we may hope to be able to provoke and study other and more complex phenomena of mediumship in the same manner, such as levitation and such things.

The present work aims less at giving an account of a particular case than at disclosing the possibility of introducing an experimental method into this new field of study. The importance of such a method cannot be exaggerated, for it is only by basing our speculations upon an experimental method that we can hope to explain these obscure phenomena which still deserve to be called "occult."

We can only applaud the efforts of the Swedish savant. Everybody can see that the credulous believers in Spiritualism do more harm to it than the sceptics, the uncontrolled assertions of the former being often of an unpardonable simplicity. But it is clear that this experience of Mme. Karin would only explain a very small proportion of the phenomena expounded in this special book on haunted houses, and would notably not explain apparitions and the like.

We might admit that by means of faculties at present unknown to science the spirit of a person asleep might have received in a dream the telepathic communication of a distant death (pp. 3, 4, 5); or seen beforehand an incident which happened the next day or long afterwards (pp. 7, 10, 12); or seen at a distance a brother killed by a train. But how can we ascribe to ourselves external events foreign to us, such as the apparition of a person who has just died in a distant country and whose death we do not know of (p. 3); or hear a deceased person whom we think alive, calling us piteously (p. 6); or see an alleged suicide protest against the accusation (p. 24); or a brother sit down beside us just when he has been killed in the chase (p. 28)? And that ecclesiastic announcing his death to the almoner by fictitious noises (p. 30)? And that cousin announcing his death for a legal declaration (p. 32)? And Cicero's traveller calling out to his friend that he has been killed (p. 46)? And Lord Brougham's vision of his schoolfellow dead in India (p. 49)? And M. Belbéder seeing the apparition of his friend's mother commending the latter to him (p. 50)? And the precentor Russell (p. 52)? And Charles who just committed suicide (p. 54)? And Mr. Tweedale's grandmother (p. 55)? And Mrs. Ram (p. 60)? And the peasant girl appearing suddenly after death (p. 61)? All these cases, accurately observed, are outside the personality of the observers. And the Athens ghost (p. 145)? And the fall of portraits and stopping of clocks (pp. 148-157)? And the parsonage with the mysterious noises (pp. 161-173)? And the Coïmbra villa (pp. 185-196)? And the case of the Brest professor (p. 214)? Why should we not seek the cause in the person who had just died? And the door burst open at Strassburg (p. 233), etc.? It is truly impossible to ascribe these cases to any faculties of the observers, who were wide awake, not "duplex," and endowed with good eyesight and cool heads. These cases are real and external to the observers, and they reveal the existence of an invisible psychic world.

My illustrious colleague and noble friend of the English S. P. R., Sir William Barrett, agrees with Aksakoff and myself that, as in mediumistic cases, animism and spiritism are associated in the physical phenomena which we are now studying. He concludes a competent study of *Poltergeists* with the following reflections:[6]

> Here we encounter the problem why a human centre of radiation is necessary in *Poltergeist* phenomena. In chemistry we find that in a saturated saline solution there is a condition of unstable equilibrium such that, if a particle of solid matter falls into the liquid at rest it produces a sudden molecular disturbance which is transmitted to the whole solution and produces an aggregate of solid crystals. The disturbance becomes general, until the entire solution has coagulated into a solid mass of crystals. All this results from a nucleus having come into contact with an aggregation of things which had been perfectly at rest. These phenomena are familiar to microscopists, and it is particularly in the development of cells that a "nucleus" shows itself to be essential.
>
> Thus we might consider the youth or any other subject in the *Poltergeist* phenomena to be the "nucleus" representing the determining factor in these phenomena. We ourselves and our world, are we anything, perhaps, but "nucleated cells" belonging to a much vaster living organism of which we cannot form an idea? It is undubitable that some inscrutable intelligence shows itself at work, in the arrangements of cells as well as the procession of

6 See *Proceedings of the S. P. R.*, vol. xxv, p. 411.

worlds and suns. And since we cannot suppose that the evolution of animate and inanimate nature is confined to the visible world, we must admit the possible existence of different types of living beings of extremely diverse intelligence, both in the visible and the invisible world. In this case the origin of *Poltergeist* phenomena might be attributed to the work of certain invisible intelligences, possibly perverse, possibly rudimentary. Why should we persist in believing that both pleasant and perverted beings cannot exist in the spiritual world? Indeed, they should be found there in greater numbers than here. In any case, we cannot explain how the combination of a given locality with a particular human organism enables them to play abominable tricks in the world of the living, just as a savage cannot explain how the combination of a dry day with a special material enables a machine to produce electricity.

Positive, direct, scientific observation of the phenomena and their normal interpretation have led us to believe that there are invisible beings which act in our atmosphere. That declaration seems bold and risky, and we could not be led to adopt it if it were compelling. Yet we cannot account for the authentic facts in this book, unless we assume that there are not only forces but *beings* which are independent of ourselves.

This experimental conclusion agrees with the philosophical theory of palingenesis and confirms it. There is no reason why general psychic evolution should stop at man. Without being confined to a single system, all thinkers know Charles Bonnet's *Palingénésie Philosophique,* published in Geneva in 1770, and his *Contemplation de la Nature,* published in Amsterdam in 1764. And who does not know the *Philosophie de l'Univers* of Dupont of Nemours (1796)?

Ballanche, Saint-Martin, Schlegel, Savy, Esquiros, Jean Reynaud, and Pezzani continued that tradition in the nineteenth century. But let us say again that this book is not written from the philosophic standpoint, but from the exclusively scientific standpoint of experimental observation.

But it is time to conclude. Everywhere in nature, in the directive force of terrestrial life, in the signs of instinct in plants and animals, in the general spirit of things, in humanity, in the cosmic universe, everywhere there is a psychic element which reveals itself more and more in modern studies, notably in the researches concerning telepathy and those unexplained phenomena dealt with in the present volume. This element, this principle, is still unknown to contemporary science; but, as in many other cases, it was guessed by the ancients. I invent nothing.

Besides the four elements, air, water, earth, and fire, the ancients did, in fact, assume a fifth, of an immaterial kind, which they called *animus,* the world soul, the animating principle, the ether. "Aristotle," writes Cicero (*Tuscal. Quæst.,* i, 22), "having enumerated the four kinds of material elements, is moved to assume a fifth essence, *quinta natura,* which gives rise to the soul. For as thought and the intellectual faculties cannot reside in any of the material elements, we must admit a fifth kind which had not yet received a name and which he called *entelechia*—that is to say, eternal and continual movement." The four material elements of the ancients have been dissected by modern analysis. The fifth is perhaps more fundamental.

Virgil wrote in the *Æneid* (Book VI.) these admirable verses which everybody knows:

Spiritus intus alit, totamque infusa per artus
Mens agitat molem, et magno se corpore miscet.

Let us also remember the *Natural Question* of Seneca and the *Dream of Scipio,* by Macrobius (i, 6).

The Latin grammarian, Martianus Capella, like all the Christian authors of the first centuries, pointed out this directive force, also calling it the fifth element, and designating it by the name ether.[7]

A Roman Emperor well known to the Parisians, Julian the Apostate, celebrates this fifth principle in his speech in honour of the Royal Sun, sometimes calling it the solar principle, sometimes the soul of the world or the intellectual principle, and sometimes the ether.[8]

This psychic element is not mistaken for God by the philosophers. It forms part of nature.

We find it everywhere. Among other examples, it figures remarkably in the trial of Joan of Arc and in that of Socrates.

I repeat it: In proposing to admit scientifically the assistance of this fifth element, the psychic element, as a conclusion of the observations studied in this work, we do not invent anything new. We simply re-establish a forgotten principle.

The human faculties are more extensive than is generally admitted. On the present question the judicious opinion of a man like Jean Jaurès (whose stupid assassination in the first days of the war is deplored by all honest people) is not to be despised. In his book *La Réalité du Monde Sensible* (1902) he wrote:

> As the brain is enclosed in a resistant organic envelope and is apparently closed, imagination easily figures it as isolated from the world. But in reality it is quite possible that the brain is perpetually mixed and confounded with

[7] See Kopp's edition, Frankfort, 1836.

[8] See *Œuvres Complètes de l'Empereur Julien,* 3 vols., Paris, 1821.

what we call the world by a continual and subtle exchange of secret activity.

If it is true, as is declared by many witnesses whose good faith it is difficult to doubt, that the human organism can develop in certain cases a magnetism capable of lifting a table, since it is particularly by the application of will-power that these phenomena are produced, and since it is without the knowledge of their own organism that these people develop an unknown motive power acting on external objects, it appears that cerebral energy can radiate far outside its focus. It seems also as if the *ego* can act upon matter without, at least consciously, having recourse to its organism, which is no longer an active instrument but a passive conductor. The phenomenon of clairvoyance in certain special hypnotic states seems proved nowadays. It is permitted to certain subjects to see and read through obstacles which to us are opaque. Thus the opacity of matter is only relative. And since, in our imagination, what most separates our brain from the surrounding world is the opacity of our organism, that opacity, on disappearing, leaves the cerebral focus and the universe in immediate contact, even to our imagination. Thus the brain can infinitely surpass the organism, and can radiate, palpitate, and act beyond its limits. The brain no longer appears like a self-contained organ, closed up in a hard cavity; we see, even physiologically, the individual *ego* grow and, without losing its necessary attachment to a particular organism, create for itself outside the organism an infinite sphere of activity.

When one subject transmits to another an idea, an impression, or a command without words, there is evidently a radiation of thought into space, and this radiation places two brains into immediate relationship. These facts raise the question of free-will in a new and acute form. But they have another and a higher significance. They show the outside man there are powers extraordinary and unknown, which are dormant or nearly so in his normal state but show themselves in certain states which we call abnormal. There is within us an *Unknown Ego* which can exercise a direct action on matter, which can raise up a strange body as if it were its own body, pierce with its gaze the opacity of an obstacle and cull across space the unexpressed thought of another *ego.*

When normal man assimilates the powers of the magnetic or hypnotic state, see how in human life the individual organism will become accessory. No doubt it would always present itself to consciousness as the necessary root of individuality, but the *ego* could stir with its own will bodies other than its own. It would therefore no longer be the exclusive soul of a particular organism, but of all things over which it could extend, and if it could expand over the whole universe, it would be the world soul.

A free and independent spirit, Jaurès was able to see and to judge, and for him the phenomena of levitation, of mental and physical action at a distance, of telepathy, of vision without eyes, were useful in making clear the constitution of the universe. The human soul is part of the world soul.

The fifth element, of which we spoke just now, contains within itself invisible and unknown intelligences, which are revealed by a certain number of cases expounded in this work. The observers and witnesses were in full possession of their senses; they were observers rather than agents.

How can we admit the precision of aim described on pp. 77-83, without recognising the existence of invisible aimers. How can we suppose that an armchair's placed against the door to keep it shut (p. 117), or that a key is taken from a door to hit the hand of a person wanting to open it (p. 120), or that medals are taken from doors where they were placed as a protection (p. 128), or chairs arranged as for a meeting (p. 129), without acknowledging the action of some spirit? Have we not seen also a glass taken from a shelf, a bellows taken from a fireplace, a broom thrown away, a plate snatched out of hands (p. 137), which are only explained by the intervention of an invisible force? Then a door locked on the inside, cords of bells pulled, portraits detached, clocks stopped, and a spoon turning by itself in a glass (p. 175)? And the anonymous companion of Mme. de Granfort (p. 182), the shutters resisting the pushing of Mr. Homem Christo (p. 192), the child carried off (p. 194), the haunting of Miss Bates at Cambridge, (p. 210), the cousin of M. Legendre (p. 214), and the manifestation of young Garnier at Frontignan (p. 222)? And Lewis announcing his crushing by a train (p. 300)? And the invisible who threw pieces of wood about a carpenter's shop without hurting anybody and without revealing his starting-point (p. 302)? And the Morton family ghost (p. 312)? And that of the Vatas-Simpson family (p. 317), etc.? These beings are generally invisible, but sometimes visible.

There we have as many manifestations of thinking forces, several of which are identifiable. Are these invisible beings strangers to the living, or are they sometimes doublings of the spirits of the experimenters themselves? All we know is that they manifest themselves.

The phenomena we study here are products of the universal dynamism into which our five senses but place us in very partial relation.[9] We live in

---

[9] There can be no doubt that there are means of perception different from our five senses (see *Lumen*), and I gave irrefutable examples of this in my previous psychical works. To those numerous examples I shall add the following very curious one, reported to one of my friends by Ch. Richet in February, 1905:

"I had asked to my house at Carqueiranne two of my friends, both psychologists, Professor William James and Mr. W. H. Myers, for a restful holiday. They were to experiment there with a very interesting medium, Mrs. Thomson. I telegraphed to one of my friends at Nice, M. Moutonnié, to join them, since those studies profoundly interested him. But as I was myself retained at Paris the middle of an unexplored world, in which the psychic forces play a very insufficient observed part.

These forms are of an order superior to the forces generally analysed in mechanics, physics, and chemistry. They have something vital about them, and some sort of mentality. This fifth element is part of the constitution of the universe. It is the link by which beings can communicate across a distance. It has some analogy with Reichenbach's and du Prel's *Od* and Dr. Javorski's *geon*. Only in the last few years have we begun to understand it, since the ether and Hertzian waves form part of scientific theories. Its universal extension enables us to conceive the existence of an immaterial principle.

Everything, on the other hand, goes to show that the purely mechanical explanation of nature is incomplete and that there is more in the universe than just matter. It is not matter which governs the universe, it is the dynamic and psychic element.

Matter itself is only a mode of motion, an expression of force, a manifestation of energy. It evades analysis, and takes final refuge in an intangible, invisible, and somehow immaterial atom.

The atom, the basis of matter, has in the last fifty years dissolved and become a sort of hypothetical and indefinable vortex.

---

he did not go to Carqueiranne. Now Mrs. Thomson, who knew nothing, had gone for a walk on the Riviera. In the gardens of Monaco she saw on a bench a lady and a gentleman with a small dog. With some surprise she distinguished with her inner eye the word 'Carqueiranne' on the man's hat. In spite of her natural timidity she decided to engage in conversation with the couple, she was so much interested. For this purpose she used the little dog as an excuse. She asked the man: 'Do you know Carqueiranne?' My friend was astonished, and exclaimed: 'Certainly, I was to have gone there myself to make the acquaintance of a medium. . . .' 'I am the medium,' said Mrs. Thomson."

I allow myself to repeat here what I have said a hundred times elsewhere: *The universe is a dynamism.* And it seems that everything is electrical. World soul, animal electricity, magnetic fluid, *Od* are diverse names for this same principle of movement. The psychic and physical worlds are associated. The universe consists of intelligences of all degres, and the cosmos as a whole is unexplored.

The manifestations in haunted houses, often so commonplace, so incoherent—like, indeed, those spiritualistic experiences in which the self-suggestion of mediums can be eliminated—lead us to consider the value of the forces and invisible intelligences producing them, and take us along another path back to the ancient parallel between man and the insect. Can it be that the hours, days, and weeks, or even the months and years which follow death, are but the stages of evolution of the human chrysalis and not those of the soul entirely freed from matter?

The spirits of all degrees which perpetually pass from the material world of life to the invisible world are of very varying intellectual values. How many remain in the earthplane? How many are reincarnated, and when?

Let us repeat, for the thousandth time, that the intrinsic nature of the human soul, in life as in death, is still entirely unknown to us. What is immortality?

One day Senator Naquet came to me vividly impressed with a conversation he had just had with Victor Hugo. "We were talking," he said, "of the plurality of worlds and about your *Lumen*. 'Are we all immortal?' he suddenly asked me point-blank. 'But, dear Master,' I replied, 'either one survives or one does not, one or the other. I admit that for my part I do not much believe in it.' 'There are differences and degrees,' said he; 'as for myself, I feel indestructible.'

"I am sure," continued Naquet, "that for him immortality was a personal certainty, but I thought that was some sort of individual pride."

"The question of the inequality of souls has already occurred to me," I replied to Naquet; "it seems worth considering. No, it is not pride in Victor Hugo, it is a sentiment of justice, for he knows well that his works prove his personal individuality."

That conversation took place about 1880. Over forty years afterwards I am of the same opinion, fortified by my psychic studies. No soul seems to be destroyed. But are many souls conscious of their spiritual existence? Are only those conscious of it which were so before death? Variety continues. Educated and ignorant, intelligent and idiotic, good and evil. The guillotine does not make an evil- doer into a saint. The incoherent phenomena of haunted houses agree with this view.

We conclude: If the universe is a dynamism, if the cosmos deserves its name (order), if the unknown world is more important than the known world, if there are intelligent forces and invisible beings—we must discard the denials of Naquet, Berthelot, Le Dantec, Littré, Cabanis, Lalande, Voltaire and the anatomists in favour of the convictions of Victor Hugo, Pasteur, Ampère, Goethe, Euler, Pascal, Newton and the spiritualists. For these penetrate the crust of appearances and discover in the final analysis of things the fundamental invisible dynamism.

EPILOGUE

THE UNKNOWN OF YESTERDAY IS THE TRUTH OF TO-MORROW

Progress surrounded by obstacles—Lavoisier's Report to the Academy of Sciences on meteorites.

THE Unknown of yesterday is the Truth of to-morrow.

We must study everything, discuss everything, analyse everything, without prejudice. The history of the sciences shows us a great number of eminent men, superior spirits, who were stopped in the path of progress by the idea that science had spoken her last word. In astronomy, in physics, in chemistry, in geology, in all branches of human knowledge, it would be easy to fill several pages with the names of famous people who thought science would not pass the limits obtained in their own time, and that there was nothing left to discover. Among savants of the present day it would not be difficult to cite a number of distinguished men who are firmly convinced that in the spheres which they have mastered there is nothing more to be found.

We must only admit that which has been proved. We must be neither credulous nor incredulous. We must study without prejudices and, above all, we must remain free and independent. It is quite natural that official bodies should be conservative. The important thing for the progress of ideas is that we should not be closed up, should not be blinded by a classical attitude to the evidence of facts. This has happened in astronomy, physics, chemistry, and medicine, in all the sciences, in "phlogistics," in steam, in electricity, and in the matter of meteorites. A great and noble spirit, the immortal Lavoisier himself, who had destroyed phlogiston and created chemistry, remained in the eighteenth century bound by the ideas of his time. Charged by the Academy of Sciences with the preparation of a report on a fall of meteorites which had been clearly observed, he wrote in 1769 the following document, which must be a lesson for us all. I shall here give a verbatim extract worthy of being preserved for our instruction. This document is historical and teaches us much. It is taken from the official edition of the works of Lavoisier (Paris: Imperial Press, 1868, vol. iv):

Report on a Stone alleged to have fallen from the Sky during a Thunderstorm.

We, M. Fongeroux, M. Cadet, and I, have been charged with submitting to the Academy an account of an observation communicated by M. l'Abbé Bachelay on a stone alleged to have fallen from the sky during a thunderstorm. There is probably no stone with a longer history than the thunderstone and thunderbolt, if we were to collect all that has been written by the various authors. We may judge of this from the large number of substances designated by that name. Yet, in spite of the belief of the ancients, true physicists have always been doubtful of the existence of these stones. We may find some particulars in a memoir written by M. Lémery, printed among other Academy transactions in 1700.

If the existence of thunderbolts was regarded as doubtful at a time when physicists had hardly any idea of the nature of lightning, their attitude seems even more reasonable nowadays when they have discovered the identity of that phenomenon with electricity. However, we shall faithfully report the fact communicated to us by M.

Bachelay, and we shall then see what conclusions we can draw.

On September 13, 1768, at half-past four in the afternoon, a stormcloud appeared in the direction of the castle of La Chevallerie, near Lucé, a small village of Maine, and a sharp thunderclap was heard which resembled the report of a gun. Then, over a space of some two leagues and a half, a considerable whistling sound was heard in the air, without any appearance of fire. It resembled the lowing of a cow so closely that several people were deceived by it. Several crofters who were harvesting in the parish of Périgué, about three hours from Lucé, having heard the same noise, looked up and saw an opaque body describing a curve, and falling on a meadow near the main road to Le Mans, beside which they were working. They all ran up to the spot and found a sort of stone about half buried in the earth, but it was so hot and burning that it was impossible to touch it. Then they were all seized with terror and ran away. But on returning some time afterwards they saw that it had not moved, but it had cooled down sufficiently to allow them to examine it more closely. The stone weighed about seven pounds and a half, and was of a triangular form—*i.e.*, it presented three more or less rounded horns, one of which had pierced the turf at the moment of falling. All that portion which had entered the ground was of a grey or ashen colour, while the rest, which had been exposed to air, was extremely black. M. l'Abbé Bachelay, having procured a piece of this stone, presented it to the Academy, and seems to have expressed a wish that its nature might be determined.

We shall give an account of the experiments we have made with this object. They will help us to determine what we must think of such a singular fact.

The substance of the stone is pale ash-grey. On looking at the grain with a magnifying-glass it is seen to be studded with a multitude of small bright metallic points of a pale-yellow colour. The part of its outer surface which, according to the Abbé Bachelay, was not embedded in the ground, is covered with a very thin layer of a black substance, inflated in some places, which appears to have been fused. On striking the inside of the stone with steel no sparks were drawn; but if the outer coating, which seems to have been exposed to fire, was struck, a few sparks resulted.

We tested the stone in the hydrostatic balance and found that it lost in water very nearly two-sevenths of its weight, or, more accurately, that its specific weight compared with water was as 3,535 to 1,000. This specific gravity was already much higher than what is usual in silicious stones, so it indicated a considerable proportion of metallic parts.

Having reduced the stone to powder we combined it directly with black flux and obtained a black glass quite similar in appearance to the crust covering the surface of the stone.

After calcination we proceeded to reduction. We only obtained a black alkaline mass, and hence concluded that the metal contained in the stone is iron, combined with the alkali.

It were superfluous to reproduce here the course of the chemical analysis of this mysterious stone, an analysis in which we find Lavoisier chiefly preoccupied with the popular belief that the stone might be a product of lightning. Let us proceed to his conclusion:

We may conclude, therefore [he writes], from the analysis alone, and independently of many other reasons which it were useless to specify, that the stone presented by M. Bachelay does not owe its origin to lightning, *that it did not fall from the sky,* and neither was it formed by fusion due to lightning, as might have been supposed; we may conclude that this stone is nothing but a sort of pyritic sandstone, which has nothing unusual about it except the hepatic smell which it gives off on being dissolved in spirits of salt—a phenomenon which does not happen in ordinary pyrites. The opinion which seems to us the most probable and agrees best with principles accepted in physics, with the facts reported by the Abbé Bachelay, and with our own experiments, is that this stone, which was perhaps covered by a thin layer of earth or turf, was struck by lightning, and thus put in evidence. The heat would have been great enough to fuse the surface of the part struck, but it would not have continued long enough to penetrate into the interior, so that the stone was not decomposed. The considerable quantity of metallic matter which it contained, opposing less resistance than another body to the current of electric substance, may have even contributed to determining the direction of the lightning flash.

It is known that it prefers to pass towards the bodies which are most easily electrified by contact. We must not lose sight of a singular fact. M. Morand, jun., has sent us a piece of a stone from the neighbourhood of Coutances, which was also alleged to have fallen from the sky; it was found very much like M. Bachelay's stone. It is also a sandstone permeated with iron pyrites, and only differs from it in not giving the smell of liver of sulphur with spirits of salt. We believe we can only conclude from this resemblance that lightning falls by preference on metallic substances, and especially those of a pyritous nature.

However fabulous this class of occurrences may appear to be, since they may contribute to the elucidation of the history of thunderbolts by means of the considerations and experiments detailed above, we consider it appropriate to mention them to the Academy.

This report of Lavoisier to the *Académie des Sciences* gives rise to reflections closely connected with the researches under discussion in this book. Witnesses *saw the stone fall,* in broad daylight, on September 13, 1768, in the open country. They picked it up; it is true. It is examined and analysed, and the conclusion drawn is that it did not fall from the sky. Preconceived ideas prevent recognition of the truth. Popular opinion associating these stones with thunder was wrong, but there was no idea of challenging the existing theory and conceiving the possibility of another explanation. Human testimony counts for nothing, and, even in our day, a certain school inclined to paradox continues to teach that witnesses, whoever they may be, can prove nothing.

Certainly, human testimony is fallible, as anyone may be mistaken, and it is not scientific to trust it blindly; but there is a great gap between that and the attitude of denying everything. Now, this was not the first time that one or several stones were seen to fall from the sky, picked up, and preserved. To cite but one instance (the most celebrated): On November 7, 1491, at Ensisheim (Haut-Rhin), an enormous stone fell in front of a whole army, near Maximilian I., the Roman Emperor. They are seen nearly every year somewhere or other. Even in 1768 another one fell at Aire (Pas-de-Calais), and another at Maurkirchen in Bavaria. Lavoisier knew this, and yet he wrote that "true physicists have always regarded as doubtful the existence of these stones." This perennial blindness towards all that is unknown has constantly hindered the progress of science. We see at the same time how imprudent it is to form premature explanatory theories, for this explanation of meteorites has to some extent negatived the judgments of the *Académie des Sciences.*

Let us distrust premature theories; this historical case enjoins it upon us.

Human beings of all degrees of intelligence who still think that metapsychical phenomena are inadmissible, because to admit them throws doubt on certain principles of classical teaching, should also remember that all discoveries began by being denied.

For thousands of years meteorites had fallen from the sky before hundreds of witnesses, a great number had been picked up, several were preserved in churches, museums and collections. But there was still lacking in 1769 an independent spirit to confirm them. This man arrived in 1794. It was Chladni.

I throw no stones at Lavoisier, nor at the *Académie des Sciences,* nor at any person, but at the tyranny of prejudice. They did not believe, they would not believe, that minerals would fall from the sky. It seemed contrary to common sense. For example, Gassendi was one of the most independent and learned intellects of the seventeenth century. A meteorite weighing sixty-six pounds fell in Provence, in 1627, from a clear sky. Gassendi saw it, touched it, and examined it, yet he attributed it to some terrestrial eruption.

The *Académie des Sciences* at last recognised, on the report of its own commissioner Biot, the reality of meteorites at the time of the fall at Laigle (Orne), on April 26, 1803. The stones had been picked up, still hot, by a number of witnesses who had narrowly escaped being stoned to death by the heavens. Since that time it has very often had to engage in the study of meteorites.[1] In spite of all, the world goes forward, and the truth forces itself upon us.

Peripatetic professors of the time of Galileo stated dogmatically that there could be no spots

---

[1] The very day that I received the proof of this page (September, 1923) I read in the *Comptes rendus de l'Académie des Sciences* of September 10 an account by Messrs. Mengaud and Mourié of the fall of a curious meteorite, weighing thirty-one pounds, which fell at Saint-Sauveur (Haute-Garonne) on July 10, 1914, near two farm labourers. The analysis has just been completed by M. A. Lacroix. Since 1803 science has made useful progress from these verifying statements.

on the sun. The Brocken spectre, the Fata Morgana, and the mirage were denied by a great number of intelligent people as long as they were unexplained. It is thought necessary to be able to explain a fact before admitting its reality.

It was not so very long ago (1890) that ball-lightning was questioned at a full meeting of the *Académie des Sciences* in Paris by the very member of the Institute who ought to have known most about it, Mascart, director of the Central Meteorological Office. He maintained that my conviction was not well founded, although I had quoted so many examples in my works.

The history of the progress of science shows throughout that great and fruitful results may arise from simple and commonplace observations. In the domain of scientific study nothing should be disdained.

We should always observe this double principle:

> Deny nothing *a priori.*
> Admit nothing without proof.

In 1831, Dr. Castel said, at the *Académie de Médecine,* after the reading of a report of a commission of this Society on animal magnetism:

> If the majority of the facts stated were true, then half the knowledge acquired in physics would be invalidated. Therefore their propagation should be guarded against in printing the report.

The advice of the Medical Faculty of Bavaria against the introduction of railways offers a typical example of this antipathy for everything new. That learned body supposed that such rapid movement would infallibly produce cerebral derangements in the travellers and giddiness in the onlookers. They recommended that at least a wooden partition should be erected on each side of the railway.

We may also remember the opposition excited by Harvey's discovery of the circulation of the blood and, that he was treated as a lunatic by the savants of his time; also the opposition to Jenner's vaccination proposals, etc. The invention of photography passed through the same ordeal[2] in the days of Niepce and of Daguerre. Yet what a world of revelations has it not opened to science! We need only think of astronomy, from the sun to the nebulæ.

The reception which the savants accorded to the discovery of Jupiter's satellites, and their refusal to look through Galileo's telescope, has not been forgotten. At the time of the discovery of the bacillus of tuberculosis, did not a well-known professor, an opponent of bacteriology, refuse to look through the microscope at a bacillus culture which his assistant wished to show him? Dr. Schrenck-Notzing has recalled the judgment given in the *Grenzboten* by an eminent savant, which indicates the same attitude of mind: "I shall not believe in hypnotic suggestion until I see a case; and I shall never see one, for I ignore it on "principle."

---

[2] Mme. Blavatsky tells (in *Isis Unveiled*) an anecdote current among the friends of Daguerre between 1838 and 1840. During a soirée at Mme. Daguerre's, some two months before the presentation of the new process before the *Académie des Sciences* by Arago (January, 1839), the latter had a serious consultation with one of the medical celebrities of the time concerning her husband's mental condition. After explaining her husband's aberration, she added, with tears in her eyes, that the most convincing proof of Daguerre's insanity was his firm conviction that he would succeed in nailing his own shadow on the wall or fix it on a magical metallic plate. The doctor listened attentively, and replied that on his part he had lately observed symptoms in Daguerre which to him amounted to an irrefutable proof of lunacy. He ended the conversation by advising her to send her husband quietly and without delay to Bicêtre. Two months afterwards a vivid interest arose in the world of science and art after an exhibition of pictures prepared by the new process, and photography, already discovered by Niepce, was recognised.

And the great physicist, Lord Kelvin, wrote the following:[3]

> I make a point of repudiating any appearance of a tendency to accept this miserable superstition of animal magnetism, table-turning, Spiritualism, mesmerism, clairvoyance, and raps. There is no mystical sixth sense. Clairvoyance and the rest are the result of malobservation, with a touch of voluntary self-deception, acting upon simple and trusting souls.

Such is the degree of blindness to which one of the greatest intellects of the age was reduced. He did not deign to notice, or examine, or try to understand.

We can add the name of Ernest Haeckel to the list of savants blinded by a false pride, who have denied the existence of unexplained phenomena. On one unfortunate page of his interesting work *The Riddle of the Universe,* after lightly and hastily touching on mediumistic phenomena, which he classes as aberrations of overwrought minds, he speaks of thought-readers in these terms:

"That which is called telepathy (or thought transference without a material medium) does not exist any more than spirits or ghosts, etc."

In spite of Haeckel and his colleagues, thought-transference, hypnotism, and many other psychic manifestations are now acknowledged by eminent men, and the psychologist has taken courage to interest himself in problems which arise in a field of study hitherto considered a mass of trickery and fraud. Let us rather reason as Jaurès did just now.

We must remark again, with Ch. Richet, that the

---

[3] See Myers, *Society for Psychical Research*, xiv, 1904, p. 365; and Richet, *Traité de métapsychique*, p. 6.

comprehension of psychic phenomena is beyond the capacity of a certain number of men.

In the first place, there are first-class men of science, high officials in education or administration, who are very competent in certain subjects, very upright, of a ripe and usually well-founded judgment, but who do not go outside their sphere, and for whom science has said its last word on everything. They are convinced that the laws of nature are known! This class of people was opposed to new discoveries throughout the ages, the movement of the earth, the telescope, the circulation of the blood, meteorites, vaccination, electricity, gas lighting, railways, photography, submarine telegraphy, the phonograph, the cinematograph, aviation, etc. They would never devote their time to these things *because they were sure they were impossible,* and they always obstinately adhere to a scepticism which to them seems rational.

Then there are the shrewd persons of business ability, false, knavish, and crooked people, given to exploiting their neighbours, convinced that it is better to rob than to be robbed, and setting unscrupulous traps for others. These people can see nothing but cleverness, falsehood, and deception in these things.

Lastly, from another point of view, but equally incapable of judging the phenomena, there are the simpletons, the credulous, who have no critical minds, who make a blind faith of Spiritualism—a religion indeed—and cannot exactly analyse the effects to be observed.

Yet there are also the Free, and they surely form a notable proportion of the human species.

Let us acknowledge, in any case, that people in general are incapable of a sustained attention, and that in the terrestrial human race, as a whole, indifference to the knowledge of truth is almost universal. This indifference perpetuates the amazing ignorance which every shrewd observer encounters in all scientific and historical fields. After so many centuries of progress, so many discoveries, this universal ignorance is truly fantastic. Nobody wants to learn. The inhabitants of our planet live without knowing where they are and without having the curiosity to ask.

The columns of the Press are occupied with material pursuits, races of all kinds, millions in bets, speed tests, sports, boxing, pugilistic matches, speculations, the theatre, the cinema, the films, new dances, the nude in the music-halls, adulteries, crimes of passion, assassinations, political speeches, advertisements. As regards scientific progress and general instruction, they are conspicuous by their absence.

It is particularly in psychic matters that this ignorance is remarkable and regrettable, for we are all personally concerned there. The psychical world is vaster and more immense than the physical world.

A last word. It is well to know this psychical world. We are far from having exhausted its study in this or the preceding volumes. We have not been able, as we had hoped to be, to include the numerous and incontestable observations concerning apparitions of the dead to the dying, which are evidence of the survival of those dead, and have their special value. Neither have we been able to concern ourselves with the phantoms themselves, those which have been seen and heard. There we have a whole field of complex studies which opens unexpected horizons. It seems to me that the time has come to devote, in spite of the apparent paradox, a special volume to ghosts, methodically discussed, in the light of observational science. That will be the subject of my next work.

Yes, the Unknown World is vaster and more important than the Known.

(1)

THE END